ADVANCE PRAISE FOR
WILD COUNTRY COMPANION

"**Wild Country Companion** *is an excellent guide to the leave-no-trace practices that every wilderness visitor should strive to follow.*"

> —David Cole, Scientist, Aldo Leopold Wilderness
> Research Institute USDA Forest Service

"**Wild Country Companion** *looks great! I am excited about having this much-needed information readily available to our staff and visitors alike. Our jobs, our resources, and our outdoor experiences will all benefit from your efforts.*"

> —Sandy Kogl, Backcountry Subdistrict Ranger,
> Denali National Park

"*You've done an excellent job of addressing the needs of all outdoor recreation user groups.*"

> —Stewart L. Jacobson, National Coordinator,
> Tread Lightly! and Leave No Trace,
> Bureau of Land Management

"*Excellent job.*"

> —Dr. Warren Bowman, Jr., President,
> Wilderness Medical Society

"As our wilderness areas and natural resource recreation areas continue to grow in popularity, the information you present will become more and more important in helping to protect and preserve our natural resources."

—Mark Butler, Physical Science Specialist,
Yosemite National Park

"Interesting book and treatment of this complex topic."

—James J. Claar, USDA Forest Service Regional Grizzly Bear
Habitat Coordinator

"Wild Country Companion *is a volume of uncommon sense for backcountry travelers. There's something here for everyone...It culls the available resources to offer good, specific advice on minimizing the impacts associated with different uses and different environments. Maybe most importantly, it tells us how to make decisions when the advice doesn't work."*

—Jim Hasenauer, President of the International Mountain
Bicycling Association

"The Back Country Horsemen of America endorse your book. We feel it fits well with our attempts to help educate the public about livestock and 'leave-no-trace use' of public lands."

—Kurt J. Dyer, National Chairman, Back Country
Horsemen of America

WILD COUNTRY COMPANION

WILL HARMON

FALCON™

FALCON PRESS PUBLISHING CO., INC.
HELENA, MONTANA

Falcon Press is continually expanding its list of books. This book is a companion to Falcon's recreational guide books. All guide books include detailed descriptions, accurate maps, and all the information necessary for enjoyable trips. You can order extra copies of this book and get information and prices for other Falcon books by writing Falcon Press, P.O. Box 1718, Helena, MT 59624. Also, please ask for a free copy of our current catalog listing all Falcon Press books.

ISBN: 1-56044-169-0

Printed in the United States of America.

Falcon Press Publishing Co., Inc.
P.O. Box 1718, Helena, MT 59624

Cover and text page design by Ginger DeWit
Illustrations by Lisa Harvey

  Printed on recycled paper.

CAUTION

Outdoor recreation activities are by their very nature potentially hazardous. All participants in such activities must assume the responsibility for their own actions and safety. The information contained in this guidebook cannot replace sound judgment and good decision-making skills, which help reduce risk exposure, nor does the scope of this book allow for disclosure of all the potential hazards and risks involved in such activities.

Learn as much as possible about the outdoor recreation activities you participate in, prepare for the unexpected, and be safe and cautious. The reward will be a safer and more enjoyable experience.

CONTENTS

LIST OF REVIEWERS

A special thank you to the following people who reviewed all or part of the text.

David Cole, *Scientist, Aldo Leopold Wilderness Research Institute, USDA Forest Service, Missoula, MT*

Kate Kendall, *Research Ecologist Specialist, National Biological Survey, Glacier National Park*

Mark Butler, *Physical Science Specialist, Yosemite National Park*

Dr. Warren Bowman, Jr., *President, Wilderness Medical Society*

Sandy Kogl, *Backcountry Subdistrict Ranger, Denali National Park*

Stewart L. Jacobson, *National Coordinator, Tread Lightly! and Leave No Trace, Bureau of Land Management*

Ralph Swain, *National Coordinator, Leave-No-Trace Program, USDA Forest Service*

J. D. Swed, *Climbing Ranger, Denali National Park*

James Claar, *Regional Grizzly Bear Habitat Coordinator, USDA Forest Service, Wildlife, Region I*

Jim Hasenauer, *President, International Mountain Bicycling Association*

Gary Colliver, *Climbing Ranger, Yosemite National Park*

Rich Brame, *Outreach and Training Manager, National Outdoor Leadership School*

Kurt Dyer, *National Chairman, Back Country Horsemen of America*

ACKNOWLEDGMENTS

Before I started writing this book, my address file was nowhere near as interesting as it is now. The people I met and talked with while researching the finer points of the leave-no-trace ethic and backcountry safety are without exception the most enthusiastic, knowledgeable, articulate, and generous men and women I have yet come to know. If, as Gilbert Highet suggests, a book is a mind alive on the shelf, then this book is a gathering of the most lively minds.

A book of this scope is necessarily a team effort, and each of the following people contributed important information, insight, and support. Any errors or omissions, however, are the fault of the author alone.

A heartfelt thanks to David Cole and Alan Watson, USDA Forest Service Aldo Leopold Wilderness Research Institute; John Twiss, Nat'l Leader for Wilderness Management for the Forest Service; Rich Brame, National Outdoor Leadership School; Connie Myers, director of the Arthur Carhart National Wilderness Training Center; Ralph Swain, National Leave No Trace Program; Linda Thompson, Wilderness Management Correspondence, Colorado State University; Jim Hasenauer, International Mountain Bicycling Association; Andrea Ash, Pennekamp State Park in Florida; Alice Ruth, Gulf Islands National Seashore; Sandy Kogl and J.D. Swed, Denali National Park; Kate Kendall, Glacier National Park; Pam Griffin, Tom Larson, and Roger Drake, Mount Rainier National Park; Jackie Skaggs, Grand Teton National Park; Jill Clayton, Gary Colliver, and Mark Butler, Yosemite National Park; Steve Morton and Jim Claar, Forest Service Region 1; Don Pfitzer, retired U. S. Fish and Wildlife Service; Dr. Warren Bowman, Wilderness Medical Society; Jean Johnson, Montana Outfitters and Guides Association; Kurt Dyer, Back Country Horsemen of America; Bill Brown, outfitter; Julie Huck, Adventure Cycling (formerly Bikecentennial); Bob McConnell, Everest Environmental Expedition; and Mark Shapley, Montana Wilderness Association.

Kudos to the production team, including Randall Green, editor, who was always on belay when I needed it; John Grassy, for his well-read eye and timely encouragement; Lisa Harvey, illustrator and constant ray of realistic optimism; Ginger Dewit, for layout and design and patience beyond the pale; and John Horton, for his photographic and darkroom expertise.

Finally, I owe a special debt of gratitude to Bill Schneider for trusting me with his idea and to Chris Cauble for encouraging creativity; to Mike Cavaness, Charlie Crangle, Kim Blommel, and Gloria Lambertz for inviting me along on so many adventures (and then to the movable feasts that always followed); to Vicki at the Montana State Library and Sara Toubman and the gang at the information desk at Lewis and Clark County Library for helping me thumb a ride on the information superhighway; to Teresa Hastings for the simple loan of a book; and last but most of all to Rose, Evan, and Ben, who make it all worthwhile.

PREFACE

It's what you learn after you know it all that counts.

— Chalkboard graffito in Advanced First Aid Course

WHY DO IT?

This book outlines the latest information on no-trace camping and wilderness safety. These are probably not the most popular subjects for bedtime reading. Instead, we prefer to plan out our dream trips and read about where to hike, how to get down a river, up a mountain, or how to catch a big trout. So why study this stuff?

First, we have a responsibility to know it. We not only have to be responsible for taking care of ourselves, but also our companions. And anybody who uses wild country has the obligation to take care of it. We are all accountable.

But there's another important reason to do it—and one many of us do not often consider.

You will enjoy your wilderness trips more—if you have within you the self-assurance that you know how to take care of the wilderness and handle any emergency. You can never forget proper preparation and good common sense, but you can leave fear behind. You will have the confidence that adds so much to the enjoyment of your wilderness experience.

It's like your fitness level. You could say it's a good idea to be in top physical condition so you won't have a heart attack. Or you could say that a high level of fitness will allow you to enjoy your trip more thoroughly. The same goes with knowledge of wilderness safety and no-trace camping.

So, there is a good reason to do it, and we certainly hope you do.

—*Bill Schneider, Publisher*

INTRODUCTION

"One learns a landscape finally not by knowing the name or identity of everything in it, but by perceiving the relationships in it."

—Barry Lopez, "Landscape and Narrative," in *Crossing Open Ground*

People who enjoy backcountry travel tend to be flexible and resourceful. We learn to cope with abrupt changes in weather, challenging terrain, equipment failure, blisters, and bugs. We adapt, or we soon cease to enjoy the experience.

Not surprisingly, this same ability to adapt comes in handy in the practices of safe travel and leaving no trace in the backcountry. Different techniques work for different environments and circumstances. The right boots for scaling an ice-clad mountain would wreak havoc on a water-logged meadow. A good tent site in a heavily visited area is far different than a good tent site in pristine wilderness. The ridge top that's risky in a lightning storm provides safe haven from winter avalanches.

Decisions and choices confront the backcountry traveler at every turn in the trail. Even going to the bathroom in the backcountry is fraught with dilemmas: a group latrine or individual cat holes? How deep? Burn the toilet paper or bury it?

How do we sort through all of the choices? Add a host of federal and state agencies and the flurry of choices becomes a blizzard of rules, regulations, conflicting expert opinions, and innumerable special policies. How do we cope? How can we learn to travel safely and leave no trace without feeling like we've been dragged through obedience school?

The answer lies not in memorizing lists of rules or creeds of conduct—there are simply too many variables and too few absolute truths. The answer lies instead in our own ability to make sound decisions, under a wide range of circumstances. How? With resourcefulness and flexibility, traits we've already laid claim to. In fact, wise decision-making in the backcountry is more a matter of attitude than skill or special knowledge. It's a frame of mind grounded in common sense and respect for the land, its inhabitants, and other visitors.

Wild Country Companion is designed to build on that frame of mind, to help you make the choices that best suit your surroundings, skills, and mode of travel. The following pages are crammed full of the best and most up-to-date advice on how to camp and travel safely, with little or no harm done to your surroundings, throughout North America's diverse wild lands. The focus here is on developing and refining an ability to make well-informed judgment calls when the "right" answer isn't clear. Rather than listing all the do's and don'ts, we give a range of options and encourage you to decide what will work best in any given situation. We won't tell you, "Don't build campfires," but we do look at situations where campfires are appropriate, and some situations where they aren't. And we explain how you can tell the difference. If you do decide to build a fire, for comfort or out of necessity, we provide step-by-step instructions for building a safe, no-trace fire with less effort and fuss than most other methods.

That's a good example of how this book works. Throughout *Wild Country Companion* we supply the facts and the know-how. Then we encourage you to hone and trust your own intuition and to bear in mind your own preferences and motives for backcountry travel. We also recognize that no-trace techniques and safety measures work best if they don't conflict with the reasons people go into the backcountry in the first place.

So why do we head for the hills? What draws us to wild country? According to USDA Forest Service surveys of wilderness visitors, the two most commonly cited reasons are "to find solitude" and "to experience nature." Surely these are important, even heroic reasons—the individual, weary of society's crush, strides alone into the wilderness for solace and renewal. People also go to face risks, to test themselves, to study nature, and to hunt, fish, or take photographs. But a more ordinary rationale (perhaps the root of all others) also seems likely: it's fun!

Of course not everyone finds fun in the same way. Backpackers enjoy suffering under heavy packs and bandaging blistered feet, horseback riders are fond of saddle sores and horseflies, canoeists thrive on sitting in cold, wet clothes and losing their shoes on long portages, and mountain bikers show a predilection for prolonged oxygen debt and collecting dents in their helmets. Yet we hold one over-riding joy in common, the pure pleasure of setting out across wild country. As a wily old statesman once remarked, "we may not be in the same boat, but we are all in the same water."

That's another important theme of this book. With so many people heading into the wilds, there's less elbow room—less of that solitude we covet—and more chance for encounters and conflicts among folks of different persuasions. All too often we divide ourselves with labels—hiker versus biker versus horsepacker, or skier against snowmobiler. In reality, few people fit such narrow stereotypes. The photographer on foot in June may turn hunter on horseback in October. The snowmobiler on Yellowstone's snow-covered roads in January may spend summer weekends birdwatching on a local wildlife refuge. Regardless of our differing modes of travel, special interests, or levels of skill, we share a commitment to preserving our wild lands and the array of recreational opportunities they offer. On the trail and in camp, we must each cultivate a healthy tolerance and respect for other backcountry visitors.

But what do no-trace techniques and safety have to do with fun? Everything. Only by working to minimize harm to the land and to ourselves can we hope to sustain these very same things for future enjoyment. Trample a mountain meadow to dust and the area may be closed to all use when you next visit; drink untreated water, and a sudden case of diarrhea may quickly end your trip. In these days of increasing pressure on our wild lands from ever growing numbers of outdoor enthusiasts, taking the sustainable approach is imperative for all.

We've tried to avoid jargon in writing this book, and the word sustainability rarely appears. But that's the primary, if unstated, theme throughout *Wild Country Companion*. Keep sustainability in mind as you read and you'll find that it ties all the details together. Of course, safety and leaving no trace often go hand-in-hand anyway. For example, anticipating foul weather and packing appropriate clothes and food reduces your risk of hypothermia and eliminates the need to build an "emergency" fire. And we've tried to make these connections as clear as possible, cross referencing similar topics, repeating crucial information as needed, and, occasionally, wallowing in a brief digression or foreshadowing. It is our hope that in this way readers will understand not only what works best, but why.

Before we talk any more about "wild" country, our choice of terms bears explaining. Throughout this book we use the words *wild lands, wild country, wilderness,* and *backcountry* interchangeably. What we mean is: land beyond road's end. Not all such land is pristine, or even necessarily remote. But many of the same no-trace and safety measures apply as well to a large city park as they do to a vast, primeval wilderness. Of course, the term *wilderness* now carries a specific legal meaning, as outlined in the 1964 Wilderness Act (and the subsequent Eastern Wilderness Act of 1975). When we address land bound by the legal definition, we use the appellation *designated wilderness area* or we refer to the area by name: the Popo Agie Wilderness in Wyoming.

Read and enjoy! Our highest hope is that your next backcountry outing will be safer—and softer on the land—for having read this book.

HISTORY OF THE
LEAVE-NO-TRACE CONCEPT

History balances the frustration of "how far we have to go"
with the satisfaction of "how far we have come." It teaches us tolerance
for the human shortcomings and imperfections which are not uniquely
of our generation, but of all time.

—Lewis F. Powell, Jr.

No-trace camping is a fairly recent phenomenon, an outgrowth of the explosion in recreational use of America's backcountry during the late 1960s and early 1970s. The short-hand version of this history is simple: Having won passage of the Wilderness Act in 1964, Americans suddenly heard the call of the wild and descended on the backcountry in droves. Within a decade, many once unspoiled places were at risk of being trampled beyond recognition. Land managers sounded the first alarm, citing overcrowded campsites, eroded trails, and a rising tide of litter, noise, and vandalism. Our wild lands, according to historian (and former fishing guide) Roderick Nash, were in danger of being "loved to death."

The initial response to the problem was to regulate and, where necessary, limit use. But only the hardest hit areas actually saw limits placed on the number of visitors; in 1973 quotas were set for boaters on the Grand Canyon of the Colorado, and by 1975 several of the more popular wilderness areas and many national parks required permits for backcountry camping.

Rules and regulations, however, quickly sprouted on nearly every trailhead sign across the nation. The USDA Forest Service and National Park Service targeted recreational visitors with educational brochures, posters, and television ads. "Leave only footprints; take only photographs" became the catch phrase of a new generation of outdoor enthusiasts, a generation whose growing sense of environmental responsibility dictated a new approach to backcountry camping and travel. The no-trace camping ethic was born.

But this short-hand account describes a mere blink in time, a glimpse too brief for us to see the whole picture. That picture is more generously framed by Roderick Nash in his book, *Wilderness and the American Mind*. Nash reaches back twenty million years to set the stage for the wilderness preservation movement of the

Much of the discussion here of the history of wilderness preservation was condensed from Roderick F. Nash's classic *Wilderness and the American Mind*, (©Yale University Press, 1982). Additional material, from Nash's "Historical Roots of Wilderness Management," in *Wilderness Management*, is used by permission of North American Press.

twentieth century. That's a long reach, but one worth repeating here. Why? Because the work of preserving wilderness has also preserved many of our attitudes about wilderness. Today's backcountry travelers carry twenty million years of intellecutal and instinctual baggage, our imaginations straining at the seams like overstuffed backpacks. We see in nature beauty and ugliness, comfort and danger, play and utility, spiritual inspiration and earthly dirt, mystery and knowledge. In the wild, we are at turns haughty and humble, and it shows in our behavior.

In other words, how we think and feel about nature determines the choices we make as backcountry visitors. To fully understand our own choices—for example, why we sometimes prefer solitude and at other times crave company—we need first to consider the history of human attitudes about nature. That will take us, briefly, back to the Miocene Epoch, so hold onto your bifocals.

SEEDS OF CONSCIOUSNESS

"Until roughly twenty million years ago," Nash writes, "our prehuman ancestors dwelt in an arboreal environment. They were at home in the trees of jungle or forest primeval—'wilderness' in the commonly understood sense of that term today.... But about fifteen million years ago it appears that climatic changes and fire began to reduce the area of forest in central Africa and other seedbeds of man. Prehumans gradually left the shrinking arboreal habitat and began to adapt to life on the plains and grasslands."

Nash explains that these new grassland inhabitants grew to rely on vision as an edge against other predators in the struggle for existence. "It followed," he continues, "that for millions of years our distant ancestors preferred open environments, where the eye and the brain could function, to the dark primeval forest." Taken as a whole, these millennia of gradual change must have left early man with a puzzled, slightly apprehensive look on his face, a creature of the trees grown fearful of the forest.

This bias against a "wilderness" that was once "home" became imprinted on our species' thoughts and behavior. The inherent ambivalence is remarkably familiar to us today. In the 1992 version of the classic fairy tale *Beauty and the Beast*, Disney animators strike an ominous chord in every child (and parent) when the heroine's father steers his horse from bright, open farmland into a dark, unkempt forest. Even the weather turns suddenly hostile. We know in our bones that Papa is headed for trouble, lost in a fearsome place where he does not belong. The scene is designed to prod us in the adrenal glands, to get the old fight-or-flight juices flowing.

Conversely, forest scenes can also soothe us. Take an overworked, stressed out stockbroker off the uptown subway, as psychologists have, and plunk her into a recliner in a dark room. Hook up a few electrodes to monitor her racing heart rate. Flash a photo of a city skyline on the screen. The heart bumps faster. Next, an ocean wave curling onto a beautiful, deserted beach. The cardiac rhumba slows a notch. Then a wall of green trees, boles and branches reaching toward a sky of leaves. The heart monitor's rhythm plummets to a slow waltz.

These same impulses and instincts well up throughout our more recent tenure on the planet, though for the first 5,000 years of recorded history our relationship to the natural world was driven primarily by fear and loathing and the need to conquer the unruly side of nature. For a representative example, fast forward to the year 1620 and the arrival of the pilgrims at Plymouth Plantation. Nash relates that "when William Bradford stepped off the Mayflower into a 'hideous and desolate wilderness' he started a tradition of repugnance. With few exceptions later pioneers continued to regard wilderness with defiant hatred." This prevailing view held sway with nary a voice raised in rebuttal until the beginning of the nineteenth century.

A CHANGE OF HEART

But between 1800 and the establishment in 1872 of Yellowstone as the world's first national park, Americans' attitudes about nature underwent a dramatic change: Explorers and pioneers found new wonders in the West, and rumors spread of natural wealth, of furs and gold, and of dark, loamy soil waiting for the plow. European aristocrats came to America and wrote or painted accounts of their adventures in a land of vast prairies, strange beasts, and "noble savages." By the 1840s thousands of farmers, prospectors, and new arrivals were ready to leave the east, where most of the good opportunities were already taken. Within a decade tens of thousands made the trip, spurred westward by the cheerful (and usually spurious) reports of guides, the railroads, and government. The West, in all its wildness, had been made appealing, at least from a utilitarian perspective. And more than a few hardy pioneers survived the heartbreak of vast distances, insufferable weather, hunger, and disease only to find that it was beautiful country, even more wondrous than its embellished reputation. The once "godless" wilderness became for some a source of spiritual renewal, a landscape where the creator's hand was everywhere in evidence.

No sooner had Americans begun to appreciate the frontier than it was nearly gone. By the 1860s the Wild West was well on the way to being tamed. Within a single lifetime all but one of the Indian tribes had succumbed to life on the reservations, the thunder of buffalo had grown quiet, the fur trade was played out, and gold rush camps turned to towns and cities rivaling those back east. As civilization spread, wilderness became scarce. And as a commodity's supply dwindles, its value often increases.

This dramatic turn of events was foreseen remarkably early in the process by George Catlin, a painter and student of native life. In 1829 Catlin traveled west and recorded in letters and on canvas the vigorous life of the frontier. What he saw of the "pristine wildness and beauty" in the upper Missouri plains led him to suggest that at least a portion of this vanishing landscape should be preserved as a "nation's

Park." Other visionaries, including Henry David Thoreau, Horace Greeley, Samuel Hammond, and George Perkins Marsh, joined the call to protect some remnant of the West and the idea soon gained widespread recognition and support. In 1864 the federal government granted Yosemite Valley to the state of California as a park "for public use, rest and pleasure." Then on March 1, 1872, President Ulysses S. Grant signed into being Yellowstone National Park, the world's first national natural preserve. Other lands were soon accorded national park status, including Yosemite (1890), Sequoia (1890), Mount Rainier (1899), Crater Lake (1902), and Glacier (1910).

Nash notes, however, that these first national parks were set aside not to preserve their wilderness qualities but to protect a few natural features, such as geysers, waterfalls, and scenic lakes, from private ownership and entrepreneurial gain. They were seen as public resorts, and park status came complete with plans for fine hotels, rail and highway systems, and other trappings of mass tourism. The wilderness quality of these early parks was largely unrecognized—despite a lifetime of eloquent pleading from John Muir—until the 1920s. And by then, two young upstarts in the Forest Service were formulating a wilderness preservation plan of their own.

In 1919 the Forest Service sent Arthur Carhart, an agency landscape architect, to survey Trappers Lake, a remote and unspoiled area in the Colorado Rockies. His job was to map out an access road and plots for several hundred vacation homes around the lake. Instead, after enjoying a summer in the wild, he returned to Denver and recommended that the region be left in its pristine condition. "Probably to his surprise," notes Nash, "the USFS approved the idea." Today, Trappers Lake is part of the 235,230-acre Flat Tops Wilderness Area.

At the same time, forester Aldo Leopold was formulating his own ideas about protecting roadless areas on national forests in New Mexico. Leopold and Carhart met and exchanged concerns in 1919, and then in 1921 Leopold issued a call for at least one 500,000-acre wilderness area in each of the eleven states west of the Great Plains. The first of these, 574,000 acres on the Gila National Forest, was set aside in 1924.

The movement to preserve pieces of the vanishing wilderness quickened, culminating with official action in 1939, when Robert Marshall, chief of the Division of Recreation and Lands within the Forest Service, established the so-called U Regulations. These administrative rules protected some fourteen million acres of national forest lands as "wilderness" and "wild areas." Certain uses, including motorized transportation, logging, and permanent camps, were prohibited.

The creation of the U Regulations coincided roughly with an upswing in the public's regard for "roughing it" in the outdoors. Throughout the Depression years, the Civilian Conservation Corps and other federal work programs had laid miles of trail and constructed numerous recreation facilities in the national forests and parks. These improvements attracted people, and as early as 1937, land managers began to recognize that too many recreational visitors could spoil an area's natural qualities.

During the 1930s and 1940s, a small publishing industry buzzed around this blossom in the public's interest in outdoor recreation. These early campcraft books and backcountry how-to manuals harkened back to pioneer days and a vision of wilderness as raw material, something to put to good use, to rearrange and shape to suit human needs. The emphasis was on making the camping experience as comfortable and convenient as possible. Books the likes of *Wildwood Wisdom* (1945) described how beds could be made of fresh pine boughs lopped from nearby trees; chairs, benches, even tables hewn from timber on the spot; and elaborate corrals erected for stock animals. (The lone exception to this approach was Aldo Leopold's *A Sand County Almanac*, first published in 1949. But *Sand County* was more a philosophical treatise about nature than a field manual. For more of Leopold's ideas, see Chapter 2.) Wildland recreation, albeit styled after a dim romantic notion of frontier life, had quietly entered the mainstream.

AN OVER-POPULATED SOLITUDE

As Americans reacquainted themselves with their wild hinterlands, the idea of formally preserving wilderness also gained popular support (enough to encourage Congress to enact legislation). But mere popularity was nothing compared to the celebrity bestowed on wilderness and the subsequent frenzy of recreational use that occurred after passage of the 1964 Wilderness Act. Nash cites one particularly telling example of the sudden surge in wilderness recreation—the number of boaters on the Grand Canyon of the Colorado. From 1869, when John Wesley Powell became the first to negotiate the canyon until (and including) 1964, some 1,521 people had run the river. Then 1,614 people floated it in the next two years. By 1972, the tally of Grand Canyon river runners had risen to more than 16,000 people each year.

Other natural areas similarly went from obscurity to overuse in less than a decade. Trails turned to trenches, campsites widened and proliferated, litter and human waste cropped up around every bend in the trail, on the shores of every pretty lake, and in the foreground of every scenic view. The "outstanding opportunities for solitude" heralded by the Wilderness Act were increasingly difficult to find. Don Pfitzer, a retired Assistant Director for the Southeast Region of the U. S. Fish and Wildlife Service recalls, "When I first hiked on the Appalachian Trail, in 1950, I traveled seventy-seven miles through the Great Smoky Mountains and saw only one other person." By the early 1970s, the trail had become what Pfitzer calls "a buffalo road," a wide, desolate ribbon of dirt, exposed bedrock, and boot prints. Indeed, according to an article in *Backpacker* magazine in 1973, a survey of Appalachian Trail use found that hikers passed the survey point on an average of once every twenty seconds, "more frequently than people pass the door of my apartment building on the corner of 96th Street and West End Avenue in New York City," lamented the article's author.

Because the growth in outdoor recreation came so abruptly, its effect on the landscape was immediately obvious. At first, land managers responded, where legally and fiscally feasible, by "hardening" heavily used sites—laying gravel (or even asphalt) on eroded trails, building bridges and boardwalks over boggy terrain, and providing hitch rails, fire grills, raised tent pads, and out houses at backcountry campsites.

But these "improvements" produced two decidedly unwanted side-effects. In once wild or unspoiled areas, they greatly reduced the place's naturalness and the visitor's sense of wilderness. And perhaps more worrisome, adding facilities to a site tended to attract even more people. Hardened sites, too, could be overwhelmed.

There were two components of the problem facing land managers: the land itself, and the people crowding onto it. In most cases, changing the land did not remedy overcrowding and consequent damage. Gradually, researchers and managers began to focus instead on changing the behavior of backcountry visitors. They soon came to realize that, in the words of Roderick Nash, "wilderness management is largely people management."

FROM SLOGANS TO ETHICS

Initial attempts at managing recreational visitors reflected a lack of knowledge about how and why people recreate, and about the landscape's response to various levels of use. The late 1960s and 1970s brought a spate of broad (and often conflicting or largely unenforceable) regulations to the backcountry. In many areas, permits were required for overnight stays, and campers were directed to designated campsites. In others, rangers tried to disperse use, establishing quota systems for their trails. Especially hard-hit places were closed to use or restricted to day-use only. Campfires were banned where the forest had been picked clean of fuel. And backcountry rangers began to preach a litany of hopeful slogans: Leave only footprints, take only photographs; Give a hoot, don't pollute; Tread lightly.

With hindsight, these actions and slogans may seem too simplistic or vague to have been effective, but they served well as a starting point. They came during a decade of growing grass-roots awareness and activism regarding air and water pollution, urbanization, and other widespread environmental problems. In general, the public was receptive to calls for more responsible behavior in the backcountry. That call had already been issued, and not merely in a slogan campaign. In 1968 Oxford University Press reprinted a paperback edition of Aldo Leopold's 1949 classic, *A Sand County Almanac*, in which Leopold lobbied for the creation of a "land ethic," an extension of morals from the social arena to the relationship

9

between people and nature. Leopold also appealed to "scholars" and experts to flesh out the details of the land ethic and teach it to others. Throughout the 1970s and 1980s, and still to this day, land managers, research scientists, park rangers, guides, and ardent recreationists have taken this call to heart.

The early codes of backcountry behavior focused mainly on pollution and harm done to the land. Guidelines addressed only the most blatant problems: erosion due to trampling, litter, careless use of fire, and improper disposal of human waste. Backcountry travelers were encouraged to stay on established trails; to heed the edict of "pack it in, pack it out"; to douse and stir fires until cold, and to bury all human waste. Setbacks from lakes and streams were recommended for campsites and waste disposal, but distances varied—anywhere from fifty to two hundred feet. Little or no management was directed at social impacts, other than to relieve serious overcrowding through quotas or permit systems. Many issues that are important today, such as the introduction of new and undesirable plant species, the visual impact of brightly colored tents and packs, and marking or blazing of unofficial cross-country routes, went largely unrecognized just fifteen years ago.

During this period, people striving for ethical behavior in the outdoors had to rely upon a seat-of-the-pants willingness to improvise. Situations frequently arose that were not covered by the known rules. Campers wondered, "How can I minimize trampling damage when hiking where there are no trails? When is building a campfire ill-advised? How should human waste be disposed of when snow or ice covers the ground?" Large gaps remained in nearly everyone's knowledge of how to reduce impacts, or even what qualified as an impact. But the vast majority of backcountry recreationists demonstrated, from the outset, an eagerness to learn.

THE LEAVE-NO-TRACE ETHIC IS BORN

Lighter tents, smaller and more efficient cookstoves, and better boots and packs encouraged many folks to voluntarily move away from some of the more detrimental "traditional" camping practices. Sewn-in waterproof tent floors (and a little common sense in tent placement) eliminated the need to trench around a tent site. Backpackers quickly discovered the many benefits of using a lightweight stove rather than cooking over an open fire, and the once compulsory campfire became a luxury, or a chore that was best left undone.

Another motivating force—the need to preserve dwindling access to recreational opportunities—began to inspire many special interest groups to higher standards of backcountry behavior. Backpackers and packstock users found that a more careful, responsible approach was required in national parks and designated wilderness areas, where the agencies were mandated to preserve each unimpaired area in its natural condition. If recreationists didn't police themselves, government agencies could regulate, restrict, or prohibit certain activities or types of backcountry use. Today, regional and national organizations, such as the American Hiking

Association, Back Country Horsemen of America, Ducks Unlimited, International Mountain Bicycling Association, the Sierra Club, Tread Lightly! (for motorized off-highway vehicle users), and others, funnel much of their funds and energies into preserving public lands and protecting access for their members by promoting low-impact and leave-no-trace behavior (see Sources on page 181). In some cases, this has been an uphill battle; adherents to some forms of "traditional" recreation are often reluctant to admit that their practices may be outdated in an age of increasing backcountry use. Vestiges of pioneer attitudes—or perhaps shadows from even earlier times—still show in some campers' habits of building windbreaks around tents, using large rocks to reflect heat from a fire, and carving blazes or initials into trees and landmarks. Even the rangers and land managers charged with protecting the resource find that old habits die hard—using nails to mount signs on trees, for instance. These practices may have had an inconsequential effect on the vast wilderness of our first twenty million years on this planet, but such behavior is simply inappropriate in today's overpopulated wilderness.

Federal agencies, particularly the Forest Service, have taken the lead in researching the range of impacts, monitoring backcountry use and how it affects the land, its inhabitants, and the recreational experience of others. Thus armed with a better understanding of the problems, and drawing on information from ongoing field experiments, Forest Service researchers (in cooperation with other federal agencies and the National Outdoor Leadership School) have developed the Leave-No-Trace Ethic—a set of eight general but widely applicable principles (backed up by detailed rationales and instructions) for eliminating or reducing the unwanted physical, biological, and social side effects of backcountry recreation. The next three chapters of *Wild Country Companion* are devoted to the theory and practice of leaving no trace, and the eight principles are more thoroughly presented there (see page 17).

Within the framework of these eight principles, the experts now advocate a host of specific no-trace techniques and practices. These, too, are described in detail in the following chapters. Suffice to say here that the recommended techniques cover nearly every conceivable activity and circumstance that can be encountered in the backcountry. Certainly, some of the details and actual no-trace techniques will continue to evolve as new information pours in, and as recreation trends shift and priorities change. But a workable ethic is available today for all recreationists.

THE FUTURE

As we enter the twenty-first century, many challenges—some familiar and others new—still face managers and recreationists. For now, at least, the crescendo in outdoor recreation has quieted down. Overall, the number of people engaging in backcountry recreation stabilized during the late 1980s, albeit at higher levels than ever seen in our history. Conversely, new forms of recreation (mountain biking, for example) continue to spur growth. Any respite from the ever-rising tide of hikers, horsepackers, and other traditional pursuits may be offset by new kinds of impacts as the types of backcountry use grow more diverse.

Few people anticipated the burgeoning popularity of mountain bicycles, heli-skiing and hiking, sea and downriver kayaking, or packing in with llamas and goats. (No kidding...by 1990, fully fifty-seven percent of all designated wilderness areas where packstock were used saw some llamas on the trails. And at least one outfitter uses goats to pack in his clients' gear.) Unfortunately, the sheer diversity in types of recreation is generating new and more frequent conflicts among backcountry users. In some places, acts of intolerance and even violence on the trails are grabbing headlines and overshadowing other important impacts to the land and wildlife.

Winter recreation is also on the rise, made more safe and comfortable due to recent innovations in synthetic fabrics and equipment design. Winter is no longer the off-season, even in places with relatively harsh climates. On New Year's Day 1994, the Associated Press reported that national park officials in Yellowstone were considering limits on the number of winter visitors allowed in the park. In just two years, winter use (predominantly snowmobilers) in the park had increased twenty percent, exceeding levels park managers had not expected to see for another eight years. As visitation increases during this historically low-use season, new impacts may emerge, particularly regarding disturbance to other recreationists and wildlife.

Another troubling development is the recent backlash in some circles against no-trace and low-impact ethics. In the early 1990s, a rash of articles and letters-to-the-editor blistered the pages of several outdoors magazines, giving voice to the sentiment that the no-trace movement has gotten out of hand. Letter writers often cited specific techniques as impractical or absurdly petty. Some folks, apparently, resent being asked to leave toothpaste at home, or to use leaves instead of toilet paper, or to fluff up the grass beneath where they slept. Others are simply tired of Woodsy Owl pointing his feathery finger from trailhead posters, and are weary of the blizzard of pamphlets enumerating no-trace do's and don'ts. At best, the no-trace message is so familiar that many of us tune it out—or mutter oaths of rebellion under our breath—even as we practice what is preached to us. But at its worst, the message rains down like a guilt-laden sermon.

The arguments against the more painstaking no-trace recommendations frequently hinge on the notion that recreational damage is minor or temporary when compared to the effects of mining or logging, and that we should be more tolerant of our own impacts. Footprints, after all, along with human waste and even the charcoal remnants of a campfire, are to some extent "natural" because humans are as much a part of nature as they are distinct from it. Besides, animal tracks, scat, and fire all occur naturally—that is, in the absence of humans. And certainly, some no-trace practices can be carried too far. Toothpaste, for example, is blacklisted in the backcountry by at least one no-trace expert, but a more reasonable (yet still effective) approach would be to use as little toothpaste as possible. Residue can be spat into a scuff made with your heel in the duff (well away from camp so as not to attract animals), and covered. Some experts suggest using baking soda instead of commercial toothpaste, or scattering the froth over a wide area by pressing tongue against teeth (say "the") while spitting. In small amounts, toothpaste can simply be swallowed after brushing. These options, clearly, are preferable to risking infections, gum disease, and halitosis (which, on the plus side, can greatly expand your opportunities for solitude), especially on prolonged expeditions.

Yet if we have learned anything from our relatively brief and sudden infatuation with wild-land recreation and managing its uglier side effects, we should know that it's easier to prevent impacts than to heal the scars, no matter how subtle they may be. Whenever possible, trade-offs between reducing impacts and enhancing comfort or convenience should be resolved in favor of sustaining the beauty and biological integrity of the land and its inhabitants. Even when brushing our teeth.

How do we cope with this roster of dilemmas, and new ones sure to unfold? Some answers can be found in this book. The eight principles of leaving no trace offer broad but useful guidelines for making ethical choices in the backcountry. These principles are reinforced by detailed, field-tested no-trace techniques devised to address the full range of environments and today's recreational activities.

Wild Country Companion also encourages the spirit of cooperation and voluntary compliance exhibited by most outdoor enthusiasts. More and more people are recognizing that the surest way to sustain the land and the recreational opportunities it affords is through self-restraint. In response, administrators and backcountry rangers are relying less on regulations and more on education and friendly guidance. At Grand Teton National Park, for example, rather than limiting campers to specific, designated campsites throughout the park, park managers have delineated zones where campers are essentially free to pitch a tent in any spot as long as it's one hundred feet from lakes and streams and out of sight from trails and other campers. Where previously used campsites exist, visitors are encouraged to use them, but in many of the Teton's trackless canyons and high basins, backcountry travelers enjoy a genuine sense of freedom in selecting a campsite. Even fewer restrictions greet visitors to the remote and wild north end of the park, where more difficult access has held visitor use to extremely low levels. In exchange for these freedoms, most folks are more than willing to accept the park's ban on backcountry campfires.

Also, building tolerance among different types of recreationists will continue to be an important job for all concerned in the advancement of no-trace ethics. But tolerance will be cultivated only if we acknowledge the historical depth and breadth of our heritage as devotees of wild land recreation, and find room—both on public lands and in our minds—for recreational pursuits and ethical concerns different from our own. If campfires, as a hypothetical example, are eventually banned as a rule rather than the exception, then perhaps some places ought to be set aside (and managed) as campfire zones, where people so inclined could still enjoy that most ancient of rites. Can any of us actually look forward to a day when the pleasures of a campfire would pass forever out of the realm of human experience? Management options are available, as shown again by Grand Teton National Park, where backcountry campfires are prohibited, yet thousands of campers each year savor the scent of wood smoke—at one of five front-country campgrounds.

Finally, the future holds hope, because this newly fledged land ethic, the leave-no-trace concept, has already shown such a tremendous propensity for growth and improvement. We should congratulate ourselves for having come so far in such a relatively short period of time. New dilemmas will undoubtedly confront tomorrow's backcountry traveler. But just as assuredly there will be new answers, fresh ideas, and a renewed respect for wild country wherever people have learned to leave no trace.

LEAVE NO TRACE:
ETHICS OR ETHOS?

> *Barring love and war, few enterprises are undertaken with*
> *such abandon, or by such diverse individuals, or with so*
> *paradoxical a mixture of appetite and altruism, as that group*
> *of avocations known as outdoor recreation. It is, by common*
> *consent, a good thing for people to get back to nature.*
> *But wherein lies the goodness, and what can be done to*
> *encourage its pursuit?*
>
> —Aldo Leopold, *A Sand County Almanac*

An ethic, according to *Webster's*, is a "group of moral principles or set of values." The definition also mentions "standards of behavior." The leave-no-trace ethic, as it is widely preached, fits well into this definition. In fact, later in this chapter we list eight principles, every one intended as a standard of no-trace behavior. Borrowing Leopold's terms, an ethic could be defined as the systematic pursuit of goodness, and *Wild Country Companion* offers just such a system. But what Leopold was really looking for was an *ethos*, "the spirit that motivates the ideas, customs, or practices of a people" (*Webster's* again). If ethics is helping a little old lady across the street, then ethos is the spirit—the compassion—that made you offer to help in the first place. But what spirit motivates people to practice the art of leaving no trace?

THE ETHOS

When people travel and camp in the backcountry, they leave a mark on their surroundings. It simply can't be avoided. Even the most careful and skilled no-trace traveler will leave footprints, a urine sample, perhaps the memory of a chance meeting with another party in an otherwise vast solitude. Many of these traces are subtle and relatively harmless; a footprint, after all, testifies simply that we exist, that a bipedal animal once walked here. But stamp a hundred footprints a day into the same alpine meadow and a path appears. Snowmelt and runoff chew the path into a trench, and the next wave of hikers takes two steps over to avoid the rut. A second, parallel path appears, and the cycle repeats until there's more dirt than meadow. Unfortunately, a century or more may pass before the meadow can reclaim these barren trenches, even if the area is closed to all use.

Of course, no one sets out to trash a meadow. As individuals, we seek out lupine-filled meadows, lakes full of fish, grand vistas, and solitude because we cherish and enjoy these things. Call it what you will—primal urge, aesthetic renewal, escape from civilization, recreation. The need for—and love of—nature is the root of our ethos, and it's as built-in as thirst or hunger.

But problems arise when the need overwhelms the supply, when many people are drawn to the same place. If an area is particularly fragile, the effects begin to show even with low use. In one study of extremely delicate desert soils, the passage of five hikers created an obvious disturbance; as few as fifteen hikers left a well-defined trail.

Footprints aren't the only concern. By now, the litany of problems created by heavy use in the backcountry is familiar to most of us: trampled plants and soil, erosion, axe-bitten trees, litter, a glut of fire rings, a lack of solitude, and water contaminated with disease organisms from human waste. These effects can be broken down into three categories:

- Physical—changes to the landscape and soil
- Biological—disturbance of wildlife and plants
- Social—intrusion on other people

Many actions have a ripple effect that extends across categories. A large group latrine, for example, overloads the soil's ability to compost waste, may attract wildlife, and, if uncovered by wildlife, presents an eyesore and health risk to the next camper. Throughout the next chapter we will examine ways to reduce or eliminate unwanted effects in all three categories.

In high-use areas, some of these problems have overwhelmed the land's ability to tolerate or recover from any additional damage, forcing land managers to regulate and restrict recreational use. Backcountry use permits are required at most national parks, and many allow camping only in designated sites. Campfires are prohibited in most alpine areas, and packstock and off-road bicycles are often restricted to certain trails. Managers of popular wilderness areas, notably in California and in the East, are increasingly following the parks' example. Truth be told, there are few places remaining in North America where outdoor recreation and access are not regulated to some degree, and the reason is that no place is safe from overuse.

Faced with tighter regulations, restricted access, and—in severe cases—outright calls for area closures, backcountry travelers have seen the writing on the wall. The wilderness is being loved to death. As people who cherish wild country, we bear the responsibility for its preservation. And we are bound by our ethos—by our need for wild country to roam in—to the pursuit of goodness Aldo Leopold wrote of.

THE ETHIC

Leopold also penned a concise definition of backcountry ethics, included in *A Sand County Almanac*. "A thing is right when it tends to preserve the integrity, stability, and beauty of the biotic community. It is wrong when it tends otherwise."

That's a good start, and it serves our purposes well, particularly if we remember that *Homo sapiens* are very much a part of that biotic community. To a large degree, learning to leave no trace is about preserving our own integrity, stability, and beauty, as individuals and as a society. But we need to add a corollary to Leopold's ethic: "In the field, the choice between right and wrong is not always clear." For these difficult choices, we need some guidelines, a simple code of behavior to preserve the land, our freedoms, and our recreational opportunities.

EIGHT PRINCIPLES OF BACKCOUNTRY BEHAVIOR

David Cole, scientist at the Aldo Leopold Wilderness Research Institute in Missoula, Montana, gives seven broad principles for leaving no trace while traveling and camping in the backcountry. We've added an eighth principle—Plan, prepare, prevent—to the front of the list.

The first five principles are universal—that is, they apply to all surroundings, from desert to mountaintop, and to all circumstances. For example, no matter where you travel it's best to pack out what you pack in (principle number 3), garbage and apple cores included. The last three principles are more specific; they also compel us to assess our surroundings and make choices. We'll look at those guidelines in greater detail.

1. **Plan ahead, prepare well, prevent problems before they occur.**
2. **Keep noise to a minimum and strive to be inconspicuous.**
3. **Pack it in, pack it out.**
4. **Properly dispose of anything that can't be packed out.**
5. **Leave the land as you found it.**
6. **In popular places, concentrate use.**
7. **In pristine places, disperse use.**
8. **Avoid places that are lightly worn or just beginning to show signs of use.**

(Adapted from "Seven Principles of Low-impact Wilderness Recreation," by David N. Cole and Edwin E. Krumpe, in *Western Wildlands*, Spring 1992, and *Leave No Trace: Outdoor Skills and Ethics*, a booklet produced and distributed by the National Outdoor Leadership School.)

These eight guidelines are the main themes of Chapter 3, which describes hands-on techniques for leaving no trace. They crop up on every page and reinforce the purpose for each technique or action we recommend.

Principles 6, 7, and 8, however, require a bit more explanation. These three principles cover most of the more difficult choices faced by backcountry travelers—what route to follow, where to pitch the tent, how best to dispose of human waste. Implicit in these three principles is the broader rule-of-thumb: *tailor your actions to suit your surroundings*. The flip side is also true: *choose surroundings that are appropriate for the type of recreation you intend to engage in*. Many of the finer details of no-trace techniques will fall into place if you keep these ideas in mind and understand how to apply them.

But how do you distinguish a "popular" place from a "pristine" one, and what about the range of conditions in between? First off, think about the region or area you are in: is it a well-used trail corridor in Yellowstone National Park, or are you wandering the trackless tundra and barren ridges of the Arctic coastal plain? These are examples of either extreme, and, in such cases, it is relatively easy to tell the difference based on two key factors.

In heavily visited (popular) areas, you would not be surprised to (1) see other people and (2) find evidence of previous use (well-worn trails and campsites). Generally, if an area is accessible by an official trail, it should be considered "popular." Conversely, in remote or pristine areas, you (1) would be surprised to see other people (although it's growing ever more difficult to completely escape the madding crowd), and (2) there should be little evidence—but perhaps some—of previous use. Obvious trails and discernible campsites should be absent or very rare.

In truth, however, most of the landscape falls somewhere in between or is a mosaic of popular, pristine, and in between. For example, away from the trails, much of Yellowstone's backcountry appears untouched, and human intruders are rare. Yet even the vast, empty Arctic has its busy travel corridors—particularly along rivers. As you travel the gamut of backcountry environs, rely on your best judgment and bear in mind the two key factors: the likelihood of meeting other people, and evidence of previous use.

Once you have determined whether the area is popular or pristine, you can readily decide where the best no-trace routes and campsites are found. In popular areas stay on trails and camp in well-worn, previously used sites. Here, it is particularly important to stay off pristine or previously unused sites because other visitors may follow in your footsteps. In this way damage from overuse proliferates.

A popular site shows signs of heavy use:

- You would not be surprised to see other people.
- Plants are trampled and soil on trails and in campsites is bare and packed down.
- One or more fire rings may be present.
- Use-created side trails radiate out from campsite.
- Trees around campsite may appear thinned out compared to surrounding forest; nails, girdling, and axe scars are often obvious.
- Campsite fixtures, such as log benches, firewood, or hitching rails, may remain from previous users.

A pristine site shows no signs of previous use:

- You would be very surprised to see other people.
- There are no visible worn spots—trails or campsites—on the ground. Plant cover is uniform, not visibly different from surrounding natural landscape.
- No blazes or cairns mark route or location of campsite.
- No saw or axe cuts are evident on live or downed wood.
- There are no human tracks, litter, or sign or scat from packstock.

Sites between the two extremes show signs of light to moderate use:

◆ Ground plants flattened, broken, or thinned out from trampling. Some bare soil may show.
◆ Trail, tent site, or fire pit may be visible; these features stand out against the surrounding natural background.
◆ A fire ring may or may not be present.
◆ Lower branches may be missing from trees; saw or axe cuts may show on trunks.

BASIC BEHAVIOR—IN PLACES POPULAR, PRISTINE, OR IN BETWEEN

Experience and practice will help you discern pristine and popular sites, and to recognize early signs of wear and tear in places just beginning to show signs of use. With an accurate assessment of your surroundings, you can choose the appropriate course of action with confidence, whether it be selecting a route or campsite, building a campfire or doing without, or dealing with human waste. A few pointers here might be helpful.

In popular places, concentrate use.

The main objective in popular areas is to confine activities and use to areas already damaged by previous use.

◆ Stay on established trails.
◆ Use existing campsites well away from water, trails, and other campers.
◆ Use existing fire rings, but build fires only if downed wood is abundant.
◆ Pack out all human waste or deposit it in cat holes at least two hundred feet from surface water and in spots unlikely to be used by others.
◆ Leave a clean camp so others will also use it and not be tempted to create a new site.

In pristine places, disperse use.

The main objective in pristine areas is to minimize trampling and other damage by spreading use over a wide area or by seeking out durable surfaces.

◆ Keep group size small; two to six people is best, no more than ten (use extra care to minimize impact).
◆ When traveling off-trail, spread out so that no one follows in another's footsteps. Or follow routes on durable surfaces such as sand, gravel, slickrock, or snow. Avoid steep slopes.
◆ Camp on durable surfaces or in areas with trample-resistant plants such as dry meadows.
◆ Move camp frequently, once a day if possible. Avoid walking repeatedly over the same terrain.
◆ Refrain from building fires. If one is necessary, use a fire pan or build a mound fire (see page 41).
◆ Pack out all human waste whenever possible. In remote regions, use a stick to smear human waste on the surface of the ground in an out-of-the-way spot (far from camp and water) and sprinkle it with dirt. If human discovery is likely, use a cat hole.
◆ Leave no trace of your stay when breaking camp. Fluff up flattened grass, cover bare areas with leaves and twigs, and pick up all litter.

Avoid places that are lightly worn or just beginning to show signs of use.

The main objectives in places just beginning to show wear are to avoid adding to the damage already done and to allow the site to recover.

◆ Stay off unofficial trails or paths that are indistinct or partly vegetated.
◆ Seek out well-worn campsites or previously unused sites on durable surfaces.
◆ To discourage others from using lightly worn campsites, dismantle any fire rings, wood piles, or other structures, and camouflage the area as you would a pristine campsite.

One final guideline, which overrides all others: where an agency or land owner has established rules and regulations, know and obey them. Rules would seem to be the antithesis of recreation, but every game—even hopscotch—has them. Their purpose is not to punish, but to preserve an equitable opportunity for all to participate. It may sound strange to talk of backcountry recreation as a "game," but hiking, trail riding, boating, and camping are most certainly forms of play. And the analogy serves well in light of the maxim, "it's not whether you win or lose, but how you play the game."

New York Times columnist Anna Quindlen has taken the old saw one step further, and the result works as well for leaving no trace as it does for a set of tennis or nine innings of baseball. "It's not even how you play the game," she writes. "It's how you value yourself when the game is over."

LEAVE NO TRACE: TECHNIQUES

"Theory informs, practice convinces."
—George Bane, *Celtic Art: The Methods*

This chapter presents the nuts and bolts of the leave-no-trace approach. Actually, leaving no trace has more to do with a lack of nuts and bolts—the emphasis here is more often on what to leave behind, how to do without. Many backcountry travelers are surprised to learn, after trying out these skills, that life in the backcountry is more simplified than before. There's less clutter (no axe, no soap, less trash), fewer actual chores, and with practice the new routines become automatic.

Remember that the procedures and skills suggested here are based on common sense as well as field research. They require no real sacrifice of comfort or convenience, but neither are they watered-down versions of some higher code of ethics. Instead, we've tried to offer a range of options whenever possible to help you cope with a myriad of natural environments, special situations, and unique challenges.

The range of options also gives each person the freedom to choose a method or style that appeals to his or her sense of backcountry behavior. If some of these techniques sound trivial, tedious, or unreasonable, then weigh the other options given. Also strive to match your chosen destination with your level of no-trace ambition for any given outing. In the mood for a campfire every night? Make sure the area you're going to has ample firewood and no prohibition on burning. Conversely, a willingness to do without a fire opens up a wider range of possible destinations.

Still skeptical? Consider making a trial run to find out whether an idea is as effective (or as bothersome) as it sounds on paper. Plan a low-mileage overnighter or day trip. Wait for good weather, and pick a familiar destination—a favorite backcountry lake or that box canyon unknown to the rest of the world. Then give some of the ideas here a try. Plan a no-cook menu, and leave your stove at the bottom of your pack. Go a night without a campfire. Use leaves instead of toilet paper. Wear a pair of comfortable running shoes instead of the old boots. But be careful. A lighter pack, fewer chores around camp, a sense of satisfaction upon leaving a clean camp...this could be habit forming!

We encourage careful tinkering, too. With a little forethought and a trial run or two, most of the suggested techniques can easily be customized. A better way to hang food in bear country? A soft, sturdy natural alternative to toilet paper? If you figure out a better way to leave no trace, write to us and tell us the details. We'll pass along any good ideas in the next edition of this book. Send your ideas to *Wild Country Companion*, Falcon Press, P.O. Box 1718, Helena, MT 59624.

TRIP PLANNING

For most of us, planning a backcountry trip is an enjoyable process, a heightening of anticipation before the appointed day. We pore over maps, air out the tent, and stomp around the house in old, worn-out hiking shoes "to break them in." These rituals, as fun as they are, are also fundamental to the success of any outing, whether you measure success on a scale of fun, adventure, destination, safety, or leaving no trace—or all of the above. To get the most out of planning, begin each trip by following the credo, "Plan, prepare, prevent."

Plan Ahead

The first step on most backcountry journeys is deciding when and where to go. In today's Information Age, there's no shortage of facts and advice. Read books and magazines, look at maps, and talk to friends, local outdoor enthusiasts, and land managers. When you've narrowed down the selection some, sit back and consider the following factors.

◆ Most backcountry use occurs in the summer and fall. Trails and campsites are busiest on weekends and holidays. Also, eighty percent of wildland recreational use is concentrated on just twenty percent of the land. These facts have prompted some land managers to distribute use by steering visitors to less popular trails and publicizing an area's off-season charms. But this tends merely to broaden the effects of overcrowding, disturbing areas (and wildlife and other recreationists) that were once largely left alone.

Wilderness researcher David Cole prefers to let people choose to go where and when they want. "The point is there is a range of opportunities out there. If people want to visit a popular area, that doesn't make them less environmentally sensitive. And no extra status should be accorded to those who prefer pristine places." Cole believes that "what's important is that visitors know what methods and behaviors work best for the conditions they encounter—how to select a campsite, for example. How and where you camp in a pristine area is very different from camping in a heavily used area."

It's best to consider what your goals are for each outing, and choose an area and time well-suited to those goals. If solitude is important, plan to go during midweek or during a less popular season, and seek out a less heavily used area. Realize, however, that low-use areas and times are attractive to other people, most of whom value solitude. Aim to keep a low profile.

◆ Avoid backcountry travel when trails and soils are wet (during spring snowmelt or prolonged rain storms) and when wildlife is more sensitive to disturbance (during nesting or calving seasons, and generally in winter). Some animals rely on specific seasonal feeding areas as well—bears feast in huckleberry thickets in the fall, for example. Take the time to learn about such animal-food relationships, and try to avoid disrupting them when in the backcountry.

◆ Consider local variations. In the mountains, snowmelt comes later in the spring at higher elevations; the high pass that beckons from the map may be closed by snow or knee-deep in mud. Better to choose a low-elevation hike, perhaps along a south-facing mountain flank where conditions are likely drier. In another instance, a sparsely used wilderness may harbor one prolific fishing lake that is popular with the locals and hence heavily used. Would a less popular lake offer a better destination? Also be alert for special hunting seasons, trails restricted to certain types of backcountry use, and scheduled group events (such as scout jamborees; skiing, running, or cycling races; packstock rendezvous; and the moveable feast known as Spring Break). Choose areas and trails specifically suited to your type of use, and try to avoid places and times where conflicts between different types of backcountry users may arise.

◆ Limit group size. Smaller groups lend themselves to greater flexibility in route choice, campsite selection, and on-the-spot problem solving. Two to six people is best; no more than ten. There is some evidence suggesting that groups of four or six are safer when traveling in grizzly bear country. Large groups should make an extra effort to leave no trace of their passing. Keep packstock to a minimum.

The key to good planning lies in knowing what to expect. The more you know about a place, the better you'll be able to respond to challenges as they arise, and to leave no trace of your visit.

Prepare Well

With the proper equipment, appropriate clothing and shelter, and adequate food, you can relax and enjoy the trip. Well-prepared travelers also do less harm to the land. For example, if wet weather is unavoidable, waterproof your boots and pack a pair of gaiters so you won't be tempted to step off-trail when the going gets muddy. Also carry a storm-proof shelter and good rain gear to avert the need for an emergency campfire. Of course, what's "appropriate" varies with time of year, weather, expected terrain, duration of the trip, and mode of travel. When in doubt, ask for advice from a local land manager or sporting goods store.

Backcountry travelers should also strive to remain inconspicuous to others. Wear muted, earth-tone colors (except during hunting season). Browns, dull greens and blues, and black blend in well with most natural surroundings. Try to purchase tents and backpacks in these same hues. Outdoor clothing and equipment manufacturers are getting better at offering a range of natural colors to choose from, but we can all use consumer pressure to further encourage this trend.

Make up a checklist of essential items for backcountry travel and refer to it before each trip. Many trail guidebooks and backcountry how-to manuals provide detailed checklists for camping gear, safety and first aid kits, and special equipment needs for travel by packstock, mountain bicycles, boats, and skis. Glean from these lists what you need, and add any other items you find useful. Leave-no-trace techniques don't require any special tools, but two items do come in handy: a small trowel for digging cat holes and, when necessary, fire pits; and a couple of plastic bags for packing out garbage. If you repack all food in plastic bags, you can use these for garbage bags as the food is eaten.

Finally, make sure your equipment is in good working condition and all the parts are in place before you leave. For extended expeditions, carry an extra stove or spare repair parts to avoid cooking over a fire out of necessity. A small sewing kit (two needles and a skein of heavy-duty thread) also comes in handy. Duct tape is unsurpassed for versatility in making temporary repairs, limited only by your imagination. Many veteran canoeists, kayakers, and rafters won't leave home without it. Use duct tape to seal the rip in a raincoat, splice a broken tent pole, or patch a canoe hull. Legend has it that one cross-country skier, after losing a ski binding deep in Yellowstone's wild northwest corner, was able to fashion a serviceable emergency binding by wrapping duct tape around his boot toe and the ski.

Prevent Problems Before They Occur

An ounce of prevention is worth even more than the proverbial pound of cure if you have to carry that extra pound on your conscience. It's much easier to prevent damage to the land and its inhabitants than it is to fix the problem after the fact. Here's a handful of easy precautions everyone should take before setting out.

◆ Call or write to the land manager. Ask about any special regulations, permits, or fees. Find out if there are recommended no-trace measures unique to that area.
◆ Check the weather forecast. Pack, or change travel plans, accordingly.
◆ Calculate and pre-pack the amount of food needed for each person. This keeps mealtime leftovers—an unpleasant item to pack out—to a minimum. Repackage food into plastic bags to cut down on excess trash (and weight). Wire twisties work great for keeping bags closed, but nearly every campsite houses its own twistie museum, with a permanent collection on display. Try not to lose twisties, or better yet, use zippered plastic bags or simply tie the open end in a knot. When traveling with packstock, determine how much feed to carry for each animal.
◆ Do a quick inventory for unnecessary weight. Some items are best left at home: bottles and cans; axes and saws; guns; radios and cassette tape or CD players; wire; nails; and pets. Many areas prohibit pets in the backcountry; most recreation areas discourage them. Where dogs are allowed, and you choose to bring one along, use a leash or have one handy, and keep the dog under control at all times. Remember that other people and wildlife may mistake Fido's exuberance for aggression.

At times, exceptions to this list are wise. Some states require packstock users to carry a shovel and bucket when traveling in the backcountry during wildfire season. And an axe or saw comes in handy to clear downfall from the trail, preventing the need to detour packstock around the obstacle, creating another trail.

In short, proper planning and preparation can help prevent a whole host of problems in the backcountry. And today's high-tech equipment—free-standing tents, efficient cookstoves, water filters—makes it easier than ever to leave no trace. Remember that each outing offers a range of opportunities—a wide array of destinations, route choices, modes of travel, levels of interaction with other people, and recreational activities. Strive to tailor your actions to fit your surroundings.

SELECTING FOOTWEAR

The most widespread type of damage caused by recreational use is trampling. Wherever our feet (or wheels, or Ol' Paint's hooves) touch the ground, we leave a smudge or scrape, sometimes worse. Plants are crushed and soil is roughed up, left vulnerable to erosion. Stride after stride, it adds up. Back in 1977 Dr. William Harlow scraped up the soil left standing on the trail in a single print from a traditional lug-soled boot. He dried it in the sun and weighed it—a total of slightly more than one ounce. Assuming an average stride of 2.5 feet, Dr. Harlow calculated that a single hiker walking one mile would raise about 120 pounds of topsoil.

Dr. Harlow's experiment may not represent typical trail conditions, but it does provide a dramatic explanation for the trenches that pass for trails in some of our more heavily used recreational areas. Thankfully, there's a relatively easy way to reduce the effects of trampling and soil disturbance: pay heed to what you wear on your feet.

What To Wear

For general, all-terrain hiking try a pair of running shoes. They're lightweight, which lessens fatigue, and they dry out more quickly than full-grain leather boots. Look for a design with good cushioning and support around the ankle to protect against twists and bruises when carrying a pack or crossing rocky ground. Several brands and models are made specifically for trail running, with narrower outer soles (the flared heel area on some road shoes tends to catch on rocks and roots, twisting ankles) and waterproof uppers. Cross-training athletic shoes also work well.

Many of the features that make running shoes well-suited for hiking have been incorporated into a new generation of lightweight hiking boots. Uppers of reinforced nylon mesh, removable sock liners, and flexible soles all contribute to increased comfort and performance over traditional stiff, heavy leather boots. The new boots also are gentler on the land, thanks to shallower tread patterns.

Features to look for in a good pair of lightweight hiking boots:

◆ A comfortable fit right off the shelf. The sole should flex across the ball of the foot, letting your toes bend as they push off for the next stride. Removable inner soles allow custom-fitting with thicker or thinner inner soles. And soggy boots dry out quicker with inner soles removed.

◆ Waterproof or water repellent uppers. Most lightweight boots are made from treated leather or sandwiches of synthetic fabrics with leather covering stress points, toes, and ankles. Be aware that sueded leather absorbs dirt and moisture more quickly than smooth grain leather.

◆ An outer sole of "tacky" rubber. The outer sole should have a satiny or matte finish, not slick and shiny. The tackiness provides better grip and traction on rocks, logs, and other hard surfaces. A shallow tread design won't clog with mud and debris and does far less damage to trails and plants than the old tractor-lugged soles.

◆ Stiff, padded ankle support. A reinforced heel cup with padding around the ankle and Achilles tendon helps prevent twists, sprains, and bruises when carrying heavy loads or scrambling on talus and broken rock.

Be Good to Your Shoes

Once you've invested in a good pair of boots, take proper care of them. Keep them clean, and dry them away from high heat or flames. Waterproof your boots (as needed), wear gaiters, and pack extra socks as incentives to stay on the trail even when it's muddy. Follow shoe manufacturer's instructions when selecting which waterproofing treatment to use. Generally, use a silicone-based dressing on silicone-impregnated leather. Silicone also works well on nylon uppers. Wax-based dressings are best on chrome-tanned leather. Avoid neatsfoot and mink oils; they soften leather and do little to guard against water. When traveling in wet climates (northwest coastal forests, southern swamps, northern tundra), consider wearing neoprene socks or waterproof boot liners to keep feet dry, or at least warm. If your boots came with cotton laces, replace them with synthetic laces. Cotton absorbs water and rots quickly. Always carry extra nylon shoelaces; they also come in handy for replacing worn out gaiter stirrups.

Slip into Something More Comfortable

A good pair of boots can help limit widespread trampling by keeping your feet on the trail despite sloppy conditions and by providing traction without roto-tilling the soil. But even the best no-trace boots can grind down wildflowers and churn up mud when they're planted again and again in the same spot. Such repeat foot traffic is especially heavy in camp—by the tent and around the campfire or cooking area. This problem can be alleviated by following one of the easiest—and most enjoyable—no-trace guidelines: take off those sweaty boots and slip on a pair of camp shoes.

The ideal camp shoe is light weight and soft-soled, a well-worn old friend that feels like a bedroom slipper after a day of hard travel. Some campers, not easily embarrassed, actually do wear bedroom slippers. The fleece-lined, leather moccasin style tend to hold up better than fuzzy flip-flops or plush fake-fur bunnies. Running shoes, sport sandals, or canvas boat shoes also work well; they pack easily and can double as wading shoes for stream crossings. Regardless of which style camp shoe you choose, make sure they have a smooth or low-profile outer sole to minimize wear and tear on the ground.

EXOTIC PLANTS

Mention exotic plants and some folks conjure up images of Venus flytraps, banana trees, and coconuts dangling from tall palms. But there's another slant to the term, denoting undesirable or invasive plants. When botanists talk of exotics they mean non-native species, plants that are introduced to an area. If the local climate proves hospitable, exotics often flourish because their new home offers little resistance: local insects and other plant eaters may not be adapted to feeding on the newcomers, and native plants typically are not well-suited to compete against the import's survival strategies. This is especially true wherever native plants are already stressed by trampling, overgrazing, or soil disturbance.

Exotics cause problems because they often out-compete native plant species, thereby changing the natural botanic community. Many exotics also are harmful to wildlife and livestock. In some cases, the plants are not as nutritious as the original forage, while others are actually toxic. Some plants are simply inedible, or so alien that browsing animals are ill-adapted to feed on the newcomers. And some, like spotted knapweed, bind up in the gut and strangle the poor beasts' intestines. Land managers spend millions of dollars a year trying to curb the spread of such noxious weeds.

28

Not surprisingly, most exotics are adroit stow aways. Many plants rely on animals to disperse their seeds, and the human animal has often unwittingly ferried a species to new shores. Burrs affix to clothes or hair, seeds sift into pockets or baggage, and whole plants are uprooted and tangled onto car axles or mufflers. Knapweed, for example, spread quickly from the Bitterroot Valley across Montana, but no one knew how until researchers plotted its course on a state map. Fingers of knapweed followed the highway system. Here was a champion hitch-hiker, taking rides on pick-up trucks, hunting rigs, stock trailers, and passenger cars, and most folks probably did not know they had a rider on board. Knapweed has since cropped up throughout the Great Plains and Pacific Northwest. Introduced aquatic plants can also cause trouble, hitching rides on bird's feet and boat propellers.

Unfortunately, limiting the spread of exotics is a difficult task, particularly once the species establishes a stronghold. Land owners and managers often respond to the threat of a weed invasion by restricting or closing access. But this can be prevented if recreationists learn to inspect for exotics on their vehicles, clothes, and packstock. Remember: a single seed can infest a whole new region.

◆ Before leaving home, check your vehicle for hitch-hiking weeds. Look for weeds on axles, bumpers, radiator grills, and tailpipes. Tall weeds are often caught as car doors are closed. At the trailhead, inspect your clothing for burrs and seeds. Look in pant cuffs, pockets, on socks and shoelaces.
◆ Carefully inspect packstock—especially tails, manes, and legs—for burrs and seeds before loading animals into trailers. Feed for packstock should be certified weed-free.
◆ Mountain bicycles can also snag weeds in spokes, chain rings, and sprockets. Keep an eye on those parts for stow-aways.
◆ Inspect boat trailers, hulls, and engines, paddles, and oars for clinging weeds when pulling out of the water.
◆ When eating fruit, vegetables, nuts in their shells, or seeds with husks (e.g., sunflower seeds), stash the pits, cores, rinds, peels, shells, husks and other scraps in a pocket or plastic bag. Pack out all such garbage. In bear country, it's best to keep all foods and garbage out of clothes pockets, so promptly put scraps in a plastic bag and hang it with other food out of a bear's reach.

ROUTE SELECTION

Think of your favorite backcountry spot—that lake full of trout, the view from a high mountain peak, a hot springs deep in the forest. How did you get there? Chances are it was on an established trail. In fact, most backcountry travelers rarely stray far off trails. There's little need to, with nearly 220,000 miles of official trails (and countless miles of user-created paths) threading through the backcountry of North America. Route selection, once a revered skill of scouts and explorers, is no longer a knack for reading a trackless landscape but a matter of reading the trail-head signs.

Some say we've squandered the freedom of the hills in exchange for the security of sidewalks, but from a no-trace perspective, that's actually good news. Trails tend to channel people through well-used corridors, leaving large areas of backcountry relatively untouched. Forest Service researcher Bob Lucas found that in some wilderness areas as much as eighty percent of backcountry use is concentrated on just twenty percent of the area's available trails. In other words, most people not only stick to established trails, but they favor the most well-traveled routes.

Another Forest Service study indicated that, when properly designed and maintained, trails can withstand fairly high levels of use, although localized problems may arise. Spots that are chronically wet or muddy and popular stopping places (at scenic views, for example) will show wear and tear more quickly than other sections of the same trail. And some trails attract so much use that nothing short of bedrock stops the erosion and soil compaction caused by sheer numbers of feet, hooves, and tires.

In Popular Places

The following suggestions will help reduce damage to existing trails, particularly around trouble spots and on heavily used routes.

◆ Avoid travel when trails are saturated with water. Snowmelt, spring runoff, heavy rains, or flooding can turn trails to aqueducts. Plants and the soil itself are most vulnerable to damage when wet. Routes on higher ground and on south-facing slopes tend to be drier than low drainages and north-facing slopes. Ask beforehand about trail conditions and alternative routes. Check the weather forecast.

◆ Stay on the trail. Resist the temptation to side step rocky, snowy, or wet sections, and detour around downed trees or other obstacles only if safety demands it. Horsepackers should carry a small bow saw or axe to clear downed trees that block the trail. Where the trail disappears beneath a snowfield, kick steps into the snow along the route for others to follow; extremely steep snowfields may warrant a detour. Wear snug-fitting gaiters or waterproof boots when wet or muddy conditions are unavoidable. Take the time at the end of your trip to let the land managers know about any trouble spots along the trail.

◆ If the trail becomes too faint to follow, stop and scan ahead for a blaze or other sign of the designated route. If the way ahead is visible, walk directly to it, single-file. When no path is apparent, have the members of the group spread out and seek the most trample-resistant route for the direction you wish to go.

◆ Walk single-file. Walking two abreast widens the tread, trampling plants and breaking down the edge of the trail. In some meadows and alpine areas, parallel trails have needlessly defaced the scene.

◆ Use switchbacks when climbing or descending a slope. On steep slopes, most trails follow an easier grade over a series of switchbacks. In some cases, adjacent paths lead straight up and down the fall line. Many hikers are tempted to scramble the shortest distance from top to bottom, which leads to one of the most common problems on backcountry trails: erosion due to short cuts between switchbacks. The resulting gully is ugly, extremely difficult to repair, and may threaten the stability of the trail. It is especially important to stay on the trail when using switchbacks. Given a choice between switchbacks and a more direct route, always follow the switchbacks.

◆ On busy trails, move well off-trail during rest stops. Look for a place where you will be unseen from the trail or nearby camps. Use established side-trails when possible and choose a durable rest site—a rock outcrop, gravel stream bank, sandy area, or dry meadow. Take care to minimize off-trail trampling.

◆ Respect private property. Ask the landowner for permission before setting out. Leave all fences and gates as found.

In Pristine Places

For more adventurous souls, nothing confirms a sense of wilderness as completely as travel beyond trail's end. But travel here also requires extra precaution and a willingness to tread lightly.

◆ In areas without trails, select routes on durable surfaces. Look for ribbons of bedrock, slickrock, sand, gravel, and snow pack. River banks lined with sand, gravel, or cobble offer good routes in some regions; try to stay below the high water line so any sign of your passing will be erased when the water next rises. Avoid game trails unless cross-country travel would likely do more damage to plants and soil.

◆ If no durable surfaces are available, have the group spread out so no one follows in another's footsteps. This is especially important on steep slopes because runoff seeks out any channels worn into the ground. Whether climbing or descending, move slowly along a gradual contour. Walk in a gentle series of switchbacks, and place your feet carefully to avoid disturbing soil, plants, and rocks. Skirt well around bogs and areas where the soil is wet.

◆ Keep party size small, fewer than ten people. A group of four works well, allowing flexibility in doing chores and providing safety in numbers (see page 114 about group size in bear country).

◆ When venturing off-trail, leave your route unmarked. The easiest way to discourage others from following the same route, or to give subsequent travelers a sense of discovery, is to leave no sign of it: no blazes, cairns, flagging, or arrows made of sticks or drawn in the dirt.

KEEP NOISE TO A MINIMUM

Silence is an almost tangible feature of the landscape in remote wild lands, especially to ears accustomed to ringing phones, chattering televisions, and the hum and throb of city traffic. Sometimes the ringing and humming seem to stay in our ears, even long beyond civilization's range. It often takes a day or two in the backcountry to recalibrate our ears, to hear beyond what one desert hiker calls "Mother Nature's dial-tone."

A recent study found day-time noise levels as low as twenty decibels in Glacier National Park and several of Utah's canyonland parks. Dinosaur National Monument ranks as the country's quietest place at eleven decibels (by comparison a whisper rattles the ears at fifteen to thirty decibels). Yet there are always small natural sounds—a breath of wind, the footfall of a deer, snow ticking into drifts—all tonics for our busy minds. To hear what you may be missing, go quietly in the backcountry. Leave radios, tape decks, and headphones at home. Remember that sounds travel well across lakes and in open areas. Noise may be more annoying to others at night and in the early morning.

There is one circumstance when extra noise is warranted—when traveling through bear habitat. Many hikers wear bear bells on shoes or packs, but bells are not selective—they jingle with every step and disturb deer and other wildlife. Other trail users may be irritated by an endless parade of bear bells. And because bells are a "fix-it-and-forget-it" answer to the problem, they may lull hikers into a false sense of security. It's better to pay attention to your surroundings, and sing, talk loudly, or clap hands as needed. (For detailed suggestions on traveling safely in bear habitat, see page 111.)

CULTURAL ENCLAVES AND ARTIFACTS

For twenty thousand years or more North America has been home to a diverse human population, with distinct cultures inhabiting nearly every corner and niche the continent has to offer. Many of these ancient cultures moved on or simply vanished as ice shields advanced and retreated and as new cultures arose to take their place. Today, backcountry travelers occasionally stumble across stone tepee rings, burial grounds, prehistoric arrowheads and spear points, petroglyphs, and—particularly in the desert canyons of the Southwest—pottery shards and ruins of remarkable stone houses and villages.

Over the millennia, these cultural artifacts have become as much a part of the landscape as wildflowers or birdsong. They depict a time when humans, too, lived close to the land, a part of nature rather than apart from it. They also provide important clues for archaeologists and other scientists trying to divine the secrets of our history. For these reasons—and so others may also enjoy a sense of discovery— we should all help preserve historic and prehistoric sites. Leave all artifacts and structures undisturbed. Hand oils can discolor stone and other surfaces so do not touch pottery, rock paintings, or carvings. Leave all artifacts as you found them; collecting is prohibited on all federal and most state lands. This same standard applies to most fossils and some types of bones, antlers, and more recent human historical items. Some areas, notably designated wildernesses and national parks, prohibit any removal of such objects. Other lands also post stringent regulations; ask a local land manager about the rules governing any area in which you plan to travel.

Camp well away from historic or cultural sites, and walk softly when passing through. If you happen upon a site that you suspect is a new find, unknown to the land managers or researchers, mark it on your map and jot down detailed directions for how to find it again. Report all such finds to the local office of the managing agency or to the archaeology department of a nearby university.

Though modern civilization has seeped (more often flooded) into nearly every outpost of humanity across the continent, a few places remain where traditional— sometimes ancient—ways of life still prevail. Native peoples across the Arctic—the Yup'ik, Inupiat, Inuvialuit, and Inuit—and other homesteaders still pursue subsistence hunting, fishing, trapping, and wild plant harvesting as a respected and preferred way of life. Among others, the Haida of the Queen Charlotte Islands off the coast of British Columbia continue their tradition as fishermen and carvers of elegant mortuary poles and sea-going canoes.

As a visitor, be courteous and show respect for others' beliefs, language, customs, and history. The same degree of respect should be accorded to every culture you encounter. Brush up on your French before venturing into Quebec's backcountry; read books about the land and its people; study the local history. Show courtesy by being interested in the people you meet rather than expecting them to be interested in you.

Ask permission before trespassing on tribal or village lands. Sacred, ceremonial, or historical sites may be off limits to outsiders; in some cases permits are required. If permission is granted, tread lightly around mortuary poles, burial grounds, abandoned villages, vision-quest sites, and tribal fishing or hunting grounds. Leave all objects and structures undisturbed. Also request permission before taking any photographs.

Where subsistence lifestyles are practiced, ask permission before harvesting wild game or other food. Obtain all necessary permits and licenses. Harvest only what you will eat; even crops of berries or other plants may be important food sources for a local family or nearby village.

CHOOSING A CAMPSITE

Wildland recreation in North America is infused by a long tradition of "rugged individualism" and an emphasis on personal freedom. It is no small irony, then, that so many of us choose to camp in exactly the same places, despite the apparent liberty to go where we will. In fact, the vast majority of backcountry campsites were carved out of the landscape not by work crews with saws and shovels, but by sheer dint of their popularity.

Of course, these sites became popular for a reason, or, more likely, a host of reasons. There's uncommon agreement over what features to look for when choosing a good campsite: level, well-drained ground; shelter from wind and weather; access to clean water; and, with any luck, pleasant scenery. In heavily visited areas, weary travelers add one more criterion to the list—availability.

These same traits come to play in choosing a good no-trace campsite, but from a slightly different angle. Convenience matters less than damage control. For example, level, well-drained ground is still a desirable feature, but not because it offers the best bet for a good night's sleep. From a no-trace perspective, a level, well-drained site is good because it requires no "engineering" (such as trenches to drain runoff away from the tent) to make it more suitable, and it is less vulnerable to erosion. Similarly, access to clean water is crucial for drinking and cooking supplies. But put the emphasis on "clean" rather than "access"; after all, what good is access if the water is polluted? The key to keeping a stream or lake free of contamination is to camp well away from it—at least two hundred feet from shore.

In other words, the no-trace ethic favors long-term good over short-term gain. Conventional wisdom may contend, "Everybody enjoys beautiful scenery. Find a pretty spot and pitch your tent to get the best view out the front door." But after the hundredth camper has followed that advice, the spot loses its luster. The no-trace approach, on the other hand, suggests, "Everybody enjoys beautiful scenery. Find a pretty spot. Now camp someplace else—preferably a site better suited to the rigors of foot traffic." The beautiful scenery stays that way, for all to enjoy.

Choosing a campsite is frequently the most difficult decision facing the no-trace camper. You must assess your surroundings, weigh personal comfort and safety against risk of harm to the land and wildlife, and consider the rights of neighboring campers. Few sites are ideal; many require making trade-offs among the above concerns.

When the choice of whether to use a site isn't clear look at the site piece by piece. (Leave plenty of time for this process at the end of the day. Fatigue or running out of daylight are poor reasons for choosing a campsite.) Evaluate the amount of previous use; the fragility of soil and plants; and the potential for runoff, erosion, and water contamination. Are there durable or trample-resistant surfaces? If you want or need a fire, is there abundant downed wood? Ask, "When I leave this place, will there be no trace that I camped here?" The following guidelines will help determine the answer to that question.

In Popular Places

In places with established, well-worn sites, the main objective is to confine tents, foot traffic, and other use to areas already damaged by previous use and to prevent additional damage.

◆ Where sites are designated, follow the rules.
◆ Look for a level, well-drained tent pad at least two hundred feet from streams, lakes, trails, and other campers. It may not be possible to find an existing site that meets all of these criteria, but look around rather than settling on the most convenient site. Pitch your tent on a patch of bare dirt, and situate the door and likely traffic patterns to avoid areas where plants still have a foothold.
◆ Stay off lightly used or unofficial sites in areas where designated sites exist.
◆ To preserve a sense of solitude select an out-of-the-way site or screen your tent from other campers.
◆ Look for animal sign (especially bears, see page 117; and rodents, see page 126). Avoid areas used by wildlife.
◆ Leave the site better than you found it: pick up litter; if there is a fire ring, clean it out, leave the rocks in place, and scatter the ashes.
◆ Walk with extra care around seedlings. One of the more serious effects of trampling is that it tends to inhibit tree regeneration. Even if mature trees are left relatively unscathed, the packed down soil and loss of ground cover offers a poor environment for new trees to grow. Eventually, the mature trees die off (of natural causes). If no seedlings survive to take their place, the campsite becomes an artifcial clearing, vulnerable to wind damage, increased runoff and erosion, and the introduction of more resistant exotic plants. In many cases, such sites are avoided by subsequent visitors, who set up camp nearby and start the cycle all over again. Even with long-term reseeding and TLC, the abandoned site will likely remain scarred for decades; in tundra and desert environments, recovery may take hundreds of years.

In Pristine Places

In places that show few signs of previous use, the main objective is to spread use over a wide area so that no one area receives heavy traffic or disturbance. Concentrate use on highly durable or trample-resistant surfaces, when available.

◆ Look for a level, well-drained previously used site on a durable surface such as slick rock, sand or bare mineral soil, or (when encounters with other people are unlikely) gravel lake shores and river banks below the annual high water line.

Below timberline, grass meadows can also tolerate some light, dispersed use. Avoid sites likely to attract subsequent campers.

◆ Leave rocks, logs, and other features in place. Downed logs are miniature forest communities, often harboring ground squirrels, mice, birds, and countless insects. Salamanders, snails, ants, and other insects rely on the shelter found under rocks. If moving a log or rock is unavoidable, return it to its original position when breaking camp.

◆ Spread out—pitch tents well apart and avoid congregating in one spot. Look nearby for a large rock, sandy soil, or other durable surface to use when gathering as a group. Use the sleeping area only for that purpose to minimize damage from other activites

◆ Cook and eat one hundred yards or more from tents. Keep foot traffic between tents and kitchen areas to a minimum. To prevent forming a path, walk a different route for each trip between high-use areas. Watch your feet to minimize trampling. (See below for a discussion of setting up a backcountry kitchen.)

◆ Look for animal tracks, scat, and evidence of feeding. Avoid areas frequented by wildlife.

◆ Minimize wear and tear on trees. Soil around roots is easily packed down by foot traffic; this reduces the soil's ability to hold moisture. Friction from a rope can girdle the bark off a tree. Refrain from tying ropes (including packstock tethers, clothesline, or tent guys) around trees. In general, seedlings and saplings (two-inches or less in diameter) are more easily damaged than older trees.

◆ Keep a clean camp so animals are not attracted by food odors. Always properly store food when it's not in use. In bear country, special precautions must be taken to keep food, garbage, and other odorous items out of the bruins' reach. See pages 118 and 119.

◆ When breaking camp, scatter leaves, pine needles, and other natural debris over any scuffed spots. With a stick or your fingers, fluff up grass where tents flattened it. Take one last look around for litter, worn spots, or other signs of your visit.

◆ Lightly used campsites can return to natural conditions if they are left unused. Folks who want to further discourage others from using such a site can dismantle fire rings (carry the rocks well away from the site and place them sooty side down), scatter firewood caches, and conceal log furniture. Spread duff and natural debris over bare ground to camouflage the site.

THE BACKCOUNTRY KITCHEN

In bygone days, most campers cooked over a fire. The rocks forming a fire ring held pots and pans close to the heat and supported sticks for hanging pots directly over the fire. But with the advent of light-weight cookstoves, campfires became a luxury. Stoves gave backcountry chefs a cleaner, more efficient tool, and also freed land managers to restrict or prohibit fires in fragile areas or when danger of wildfire was high.

Today's backcountry kitchen is highly portable—a small stove and fuel bottle, a set of nesting pots and a lid that doubles as skillet, basic utensils, and a water bottle. Larger stoves can be carried by packstock or in canoes and rafts, but the basic outfit remains the same. This self-contained kitchen bestows considerable freedom on the backcountry traveler in choosing a site for cooking, whether in popular or pristine areas.

In Popular Places

In a popular area, set up the kitchen around an existing fire ring or in the middle of a well-worn campsite. Old fire rings often include one big rock that can serve as a low table for food preparation and as a windblock for the stove.

In Pristine Places

In pristine areas look for a durable surface such as a rock large enough to stand on, patch of sand or gravel, or beach below the high water line. For groups of four or more people, consider limiting the number of cooks using the kitchen to reduce trampling, or set up separate kitchen areas and divide the group into pairs or trios.

In bear country, the cooking site should be at least one hundred yards downwind (and preferably downhill) from camp, in open terrain where any approaching bears can be seen at a distance. In popular camping areas within grizzly bear habitat it is wise to cook around an existing fire ring and pitch the tent at a pristine site at least two hundred yards distant. (See page 117 for a complete discussion of camping in bear country.)

Other Helpful Hints

Meal time usually entails a fair amount of unpacking, sorting, and spreading out; the military doesn't call it a "mess" without reason. Try to contain your mess in the confines of the hardened site, and keep the noise down (especially at breakfast when others may still be sleeping nearby). Several companies now sell stoves that produce good heat without roaring like the space shuttle at lift off. Also keep the clatter of pots and pans to a minimum or the neighbors may think you're trying to scare off an inquisitive bear and come over to help (we're speaking from personal embarrassment here).

Always set the cookstove in a stable, level place, out of the wind and well away from flammables including clothes, tents, and dry plants.

When drawing water for cooking or washing use only clean pots to dip into any natural water source. Use a water bag to reduce foot traffic to and from the water source. For cooking, boil untreated water for five minutes to kill any micro-organisms before adding food ingredients.

Clean pots and pans with a plastic mesh scrubber; soap is not necessary. Use warm water for stubborn, stuck-on food. Pick out food particles and residue and pack this out in a double plastic bag. Dispose of wash water by pouring it in an out-of-the-way spot at least one hundred yards from any likely camp site and two hundred feet from any water source. Wash water can also be emptied into an established fire ring if a fire is later built there to burn away any food residue. This practice may not be wise when camping in bear habitat. See page 118 for more suggestions about dealing with cooking and waste water in bear country.

Finally, consider leaving the stove at the bottom of your pack (or at home if you're sure you won't need it to boil drinking water or heat a meal to ward off hypothermia) and eat only ready-to-eat food. Grandma Emma Gatewood, who first hiked the two thousand-mile Appalachian Trail—solo—at the age of sixty-seven, never carried a stove or cooked her food. She filled her pockets with nuts, raisins, sunflower seeds, and dried oatmeal, nibbling as she walked along. Backcountry travelers who prefer heartier fare can try bagels, tortillas, pita bread, cheese, peanut butter, apples, oranges, dried meat and fruit, chocolate chips, and powdered protein or carbohydrate drink mixes. Minus a stove, fuel, pots, and utensils, your pack will be lighter, and meals require little or no preparation time. Clean up is a snap. Just remember to bring a filter for treating drinking water, since boiling won't be possible.

CAMPFIRES

Ever since our species discovered how to tame fire, to use it for our own purposes, we have, in turn, been captivated by its blaze. No doubt the earliest cave dwellers sat mesmerized by the flames as night turned black around them just as countless campers do today. And perhaps because fire eats, breathes, dances, and dies just as we do, we feel kinship to it as with no other element. When we stare into a fire, we see into ourselves, as well as into our primordial past.

Roderick Nash, in *Wilderness and the American Mind*, calls fire "that magic circle of light" offering comfort and security—comfort in life-sustaining warmth and heat to cook by, and security in its power over wild animals, its brilliant light that pushes back the darkest night. No wonder then, that for eons people have built campfires, often out of necessity, and never without a sense of ritual.

So how did campfires come to be maligned, banned outright from the backcountry in many national parks, and looked upon as taboo by so many of today's land managers and no-trace gurus? Take a look around almost any well-used backcountry campsite (wherever fires are still permitted) and the answer becomes obvious. Too many people built too many fires, and paid too little attention to the mess they left behind. The result: popular campsites sprouted dozens of fire rings like a crop of mushrooms after a spring rain; forest floors were swept clean of any and all downed, dead wood; and once-wild lands took on the ragged face of a poorly managed woodlot. Blackened rocks, axe and saw cuts, trees stripped of branches as high as a person can reach—these scars and more became the mark of popularity in the backcountry.

Of course not every site was hit this hard, but tales abound in the research literature of one hundred, two hundred, even three hundred fire rings surrounding individual lakes in places once famed for their scenic beauty—Oregon's Eagle Cap Wilderness, the San Gorgonio Wilderness in California, and Yosemite National Park. Even less popular sites had their problems, as campers frequently moved the existing fire ring or built new ones in "more convenient" locations.

Clearly, it's time to re-evaluate our penchant for campfires, and to renew our sense of ritual when we do build a fire. No longer can cozying up to a campfire be taken for granted.

Camping by Starlight

Most backcountry travelers have already switched to stoves for cooking, and many of these campers treat fires as a luxury, to be enjoyed only when appropriate. By going without a fire, however, these folks also forego a fire's warmth, utility, and charm. But just as one person's vice is another's virtue, there are two sides to every facet of a fire.

◆ A fire provides heat against night's chill, but it also anchors you to the spot. Several layers of warm, dry clothing allow you to take a moonlit stroll and still retain ample body heat. Fires are also notorious for scorching your face while your backside freezes.

◆ In the backcountry, the fuel for a fire is free for the taking, but the taking is work. Doing without a fire may provide a welcome rest at the end of a hard day on the trail.

◆ Cooking over an open fire adds flavor, but not all foods are enhanced by the tang of woodsmoke. A cookstove is more efficient, offers better control of heat, is easier to start regardless of the weather, and a gas flame won't blacken your pots and pans.

Candle lantern

◆ A campfire's glow is at once cheerful, useful, and reassuring. It illuminates our smiles, the lines on a map, and the shadows that would otherwise engulf camp. Light—perhaps no other aspect of fire is so dear to us. Admittedly, the beam from a flashlight lacks a fire's personality, but it's portable, can be aimed precisely, and turns on or off with a snap. For doing chores, a gas lantern outshines any fire, and a two-ounce candle lantern provides plenty of light for cleaning dishes or reading.

◆ Finally, while woodsmoke may be the incense of memory to some folks, the tears in their eyes are probably due to simple irritation. And the same flames that hypnotize us also blind us to the surrounding night world, the blaze of stars, the approach of wildlife.

When Fire is Appropriate

Despite the advantages of going fireless, nearly everyone feels that primal urge now and then. And even well-prepared, expert backcountry travelers aren't immune from emergencies, when a fire may provide life-saving warmth, hot food, or dry clothes. As long as people are drawn to wild country, at least some of them will kindle campfires.

The key to building a no-trace campfire is to know when a fire is appropriate, and when it is not. Bear in mind these two objectives:

◆ Leave the site as natural and pleasant looking as you found it (or better).
◆ Minimize the effects of wood gathering and of the fire itself on local soil, plants, wildlife, and other visitors.

Here are some general guidelines to help you meet these goals. Also rely on the step-by-step instructions for building a fire in popular or pristine places, matching your actions to your surroundings.

◆ Build fires only when it is safe to do so. Do without a fire during dry or windy weather, especially if nearby groundcover and trees are dry. Remember that a single hot ember can set ablaze thousands of acres of wild country; never leave a fire unattended. Also, ask beforehand about area restrictions or prohibitions against campfires. Plan accordingly and pack a stove for cooking.
◆ Build fires only where downed, dead wood is plentiful. Use only sticks that can be broken with your bare hands. Leave logs and branches larger than wrist diameter where they lay. Large downfall provides important food and habitat for fungi, microorganisms, insects, and even small birds and mammals. Nutrients from decaying wood eventually return to the soil, nurturing new plant growth.
◆ Gather firewood over a wide area, well away from camp. Pick up sticks as you walk so no one area appears picked clean. Break sticks only as needed to add them to the fire—if wood is left over after the fire is out, the unbroken sticks can be scattered and will blend in naturally.
◆ Keep fires small and brief. Conserve nature's supply of downed wood. Small fires burn more efficiently, with less smoke, and are easier to control.
◆ Protect plants, soil, and rocks from heat generated by the fire. Heat can wither nearby plants and sterilize the soil, as deep as four inches beneath a big fire. Plants may not grow again unless fungi are reintroduced. Soot-stained rocks are unsightly reminders of human use, and stones can explode when heated.
◆ Do without a fire in environments where plant growth is slow (such as in deserts, above timberline, and on the Arctic tundra). Even in low-use areas, fuel can be depleted more rapidly than trees and shrubs regenerate it. Nutrients in dead wood are essential for soil building and plant regrowth.
◆ Leave existing fire rings clean and attractive for other campers. When building a

1. Gather only downed, dead wood and only as much as you will use. Sticks should be no thicker than your wrist, small enough to be broken by hand. Keep fires small and brief (use a stove for cooking, and then build a fire for drying clothes, etc.)

2. Make a six- to eight-inch mound of mineral soil in fire pan or on other fire-resistant surface.

3. Or, with a trowel, dig a twelve-inch diameter pit down through the duff and top layers of organic soil to the mineral soil. Pile the fill off to one side; if the top layer includes sod, plants, and root systems, try to keep it intact. Water this lid immediately to keep it moist and set it well away from the fire's heat.

4. Put kindling (paper, dry pine needles, or leaves) in the center of the mound or pit. Build a small tepee of twigs around the kindling. Light the kindling; once the tepee is burning, add wood as needed.

5. Burn firewood down to a fine white ash. Use a stick to push embers and charcoal toward center of fire to burn it down. Fan or blow on coals if needed. Soak ashes with water and stir to make sure they're cold. With your fingers, crush any remaining chunks into powder.

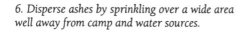

6. Disperse ashes by sprinkling over a wide area well away from camp and water sources.

7. Mound fire: return mound of mineral soil to the hole it came from. Sprinkle rock or ground surface with water to rinse away any remaining ashes or dirt. Pit fire: backfill pit and replace sod lid. Tamp disturbed soil lightly into place. Sprinkle water over area to replenish plant and soil moisture. Camouflage site by sweeping duff and pine needles or leaves over soil.

fire in a pristine area, do not build a fire ring. Return the site to its natural appearance so no one else will find and use it later.

◆ As you gather fuel, build the pyre, and light the tinder, enjoy the age-old ritual and the magic of that first spark. Build your fire carefully, as if our species' continued enjoyment of campfires—and of wild country—depends on a job done well. It does.

How to Build a No-trace Fire

In Popular Places

Forest Service researcher Bob Lucas found that most backcountry visitors don't mind finding a fire ring at established campsites. What people do object to is a dozen fire rings scattered around one campsite or piles of garbage clogging a fire ring.

In popular areas, build the fire in an existing fire ring. Gather wood from a wide area so that no one spot appears picked clean. Step lightly to minimize trampling while collecting fuel. Follow steps 1, 4, 5, and 6 as illustrated on page 42. Watch your footing around the fire—stay on the patch of bare soil that usually surrounds such a fire ring and avoid trampling nearby plants and seedlings. Burn the fire down to ash and pick out (and pack out) any litter left by previous campers. Leave a clean, attractive fire ring so the next party won't be tempted to build a new one.

Backcountry users can play an active role in rehabilitating popular areas by dismantling excess fire rings. Disperse the rocks over a wide area and turn blackened sides down. Leave one fire ring for each obvious campsite.

In Pristine Places

Choose a level site with as few plants as possible, well away from trees and surface roots. Also build at least ten feet from any large rocks that could be blackened by smoke or cracked by heat from the fire. Avoid sites where rain and runoff could later drain soil and ashes from the fire site into nearby surface water. Gently clear away plant debris that might catch fire from errant sparks. Avoid any site that looks like it has been previously used.

In pristine areas, there are two ways to build a no-trace fire: on a mound of mineral soil, or in a pit. With either method, there's no need to build a rock fire ring.

Mound fires are the best choice in most circumstances because they can be built on a variety of surfaces (in a fire pan, on a large rock, or on a bare patch of ground) and they cause the least disturbance to soil and plants. The fire is built on a six-inch mound of mineral soil, which insulates the surface underneath from the heat.

To build the mound, scoop up some sand or mineral soil from an inconspicuous place. Good sources are streambanks below the high water line or holes under the root wads of recently uprooted trees. Carry the mineral soil to the fire site in a stuff sack, turned inside out to keep the inside clean. Build the mound in a fire pan if possible. An old pie tin works well, or a sheet of aluminum foil. Even a scrap of flame-retardant canvas, cut from a discarded wall tent, will do the job. Commercial fire pans are also available. On the fire pan, rock, or other surface, shape the mineral soil into a six-inch mound about twelve inches in diameter. Follow the steps illustrated below to build a small fire on the mound.

The pit fire is appropriate when a good source of mineral soil is unavailable. Use a small hand trowel (also handy for digging cat holes) to excavate the pit. DO NOT dig a pit in dense plant cover; the upheaval usually kills plants despite all efforts to the contrary. Follow the steps illustrated below to build a small fire in the pit.

WASTE DISPOSAL

"Anyone who's been responsible for the maintenance of a cat's litter box understands how turds have an inherent tendency to pile up like junk mail." So writes Kathleen Meyer, author of the lively and informative book, *How to Shit in the Woods.* And pile up it does, mounds of the stuff—often flagged with fluttering white banners of toilet paper—sprouting around every backcountry campsite in the land.

Adding to the simple bulk of the problem is the fact that even under ideal conditions, human waste may take a year to decompose in the wild. Plop it down in a desert or atop a frozen mountain and your coprolith weathers remarkably well. In fact, studies in the Sierra Nevada and in the Northern Rockies have shown that fecal pathogens remain viable (that is, ready to infect any unsuspecting victim) for more than a year, even after being properly buried in a cat hole.

Take It With You...Or Leave It Behind?

In places where heavy recreational use threatens to overwhelm Mother Nature's composting ability, land managers often require all human waste to be packed out, just like trash. Such is the rule on the Colorado River in the Grand Canyon, where 15,000 people a year feel the roar of impending rapids reverberate in their bowels. Rafting outfitters carry portable bucket latrines, and all waste is ferried out. In Mount Rainier National Park, the waste from countless climbing parties was filling glacial crevasses and piling up like lateral moraines along popular routes. Now the park service issues blue, double-lined plastic bags to each climber; when filled, these are dropped into fifty-five-gallon barrels at high camps and other popular bivouacs on the mountain. The park service then empties the barrels and a contractor hauls the waste to an industrial incerator in Bellingham.

As more people go into the backcountry, similar restrictions on waste disposal are likely to spread. We can forestall these regulations by voluntarily packing out all waste now. Boaters and packstock users can easily carry portable latrines. The newest style—soon to be required on some heavily used rivers—is an aluminum box with an o-ring lid that can be tightly sealed. A toilet seat replaces the lid when in use. Waste goes directly into the box, eliminating the need for plastic liner bags (which foul pumping systems and resist decomposition at landfills). At the end of a trip, the box can be emptied at an RV dump station or city sewage treatment plant. Lightweight, collapsible containers are also available for hikers and backpackers, or you can carry a "poop tube"—a four-inch diameter piece of plastic pvc pipe capped at one end and threaded for a screw-on lid on the other end. Simply scoop waste from the ground into a paper bag. Sprinkle a little kitty litter or powdered chlorinated lime (available at hardware stores or sporting goods suppliers—they use it to mark playing fields) in the bag after each deposit to control odors. Then roll up the bag, slide it into the tube, and screw on the lid. The poop tube can be strapped to the outside of your pack for easy access (see page 70 for more details). Also keep urine out of the bag; it adds weight and increases the opportunity for anaerobic composting, which smells worse. (See page 47 for ideas about where to pee.)

Portable latrine

Poop tube.

Ask at the district office or ranger headquarters for the best place to dispose of collected waste once you are out of the backcountry. Most national parks have a sewage treatment plant; on national forests and BLM lands, a drive to the nearest town with a sewage plant may be required. Please do not put waste into outhouses at trailheads unless instructed to do so; there's too big a risk of spillage, and most outhouses are maintained (and drained) on a regular schedule with little room for excess waste. Finally, never put human waste into trash cans or dumpsters. This creates a health hazard—both at the trash can and later at the landfill—and is illegal in most states.

When human waste is left in the backcountry, two potential offenses arise. It is unsightly, especially when discovered in prolific quantities, and it presents a health hazard. The aesthetics—or lack thereof—are apparently dictated by the particular breed of scat. A fresh pile of bear scat in the trail piques our curiosity and heightens awareness of our surroundings. But if the same pile were human in origin, our response might range from disgust to actual physical revulsion.

The hazards posed to human (and wildlife) health raise more serious concerns. Human waste often harbors intestinal bacteria, notably *Escherichia coli*, and sometimes nasty disease organisms that cause diarrhea and illness if ingested by others. In the backcountry the two most common avenues for germs to travel from feces to ingestion is through untreated drinking water or food prepared with unclean hands. How to safeguard our water supplies is part of the bigger riddle over where (and how) to dispose of human waste. Before we get to that, let's look at the relatively simple puzzle of backcountry personal hygiene.

Clean hands...without soap

At home, with all the comforts of hot running water, a soap dispenser next to the sink, and a handy clean towel, nearly everybody above the age of six washes their hands after going to the bathroom or before preparing a meal. Ingrained as it is, this habit is remarkably fast to disappear as soon as we wander beyond reach of indoor plumbing. It's too much fuss, some say, and clean hands don't stay that way for long in the backcountry. Besides, the wash water is too cold (or too hot after neglecting it on the stove), and isn't the no-trace camper supposed to leave the soap at home?

Well...yes. But there is another way, actually two ways: pre-packaged hand wipes, or waterless hand cleanser.

Wipes are sold in grocery stores everywhere; look in the diaper aisle (ok, so they're not exactly hand wipes...but if they can clean a toddler's rump, they can certainly tackle a pair of sweaty palms). Some come in handy, reuseable travel cases that will hold a dozen or so wipes. Most brands offer several styles with different ingredients. Look for alcohol-based wipes, which disinfect fairly well, and that are also fragrance-free. The fruity or flowery smells of some wipes may attract animals or insects (read: bears and bees). One wipe should suffice to clean both hands— that's a single wipe for each trip to the cat hole or before each meal. It doesn't amount to much; figure five wipes for each day of your trip. If you buy wipes in bulk, carry only as many as you need in a sealed plastic bag to retain their moistness. Pack out all used wipes in a plastic bag with the rest of your garbage.

The other option, waterless hand cleanser, comes to us off the shelves of auto-parts stores. Mechanics need a strong grease-cutting cleanser that won't hurt their hands (as the old standby, gasoline, can do). Again, there are several brands to choose from, most in the form of gels or creams, but the key ingredient to look for is zinc pyrithione, an anti-microbial agent. Also read the instructions to make sure water isn't required. Generally, all that's needed is a dab of cleanser in the palm and then you rub your hands together until all the dirt is lifted off. Wipe off the excess cleanser on a hand towel and you're done. Look for pocket-sized tubes of cleanser at the store—a little goes a long way—or if only large containers are available, repackage only as much as you need in a small, empty hand-lotion dispenser. Carry the cleanser in a separate plastic bag, preferably in an outside pocket where it's easy to find yet won't make too big of a mess if it leaks. Use extra care to keep such cleansers from getting loose in the environment, particularly in backcountry waters.

Proper Disposal of Human Waste

Fifteen years ago few people worried about getting sick from drinking out of remote streams and lakes in North America, but today the names on the list of backcountry pathogens are all too familiar: *giardia*, *campylobacter*, *E. coli*, hepatitis A and B. Each of these bugs causes its own peculiar brand of illness, ranging from diarrhea to serious damage to vital organs. All require medical attention; if you get sick from dipping your cup in a stream, see a doctor immediately. (See page 140 for more information about these backcountry diseases.)

The truth is, no water is safe to drink untreated. That's due, at least in part, to the spread of disease through improperly disposed of human waste. And as Kathleen Meyer acknowledges in her treatise on the subject, "the amount of the waste can often have less to do with the problem than the manner in which it's discarded."

When searching for the perfect backcountry dump site, the objectives are to:

◆ Keep waste from entering surface water.

◆ Prevent waste from being discovered by other people or wildlife.

◆ Hasten decomposition.

To meet these objectives, heed the following guidelines.

◆ Anticipate. Keep an eye out for likely sites before the urge hits. Keep a trowel, toilet paper (if not using natural wipes), and a hand cleaner in a convenient pack pocket.

◆ Find an out-of-the-way site in stable soils at least two hundred feet (about seventy paces) from surface water. Avoid places that show evidence of flooding, carrying runoff, or groundwater seepage.

◆ Make sure the site is at least two hundred feet from established campsites, trails, and other centers of human activity. Also avoid game runs and nesting or burrowing grounds.

◆ Look for a site with an active layer of organic topsoil. The ground should be moist (but not saturated), fairly easy to dig in, and the organic layer should be at least six inches deep. (Techniques for waste disposal in snow and in environments where topsoil is scarce or nonexistent, such as deserts, tundra, and sandy coastal areas, are discussed in Chapter 6.)

◆ With a small hand trowel, dig a cat hole six to eight inches deep. Keep the sod lid intact. Set it aside, and pile all the dirt right next to the hole.

◆ Once the hole is dug, slip off your knickers, use whatever posture works for you (see Meyer's book for suggestions), and let the chips fall. (Some people prefer to dig the cat hole after defecating—it's easier

Cat hole.

than aiming for a wee hole in the dirt. Simply dig the hole under and around the feces, making sure that none remains on the surface. This reverse-procedure works best where the ground is easy to dig and leaf debris is plentiful for concealing the site, since no sod lid is available.)

◆ Ideally, no-trace campers should rely on leaves, pine boughs, snow, or even smooth stones instead of toilet paper. These natural wipes can go right into the cat hole before covering it. Toilet paper degrades slowly and is unsightly if dug up by animals. Use as little as possible. It's best to pack out all used toilet paper (in a double plastic bag). If you choose to burn it, use a campfire rather than lighting the paper in the cat hole. Burning toilet paper is risky at best, as one poor soul discovered after his flaming tissue paper ignited a 450-acre wildfire in Washington state during the summer of 1989. The lesson was expensive: a federal judge held the man liable for $132,700 to help pay for the fire-fighting effort.

◆ When covering the waste, use a stick to stir in the first handful or two of soil. This puts microbes in the soil in contact with the waste and quickens decomposition. Add the remaining topsoil and the sod lid. Rake leaves and duff around to camouflage the site.

◆ When urinating, seek an out-of-the-way site far from water. Pee onto mineral soil or a patch of sand if possible. Urine can burn plants, and the salt it contains attracts animals who may chew or paw doused plants and soil. Try to pee in a sunny spot so it will evaporate more quickly. On some high-use rivers, such as the on the Colorado River in Grand Canyon National Park, rangers recommend peeing directly into the water to avoid urine build-up (with attendant odors) in the sand. But don't do this unless local authorities recommend it.

◆ Clean your hands with cleanser or a hand wipe, and you're done.

That's the general procedure, and it works in almost every circumstance. Here are a few options for modifying the technique when appropriate.

In Popular Places

◆ Take extra care to choose a site ill-suited for any other use. Dense stands of trees or shrubbery are low-use areas and also offer privacy.

◆ Decomposition is slowed when waste is concentrated in one place, as in a group latrine. Unless regulations dictate otherwise, it's usually best to dig individual cat holes.

In Pristine Places

◆ Despite the prevailing wisdom that recommends always digging a cat hole, human waste decomposes rapidly in the open air. In truly pristine areas (where few if any people tread), waste can be scattered with a stick into small pieces on the surface of the ground. Select a dry site at least four hundred feet from water sources, in terrain unlikely to attract other country travelers. When in doubt, dig a cat hole.

Litter

Another kind of human waste—litter—is the number one problem cited by backcountry visitors overall. The no-trace response to litter follows the time-tested notion that if you "pack it in, pack it out." To this we add, "pick up what others left behind." Leave a little space in your pack, saddle bag, pannier, or stow sack for extra trash found along the way. Put trash in a plastic bag to protect your gear from dirt, germs, or the mystery ooze that grows in discarded beer and pop cans. The beauty of cleaning up after others is that it encourages those who follow to keep it clean, too. A single gum wrapper goes unnoticed on a trail strewn with jetsam, but if it's the only, lonely blemish on an otherwise natural scene, the owner will likely think twice about littering.

In camp, bag garbage as soon as it's generated. Better to contain it right away than to let a squirrel, raven, or williwaw carry it off. Set aside a plastic bag just for trash, and pack out every scrap. In bear country, hang garbage with food and other odor-producers well out of reach. In grizzly country, it may be best to burn food scraps in a hot fire. Scorch any empty cans, then smash them flat for packing out. Always take a last look around when breaking camp to make sure no litter is left behind. Upon your return to civilization, think twice before unloading your garbage in the first available trash can. Many outposts and small towns do not have official landfills or waste hauling services. Take the garbage home with you to make sure it's disposed of properly.

BATHING AND LAUNDRY

Most backcountry travelers are content to forgo regular bathing for several days or even a week or two. After all, sweat is a badge of accomplishment, and most wild country dirt is relatively wholesome stuff. But even the crustiest, trail-hardened adventurer eventually feels the need—or itch—for a bath.

No one has yet devised a way to get truly clean (waterless hand cleansers notwithstanding) without water, primarily because water is the universal solvent—it loosens and dissolves just about any kind of grime you mix it with. But here also lies the hazard in taking backcountry baths: anything added or rinsed into the water—soap, body oils, or dirt—is carried back into the environment, wherever the water goes. In other words, water disperses pollutants. This can be good or bad, depending on the ratio of pollutant to water. One thousand swimmers oozing sun screen, sweat, and sand may not make a dent in the water quality of the waves at Daytona Beach, but a single person soaking his feet in a desert puddle may drastically alter the pH and nutrient balance so crucial to aquatic life there. And the next person to come along will likely dip into that same desert puddle—never suspecting its role as foot bath—to slake his thirst.

In general, large lakes, rivers, and the ocean can withstand liberal amounts of skinny dipping without harm to water quality. But do not use soap or any other solvents. A good soak or swim in plain water does a passable job of unsticking hair and knocking the external bacteria count down to tolerable levels. If you're wearing sun screen, bug repellant, or a splash of fuel from the cookstove, wash it off following the guidelines listed below *before* entering the water. Also, try to minimize the amount of silt stirred up while in the water. Wade in on rocks or along a sandy or gravel bottom. As suspended silt resettles it may smother fish eggs and other aquatic organisms.

For smaller lakes, pools, and streams use a clean pot to scoop out some water. Carry the water two hundred feet from the source and find a large rock or patch of sand to stand on. Douse yourself and scrub with your hands or a clean, unadulterated washcloth. Rinse with a second dousing. Some people favor sun-heated shower bags to lessen the shock of their open-air ablutions. Be sure to hang the shower bag over a large rock or other surface that will resist erosion. If more than one person will use the shower, move it periodically so the shower stall doesn't become water logged or eroded.

If you must use soap, make sure it is biodegradable. Carry water at least two hundred feet away from water source to a resistant surface. Lather up, using as little soap as possible, and rinse. Rinse the ground with more water to disperse suds.

The surest way to avoid harming water quality is to wait for a shower upon return to civilization. It's a small sacrifice on shorter trips, and where water is scarce or available only in small rations (as in the desert), it's best left for drinking and wildlife. Besides, the anticipation of a real shower, with steaming water, squeaky clean skin, and a warm towel helps to lift even the weariest legs on the long trudge out at the end of a trip.

Think of toothpaste as another form of soap—use as little as possible and keep it out of streams and lakes. The prefered methods are to spit toothpaste into the plastic bag that's hauling all your garbage, or swallow it. (Note: in higher concentrations fluoride is toxic. It's best to use non-fluoridated toothpaste if you make a habit of swallowing the suds.) If you spit toothpaste onto the ground, spray it over a wide area by pressing your tongue against your teeth. Where soils are stable and runoff will dilute it, toothpaste can be spit into a scuff mark made with the heel of a shoe. Dillute the suds with a splash of rinse water and cover with soil. Do this well away from water sources (and from camp to avoid attracting animals). Pack out all dental floss and toothpicks with other garbage.

Clothes can usually go weeks without a wash. To keep them as fresh as possible, change into camp clothes after the day's exertions. Shake the dust out of the trail clothes and spread them in the sun for an hour or two. Air dry damp socks and sweat-soaked clothes as needed. On long trips when clothes must be washed, carry a tub of water at least two hundred feet from the water source. Soak clothes in the tub (a plastic bag with a twistie also works) for ten minutes. Do not use soap. Knead the clothes until the water is dirty, then rinse. Don't pour wash water all in one spot—scatter it gently over the ground well away from the water source. Sturdy clothes can be hand-wrung to get rid of excess water. Shake water out of pile and other delicate fabrics. Spread clothes on rocks or tree branches to dry. Hang clothes discretely when other parties are nearby.

WATCHING WILDLIFE

People are designed, at least in part, as predators—canine teeth for tearing meat, two eyes forward for good depth perception and motion tracking, and a tendency to walk around upright on two legs like we own the place. Even in people who never hunt, the human mental make-up reveals ties to our ancient hunter-gatherer heritage: we have a penchant for following tracks, we stalk birds and chipmunks and bison with cameras, and we love to simply watch animals.

In fact, seeing wildlife is often the highlight of a successful backcountry outing. A recent survey of visitors in Yellowstone National Park found that watching wildlife was the number one reason people come to the park, more important than viewing geysers or scenery.

Of course, wildlife watching has grown more sophisticated since the grunt-and-hunt days of our Cro-Magnon ancestors. Not only has technology come to the aid of our eyes and ears, but many nature fans are also becoming keen naturalists, highly knowledgeable in the habits and habitats of the creatures they watch. For these folks, watching wildlife is all the more rewarding if the animal remains unaware of any human presence and behaves naturally.

When watching wildlife, follow this general rule of thumb, adapted from the American Birder's Association Code of Ethics: *you are too close if the animal changes its behavior because of your presence.* Problems arise when we disturb wildlife because most animals are constantly engaged in an effort to survive. In other words, wild animals spend most of their time doing important things—looking for food, eating, resting, watching for predators, mating, nesting, and rearing young. When humans interrupt, the animal has to drop what it's doing. Vital calories go uneaten, more are burned in fleeing the scene or blustering a defense, and sometimes young or weak animals are left exposed to harsh weather or predation.

According to David Cole and William Hammit, co-authors of *Wildland Recreation*, the major cause of distress to wildlife by outdoor enthusiasts is "unintentional harassment." This occurs when people "unknowingly and innocently produce stressful situations" for wildlife; in many cases the people never detect the animal's presence. Some of these encounters are probably unavoidable, but many could be prevented simply by bearing in mind that we are traipsing, uninvited, through someone else's neighborhood. Stay alert to the signs of wildlife and avoid camping and unnecessary travel near solitary watering holes, feeding areas (such as berry patches in bear country), breeding and birthing grounds, and nest or den sites, particularly during critical seasons. The same precautions apply when the wildlife encounter is no accident, that is, when people seek out wildlife to watch.

Preparation for careful wildlife watching begins at home. Read up on the species you hope to see; learn their habits, preferred foods, and habitats. It helps to know what time of year mating occurs and when young are born. Most animals are more sensitive to human intrusion during these seasons, becoming either more aggressive or more skittish. Nesting birds, animals with young, and predators feeding on a kill deserve extra caution; do not go near them, for their safety and yours. Causing animals to exert energy during extreme heat or cold also puts them at a disadvantage in the struggle for survival.

In the field, wear muted colors that blend into your surroundings (except during hunting seasons, when safety orange is a wise addition to your fashion palette). Approach all wildlife slowly and quietly, constantly monitoring the animal's behavior and location. Pay heed to wind direction, which may carry your sounds and smells to the animal over a great distance. Hide behind foliage and terrain, or try to blend in with the background. In most situations, natural cover is preferable over building a blind. If a blind is used, however, dismantle it and return the site to its natural condition.

Most species have a "comfort zone" within which intruders are considered a threat. But even within a single species, individuals' responses to intrusion may vary widely. In his book, *Bears of the World*, Terry Domico relates an encounter with an Alaskan grizzly bear and two cubs that tolerated his (accidental) approach to within forty feet. The bear "ignored" Domico and a companion and let them proceed on down the trail. Yet Stephen Herrero cites one case in *Bear Attacks: Their Causes and Avoidance* of a mother grizzly with cubs that charged a man unprovoked from an initial distance of six hundred yards. These examples make it painfully clear that it is better to err on the side of caution—to keep a respectful distance—than to risk infringing on an animal's circle of safety. This holds true for watching pelicans, raccoons, or mule deer no less than bears, for ultimately the animal is the one who suffers from the intrusion.

The best way to get close to wildlife is through binoculars, spotting scopes, or a telephoto camera lens. For binoculars, seven- to ten-power (7x - 10x) magnification works best. Anything stronger jiggles too much when hand held. Spotting scopes can be steadied on a tripod, allowing much greater magnification. But scopes stronger than 45x pick up atmospheric heat waves or haze over long distances, distorting the view. Several companies make excellent scopes with zoom lenses that range from 15x up to 45x.

Good wildlife photographs require a decent 35mm SLR camera and at least a 300mm telephoto lens. Most serious photographers prefer lenses in the 400mm to 500mm range and are willing to pay extra for the low-light capabilities of a large-aperture lens. Video cameras, for the most part, are not well-suited to wildlife photography because the lens magnification is too low. All too often, the videographer compensates by getting too close to wildlife. Anyone serious about taping wildlife should look for a camera with a digital zoom feature, which enlarges the image electronically. Reasonably priced models are available with up to twenty-power (20x) digital zoom.

Hunting and Fishing

It might seem odd (to some) to talk about no-trace ethics and hunting and fishing in the same breath—isn't "disturbing" an animal a prime objective here? Certainly, killing a bird, game animal, or fish causes a rather abrupt change in the demographics of the backcountry neighborhood. But hunting and fishing predate all other recreational pastimes, and the thrill of taking wild food continues to draw many people into the backcountry today. What can hunters and anglers do to leave no trace? The general principles are the same: show respect for the land, its inhabitants (particularly the ones you find in your cross hairs or tugging at the other end of the line), and other people; and tailor your actions to fit your surroundings. A few additional guidelines are specific to hunting and fishing.

Guidelines for fishing

◆ Know and obey the regulations.
◆ Keep only what you can eat; practice catch-and-release. Use barbless hooks. Land the fish quickly rather than playing it to exhaustion. To release a fish, cradle it in the water facing into the current—this helps water flow through the gills—until the fish recovers and swims away.
◆ Lead sinkers, when ingested, are toxic to waterfowl and other wildlife. Use steel or other metals for weights.
◆ Make an honest effort to recover all snagged flies, lures, and fouled line. Pack it in, pack it out.
◆ Respect other anglers' territory.
◆ Follow local regulations for disposing of fish entrails. If a method is not specified, weigh the following options:
   Pack entrails out in a plastic bag (not recommended in bear country).
   Burn entrails in a hot fire. If any residue remains, pack it out in a plastic bag.
   If local regulations permit it, and other options are not viable, pierce entrails, deflate, and toss them far out into deep water. Take care that entrails do not wash ashore near a likely campsite.
   Bury entrails only as a last resort (and never when in bear country), or when regulations require it.

Guidelines for hunting

◆ Know and obey the regulations.

◆ Grazing waterfowl and other wildlife sometimes inadvertently swallow spent shot pellets. Lead shot is toxic; use steel shot.

◆ Take only clear, sure shots. Shoot only when certain of the target's identity.

◆ Know your weapon's range and verify a clear field of fire near and behind the target before shooting.

◆ Follow local regulations for disposing of unused remains. In most areas, dressing the animal in the field is satisfactory, and unused remains can be scattered in an out-of-the-way place. Make sure all parts of the carcass are far from any campsites, trails, or other sites likely to be used by people (this is especially important in bear country). Nature's recyclers will quickly take care of it. And remember: ask first for permission to fish or hunt on private land.

Beyond Fair Chase, a Falcon Press book by Jim Posewitz, offers additional ethical guidelines for hunters.

For more information about leave-no-trace techniques, or if you are interested in participating further, contact the National Leave No Trace Skills and Ethics Education Program at 1-800-332-4100.

LEAVE NO TRACE: TAILORED TO DIFFERENT MODES OF TRAVEL

All of the leave-no-trace guidelines discussed in the previous chapter can be put into practice by anyone who sets foot in the backcountry, regardless of the actual mode of travel used. Those principles and precautions apply equally well to hikers; equestrians; people leading mules, llamas, or goats; sled dog mushers; mountain bikers; motorcyclists; four-wheelers; skiers; snowshoers; snowmobilers; ice and rock climbers; and paddlers who travel by canoe, kayak, and raft.

In fact, the same no-trace guidelines even apply to those who drive into remote areas in 4x4 cars, jeeps, and trucks. (Heck, while we're at it, we might as well include power boats, bush planes, and helicopters.) Just modify the specific techniques slightly to better suit the mode of travel, and anyone can learn to tread lightly. For example, motorcyclists can follow the same advice hikers do for selecting a travel route in popular places: stay on the trail, or road, as the case may be. Ride single file, and avoid wet or muddy routes. On foot, hoof, or wheel, off-trail travel tramples plants, disturbs the soil, and leads to erosion.

Many of the modes of travel examined here are more regulated and restricted than foot travel because there is a greater potential for damage to the land from packstock and vehicles. The vast majority of regulations are aimed at reducing impacts; please know and obey regulations at all times. In some cases, they override one or more of the no-trace principles. For example, few pristine areas allow access to motorized vehicles; rather than dispersing use, motorized users should avoid such areas altogether. Other, more suitable places are available for motorized recreation.

CONFLICTS AMONG TRAIL USERS

It's important to note here that few of us are purists when it comes to backcountry recreation and our chosen modes of travel. There are simply too many interesting, fun options available. Increasingly, Saturday's hiker is Sunday's equestrian, and the mountain bike comes out of the garage on Wednesday evening. And most hikers use vehicles to get to trailheads. Such diversity tends to blur the accuracy of old stereotypes...it's wise to avoid labeling people based on nothing more than their given mode of travel on any one day. We are no longer purely hikers, trail riders, bikies, 'beelers, skiers, or any of the less flattering epithets sometimes heard on the trail. More often, we are some or all of the above.

But sadly, the stereotypes persist and multiply. According to recent research (if the proliferation of headlines isn't proof enough), conflicts among different types of trail users are on the rise. And with the explosion in new types of recreation, the *types* of conflict are also now more varied. From the age-old battle between hikers and horsepackers, we have "progressed" to territorial wars between skiers and snowmobilers, llama packers and horsepackers, people with dogs and those without, gun toters and those without, trail runners and anything wide enough to block the path, and just about everybody versus the beleaguered mountain bikers.

In what may be a sign of worse things to come, USDA Forest Service social scientist Alan Watson cites several new types of conflict that border on the bizarre. Visitors to the Desolation Wilderness in California complain of quiet evenings shattered by bursts from semi-automatic weapons, when no hunting season is in effect. Is this, Watson asks, a mere expression of "unconfined...recreation" as defined in Section 2, (c)(2) of the Wilderness Act? What then of the army of nude sunbathers, free of Michigan's cities, that descends on Nordhouse Dunes Wilderness only to bear the scrutiny of gawkers and red-faced tourists? Finally, there's the understandable frustration of cross-country skiers up and down the Rocky Mountains, who after toiling uphill all day, arrive at some nameless powder-filled cirque only to watch a crew of heli-skiers carve effortless figure-eights down the once-trackless slope. And skiers aren't the only ones hopping chopper rides—heli-fishing is gaining popularity on remote western lakes and streams.

BACKCOUNTRY ETIQUETTE

Clearly, conflicts do arise between different types of visitors. Can a resolution be found within the guidelines of the no-trace ethic? We believe so. All it takes is a healthy mixture of one part tolerance plus two parts courtesy.

◆ As far as is safe and reasonable, be tolerant of other people in the backcountry. Remember that they are pursuing the same goal of having fun in the outdoors and enjoying nature, however peculiar their chosen pursuit may seem. Watson's research and other studies show that most outdoor recreationists have more in common than they realize. This is true for hikers and bicyclists, stock users and non-stock users, and even motorized and non-motorized recreationists.

◆ Practice the gentle art of diplomacy. A friendly manner and the willingness to see the other person's point of view are the best encouragements for cooperation.

◆ When tolerance is stretched thin, consider moving to a different area to get away from the offending party. Save your righteous indignation for the letter you will write to the Backcountry Association of _____ (just fill in the offending party's likely affiliation). Let the local land manager know about any unduly obnoxious, unsafe, or illegal behavior encountered while in the backcountry.

◆ To foster tolerance in others, strive to be courteous and considerate toward fellow backcountry travelers. Realize that some folks are annoyed or offended by noisy, rowdy, or overtly risky behavior. Save the showing off and competitiveness for your close friends—they're more likely to forgive you in the morning.

◆ When meeting other groups on the trail, yield the right-of-way even when it's not expected of you, unless it's unsafe to do so. This one simple act generates an amazing amount of goodwill, which tends to spread up and down trail as passersby meet other parties. In the following pages we give right-of-way guidelines for specific situations, but when in doubt, yield.

◆ When meeting packstock (regardless of species) on the trail step off to the downhill side and remain quiet and calm. Loud noises and sudden movements can startle even the most mild-mannered animal, causing an unnecessary and dangerous pack animal rodeo. Courtesy to packstock ensures their safety and yours.

◆ Bear in mind Principle 2 of the Leave-No-Trace Ethic: Keep Noise to a Minimum and Strive to be Inconspicuous (see page 32).

◆ Many areas rely on volunteers to help out with trail maintenance and repair. If you use trails, you can help preserve them. Contact your local Forest Service or BLM district office, park manager, or city recreation department to offer your services. Join a hiking, equestrian, biking, skiing, snowmobile, or ORV club and initiate a trails upkeep program if they don't already have one.

◆ Also remember to plan ahead, choose a destination that's appropriate for the type of recreation you intend to engage in, and once in the backcountry, tailor your actions to suit your surroundings. Enough said.

Throughout the following sections we have relied on information and advice from a wide range of experts in each field. Special thanks here are due to the American Alpine Club, Back Country Horsemen of America, the International Mountain Bicycling Association, Montana Outfitters and Guides Association, Tread Lightly! Inc., and the National Leave No Trace Skills and Ethics Program. By seeking out organizations that represent the various types of backcountry users, we hope to avoid preaching ideas that sound good on paper but don't work in the real world. You can use the following techniques and suggestions with confidence because they are the same ones practiced and recommended by expert horseback riders, animal packers, mountain bikers, skiers, climbers, boaters, and backcountry motorists.

PACKSTOCK

In bygone days, the word packstock referred only to horses and mules. No longer. Noah's ark has landed at North America's trailheads, and the animals have disembarked. The packtrain menagerie now includes burros, llamas, dogs of all shapes and sizes, goats, and at least one instance of a pack ox. Overall, horses and mules still outnumber their more exotic co-workers, and their use—always a strong component of backcountry travel in the West—is increasing, particularly in the South. Hence, our focus under this heading will be on horses, mules, and burros;

Horsepacking

but much of this information is also relevant to other pack animals. Specific recommendations for no-trace packing on llamas, goats, and dogs are found on pages 60 and 61.

Five general guidelines that apply to all packstock will also help prevent many problems before they occur:

◆ Know your animals. Ideally, all pack animals should be healthy, reliable, calm, and well trained. High-strung, mean-spirited, or sick animals have a greater tendency to injure the land, themselves, and anyone who gets too close.

◆ Take the time at home to familiarize your animals with the packs, restraints, foods, and other equipment they will encounter in the backcountry. A storm on a remote, rocky ridge is no place for your packstock's first skirmish with a wildly flapping tent fly.

◆ Before you go on a trip ask about local regulations or restrictions concerning pack animals. Some areas limit packstock to a specific ratio of animals to people; other places require pack trains to carry their own feed. Trails or portions of some areas are closed to packstock use seasonally or year-round. Know the rules and please obey them.

◆ Pack lightly and keep the number of packstock to a minimum. Lightweight gear—such as backpacking tents and stoves—saves wear and tear on the animals and, consequently, on the trails. Fewer animals means fewer hooves or paws hammering on plants and soil, fewer mouths to feed, and less manure.

◆ Keep packstock out of campsites. This reduces campsite damage, keeps manure from underfoot, and curtails the number of flies and other pests in camp.

Horses, Mules, and Burros

◆ Keep packstock to a minimum. Horses, mules, and burros are big, heavy animals. Their weight and power can cause serious harm to plants and soils. Such scars heal slowly, and the damage is often cited by land managers when new restrictions or area closures are imposed. Check area regulations before you go; some areas limit packstock to a specified ratio of animals to people. Generally, one average-sized mule or horse can carry 150 to 200 pounds of gear, regardless of terrain. One pack animal for every two people is more than adequate on summer trips of a week or less. Longer trips may require additional packstock.

◆ Use lightweight nylon tents instead of canvas wall tents. Several companies make nylon tepee and dome tents designed specifically for large packstock groups. Smaller groups can easily use standard nylon backpacking tents. The weight saved (up to one thousand percent when compared to canvas tents) helps lighten the pack animal's step, reducing the impact on trails. Such tents are often self-contained (no wooden poles to cut), take up less ground space, and may be free-standing, allowing greater flexibility in choosing a tent site. A sewn-in tent floor helps reduce wear and tear on plants and soil. Because nylon is less resistant to abrasion than canvas, put the tent in a heavy-duty stuffsack to protect it from rope burns, sharp objects, and constant rubbing while packed on the back of a mule.

◆ Carry certified weed-free feed. Some areas require it; ask beforehand. Carrying your own feed gives you freedom to roam and is particularly important in areas where forage is scarce or packstock use is heavy. An overgrazed meadow is a sign to others of careless packstock use (and not much of a welcome to the next pack train that pulls in). The meadow also will be more vulnerable to erosion and provide less forage, at least for a while, for resident wildlife. Using certified weed-free feed ensures that no undesirable plants will be introduced to the backcountry. Remember to feed your stock on it for several days before the trip so their manure will also be weed free.

◆ Carry a fire pan. Even if existing fire rings are available, a fire pan allows greater flexibility in selecting a campsite. See page 42 for a description of how to use a fire pan.

◆ Outfitters should pack a portable latrine, especially when traveling with a large group. See page 44 for more information.

◆ Consider using the flat plate style of horseshoe. Heel and toe caulks give the horse better traction on rocky, icy, or steep trails, but they also cause more trail damage than flat plates. Flat plates work well in most conditions and also cause less damage to the home pasture if horses remain shod between outings.

◆ Trailing packstock—leaving the pack train untied, trusting the animals to follow one another down the trail—was once a popular method, but loose animals cause too many problems. They stop to feed, cut switchbacks, and wander off trail; they may impede other trail users. Instead, pigtail all stock. Tie the lead rope to a break-away loop on the pack saddle of the animal in front. Keep packstrings short to reduce the tendency for animals to stray wide of the trail. You will also travel faster with fewer problems.

Pigtail knot.

◆ Yield the right-of-way whenever it's safe and sensible to do so. In their book, *Packin' In On Mules and Horses,* Bill Brown and long-time outfitter Smoke Elser take an intelligent and admirable stand on the question of right-of-way among packstock users. "When you meet another packer on the trail," they write, "which of you is entitled to the right-of-way is less important than how you work things out between yourselves." The rule-of-thumb is that strings going uphill have the right-of-way in the morning; strings going downhill have it in the afternoon. Longer strings generally have right-of-way over shorter strings, and riders without packstock should generally yield to packstrings. When in doubt, yield to the other party and enjoy a break from the trail.

◆ Elser and Brown also provide some sage advice for when trail riders overtake hikers. They recommend calling out a friendly "howdy" so you don't sneak up on them. Realize that not all hikers know how to react when meeting packstock on the trail. Be helpful, and remind them that you're concerned as much for their safety as for your own. Hikers should all stand on the same side of the trail, and downhill from it. Horses and their kin have a long history of being prey animals; they're wary of predators attacking from above. Standing on the downhill side is perceived as less of a threat. Keep noise and sudden movement to a minimum; talk in low, reassuring tones to stock as they pass by.

"Perhaps the greatest rudeness you can direct at hikers," say Elser and Brown, "is stopping to visit without dismounting. This is an unconscious thing for most riders." Hikers may feel intimidated looking up at a rider on horseback. Take the opportunity to get out of the saddle and stretch your legs.

◆ When watering your animals, look for an established ford or low, gentle banks with firm footing. Steep banks are more difficult for stock to negotiate and are easily eroded by heavy hoof traffic. Avoid wet ground and lush vegetation. Refrain from building dams or rock pools as this disturbs the streambed.

◆ As much as possible, avoid tying stock to trees. The rope can girdle a tree's bark, and the animal's hooves will quickly trample and pack the soil around the tree's base. If you do temporarily tie up choose a sturdy tree at least eight inches in diameter (about as big around as your thigh).

◆ For longer rest stops along the trail, find a dry meadow or other trample-resistant site and either hobble the stock or set up a quick high hitchline between two trees. Use webbed slings around the tree trunks, and attach the hitchline to these with a swivel to reduce chafing on the bark. Tie the hitchline about seven feet above ground so horses can walk under it; this helps minimize pawing. Keep packstock out of wet meadows.

◆ When choosing a campsite, look for pasture that will hold your stock without damaging the country. Dry grass meadows are best, preferably in sight of camp so you can keep an eye on your animals and put a quick stop to any damaging or dangerous behavior.

◆ At camp, hobble packstock or use a movable picket line or high hitchline. A hitchline between two trees is better than tethering directly to a tree, picketing individual animals, or building a corral. Some members of Back Country Horsemen

Hitchline.

of America have found that portable, one-wire electric fences work well. The wire runs in a half-inch tape and is charged by six to eight D-cell flashlight batteries, which put out an average of seven thousand volts. One set of batteries can charge up to 1.25 miles of fence. Some models are available that run on solar power. Set up the fence on pasture at home so livestock is accustomed to it before trying it in the wilds. In the backcountry, make sure the enclosure is big enough to allow stock to move if spooked. Limit the number of animals enclosed. Know your stock. If they will stick around as long as Ol' Paint stays put, then lead Ol' Paint into the enclosure and let the others roam nearby. Studies also are being done to see if multi-wire electric fences can be used to keep bears out of feed supplies at back-country camps.

◆ Move stock frequently to avoid overgrazing of any one area. Make sure enough feed is available to leave plenty for elk, deer, and other wildlife. If possible, graze stock on north-facing slopes, where, come winter, forage will be buried beneath snow. Leave plenty of forage on south-facing slopes, where snowcover is typically thin and wildlife can feed throughout the winter. Use a nose bag when feeding pellets; very little feed is wasted and grazing damage is eliminated. Also scatter any manure piles when breaking camp.

◆ Riders on horseback should carry an axe or saw to clear downfall when traveling forested trails. Given the number of trails (and the paucity of funds for trail maintenance), crews sometimes cannot keep all trails clear, and blow-downs can happen at any time. Clear downfall only if it blocks the trail itself; this will prevent a detour path from forming around the obstacle. Resist the temptation to use the axe or saw for chores (such as gathering firewood) around camp. Aldo Leopold, forester and expert with an axe, knew the value of restraint. In *A Sand County Almanac* he wrote, "I have read many definitions of what is a conservationist, and written not a few myself, but I suspect that the best one is written not with a pen, but with an axe. It is a matter of what a man thinks about while chopping, or while deciding what to chop. A conservationist is one who is humbly aware that with each stroke he is writing his signature on the face of his land."

Llamas and Goats

According to the Forest Service, llamas and goats make up about five percent of all packstock use in designated wilderness areas. A number of llama outfitter businesses have sprung up around the country, and as of 1988, at least one commercial outfitter was using pack goats.

Llama and goat advocates claim that these animals are lighter on the land, causing less damage through trampling and grazing. In their book, *Llamas on the Trail: A Packer's Guide*, David Harmon and Amy Rubin say that a llama disturbs the soil less than a horse, but more than a backpacker. A llama's track is similar to an elk's, but the foot pad is softer so the hoof typically does not penetrate as far into the dirt, even in mud. Harmon and Rubin also note that llama manure is nearly indistinguishable from elk scat and attracts few if any flies. And most llamas have the admirable habit of stepping off trail before doing their duty. When breaking camp, scatter any piles of llama manure.

◆ Most llama packers do not carry feed with them. Even a big llama (around 400 to 450 pounds) will eat only about eight pounds of grass a day, sixty to seventy percent less than a horse. Nonetheless, some areas require feed to be packed in. Obey the regulations, and when traveling without feed, be considerate of wildlife foraging needs.

◆ Picketing and hitchlines are the two most popular ways to keep llamas in one place, and the same guidelines as for horses apply here. Llamas are highly social animals, though, so it may be possible to tie up a single animal and let the others roam nearby. This prevents trampling and grazing damage from being concentrated in one area. Keep an eye on your llamas and move them as needed to prevent overgrazing.

◆ Goats, being lighter and less able to carry heavy loads, cause even less trampling damage. But goat packers must closely monitor their stock to prevent a unique type of grazing damage. Goats display eclectic tastes when feeding, and non-food items such as packs, tents, clothes, plastic bags, and garbage are fair game. Keep goats out of camp, especially other peoples' camps, and don't let them nibble on trail signs, hitch rails, or other administrative facilities.

◆ Some land managers have expressed concern that llamas and goats might transmit disease to wildlife. Though studies are as yet inconclusive, these animals may be prohibited from some backcountry areas.

◆ Give horses and mules a wide berth when passing; some horses get skittish when llamas and goats are around (perhaps because the animals' odors are new and strange to them).

Dogs

The dog may be the earliest pack animal ever used, harnessed to drag a light travois. Some archaeologists speculate that dogs helped carry loads when Siberian tribes crossed the Bering land bridge into North America fifteen thousand to twenty thousand years ago. Their canine descendants are still pulling their weight today, either saddled with doggie panniers, or hitched to the traces of a dogsled. And some folks just enjoy their hound's companionship.

Many backcountry areas do not allow dogs because they can be a nuisance or threat to wildlife and other people. Even in areas where dogs are permitted, managers often discourage owners from bringing them (in 1976 three park rangers were attacked in separate incidents while trying to get owners to leash their pets). The problem is that even the most loyal and imperturbable dog can turn dingo and run amuck at the first whiff of wild rabbit or a whole forest of waiting trees. So if you elect to take Rover along on the next outing, heed the following guidelines.

♦ Keep your dog under control at all times. Don't let your dog chase wildlife or harass other people. Carry a leash and use it when trails are busy or wildlife is nearby. If other hikers appear nervous or alarmed, hold your dog by its collar until they pass. Do the same when encountering packstock.

♦ Keep your dog in sight when not on the leash. A dog unseen may be getting into trouble or harassing an innocent victim. Train your dog to obey verbal commands or hand signals. But also keep shouting and whistling to a minimum in the backcountry.

♦ Keep your dog quiet. Barking is an unnatural sound (coyotes and wolves yip and howl, but rarely if ever bark). Continual barking is especially annoying. If you can't control barking, leave the dog at home.

♦ Carry adequate dog food and a bowl. A well-fed dog is happier and more obedient. Lead your dog to drink downstream from any source likely to be used by people for drinking water.

♦ Lead your dog well off trail and away from water when it needs to defecate. If you're too late, scoop the pile up with a stick or rock and deposit it in an out-of-the-way spot where no one is likely to step in it. Using a cat hole (after the fact—don't expect Fido to squat over the hole you just dug) helps prevent accidental discovery by others. Don't let your dog defecate in camp.

♦ When mushing sled dogs on an established road or trail, slow down when approaching other travelers. Use extra care rounding blind curves. And yell out a warning when overtaking skiers or snow-shoers.

MOUNTAIN BICYCLES

The Forest Service reports that mountain bicycling and cross-country skiing are the two fastest growing forms of recreation on national forests. By default, mountain biking is suffering the poorer acceptance of the two among other backcountry recreationists. The reason? Skiing is done primarily when few other people are out in the backcountry, and thanks to the buffer of snow, skiing causes little or no damage to the landscape. Mountain bikes, on the other hand, are hitting the trails during the same seasons as hikers and packstock users, with scant awareness on anyone's part of the best protocol for coping with the encounters. And with their knobby tires and propensity for speed, mountain bikes have garnered, perhaps undeservedly, a reputation for damaging trails. In one California park, a few "kamikaze" cyclists have actually crashed into hikers, causing serious injury and no end to the wrathful sermons directed at even cautious cyclists on the same paths.

The reasons for retaliation against bikes in the backcountry may run even deeper. Traveling faster than other muscle-powered visitors, they appear out of nowhere, too often without warning. This can rattle even the most alert hiker or trail-wise mule. Some people object to mountain bikes simply because they are machines, all metal and whirring chains and gears, reminders of the very civilization we're all hoping to temporarily leave behind. And finally, a few folks take a gander at the flaming neon spandex, the funny shoes, high-tech accessories, and a styrofoam mushroom growing where the head should be, and they forget that a fellow human being—most likely a nature lover—dwells therein.

Bear in mind, mountain bikes became so popular precisely because they appeal to such a wide range of people. Having wrapped up eighty to ninety percent of all bike sales in this country, mountain bikes are here to stay. So what can we do, when aboard our own sprocket rocket, to prevent unpleasant encounters and harm to the land?

◆ The most important goal for the conscientious mountain biker is to minimize conflicts with other trail users. The easiest way to do this is common courtesy. Slow down when approaching others, and give a friendly greeting. Yield the right-of-way to all other trail users; give hikers plenty of room to pass.

◆ Ride in single-file when passing others. When meeting packstock head on, bikers should dismount and move to the downhill side of the trail. If overtaking a packtrain, speak out and ask for instructions. The horse riders may ask you to wait until they can find a wide spot in the trail, or they may request that you walk your bike past while the packtrain pauses.

◆ Anticipate encountering other people and wildlife on the trail. Slow down for blind corners or where terrain or vegetation causes limited-sight distance. Try to ride during low-use periods; avoid busy trails. Avoid spooking livestock and wildlife.

◆ Ride in small groups. A large pack of bikers is more likely to disturb other people, packstock, and wildlife. And when riders bunch up, there's a greater tendency to hit the brakes hard or veer off trail.

◆ Stay in control at all times, especially on descents. Slower speeds also prevent rocks from being thrown by tire treads—reason enough to slow down when approaching other people.

◆ When resting, carry the bike off trail so others may pass.

◆ Be discrete. Realize that a party of backpackers may have walked all day to reach their camping destination, though it took only three hours to cover the same ground by bike. The sudden arrival of a cyclist (likely traveling with no overnight gear) may destroy their illusion of remoteness.

◆ Wear a helmet. Not only will it protect your head, but land owners and managers don't get so anxious about liability when they see people taking responsibility for their own safety. Cyclists who dislike wearing helmets on long, hot ascents can strap one on the rear rack or into a day pack for later use on the way down.

◆ For all-around riding, keep the tires inflated to the maximum pressure recommended on the sidewalls. This provides the most efficient contact between tread and ground, reducing soil disturbance. In deep sand, gravel, or snow, you may need to let some air out for better traction.

◆ Check the bike for loose or damaged parts before each ride. Other trail users don't enjoy picking up hi-tech litter. Commonly lost parts include wheel and pedal reflectors, tire pumps, and pulley wheels and other pieces of broken rear derailleurs. Also plan ahead to recycle grease and oil (from shocks); don't pollute your local landfill.

◆ Stay on roads and trails, and only ride on trails open to bicycles. Riding in closed areas serves only to heighten antagonism between cyclists and other recreationists. Riding off-trail crushes plants and carves ruts in the soil, leaving unnecessary damage and fuel for the anti-bike crowd's ire. Ask for permission before riding on private property; leave gates as you found them.

◆ On trails, cyclists commonly follow the same "line" through corners and around obstacles. Wheel after wheel travels the same route until a rut develops. Soon the trail channels water instead of shedding it as it was designed to do. Remember that ruts will form more readily in soft or muddy soil. When safe and reasonable to do so, ride out of the obvious line while still staying on the road or trail.

◆ On dry ground, even the knobbiest bike tire does little or no damage to the soil, unless it is locked in a skid or spun in a hard push for traction. To avoid skids, control your speed and use both brakes, applying pressure gradually. On steep descents, shift your body weight behind the seat and over the rear tire to increase braking power on both wheels. You may want to lower your seat before beginning a descent. It's possible to "spin out" the rear tire during a steep climb on loose, rocky terrain. Learn to anticipate, and keep your weight over the rear wheel to increase traction. Standing up can shift weight forward over the handlebars, causing the rear wheel to spin out. If a slope is too steep to ride without skidding or spinning out, dismount and walk.

◆ Avoid riding in muddy conditions. The soils on south-facing slopes generally dry out faster than other areas; look there for places to ride in the spring or after snowmelt or rain. When riding through mud is unavoidable, the next best tactic is to slow down. Avoid skidding or spinning out. If wet or muddy sections are short and infrequent, dismount and walk through them, carrying the bike.

◆ Ride directly over water bars (logs or rocks placed in the trail to divert runoff), or dismount and carry the bike over them. Riding around the ends of water bars widens the trail and carves ruts that often reroute runoff back onto the trail. Most water bars slant across the trail, directing water to the downslope side. You may have to meander a bit (within the trail) to meet the water bar at a right angle—less of an angle and the bar may deflect your tire and cause a crash.

◆ Learn to ride switchbacks, uphill and down; do not shortcut them or skid around the turns. Most shortcutting and skidding is done by bikers heading downhill. To negotiate a switchback going downhill, ride slowly but keep your wheels rolling. Shift your weight back, sit upright (don't lean into the turn), and guide the front wheel through the middle of the turn. It takes a little practice, but your biking buddies will be impressed with your new-found agility.

CANOES, KAYAKS, AND RAFTS

The strong draw that water has on us, and the peculiar traits of water-borne recreation, call for a few special considerations among boaters of all kinds. (See pages 167 and 172 for additional guidelines for travel and camping along coasts and rivers and lakes.)

◆ The most important aspect of no-trace boating is protecting the water from contamination. This means making a concerted effort to keep litter contained and in the boat. Put all garbage in a plastic bag and secure it to the boat. Do not toss trash, food scraps, or cigarette butts overboard. Keep soap, beverages, bug repellent, human waste, fuel, and other foreign matter out of the water and in tightly-sealed, waterproof containers. Try to leave shoreline, streambed, and lake-bottom soils undisturbed; stirred up silt can smother fish eggs and other aquatic life when it settles. Look for sandy or gravelly landing sites, and keep commotion to a minimum wherever a silty or muddy bottom is easily churned up.

◆ Rafters, thanks to the large cargo capacity of their crafts, have earned a reputation for packing inordinate amounts of thirst-quenching beverages—ok, we're talking about beer, maybe the occasional soda pop. And nobody (this side of the Atlantic, anyway) likes lukewarm beer. So rafters also have developed a penchant for caching their beer under water. No problem—as long as you don't use glass bottles, lose your stash in the current, or forget it when leaving. Also, refrain from building dams to form a pool. This disturbs the streambed and sends a sediment plume far downstream. Pack out all your empties.

◆ In pristine areas, camp below the high water mark when possible (and safe). Look for a site on sand, gravel, or exposed bedrock. On popular rivers, find a less visible site on the backside or downstream end of islands or a short ways up a tributary stream. On lakes, look for coves and inlets, which will also offer protection from wind and weather.

◆ Lash gear securely to the boat to prevent loss in case you capsize. Unrecovered equipment is an expensive form of litter.

◆ Carry a fire pan and portable latrine. Many popular rivers now require these items for all boating campers.

◆ When hiking along or away from a river or lake, use established trails or walk below the high water line. When hiking as a group where there are no trails, spread out and avoid repeated use of the same routes. Skirt around boggy areas and communities of succulent plants.

◆ Give wide berth to people on shore or in the water, especially anglers, swimmers, snorkelers, and divers.

◆ Remember that sounds carry well over open water. Keep noise to a minimum.

CROSS-COUNTRY SKIING AND SNOWSHOEING

With a deep blanket of protective snow between themselves and the ground, cross-country skiers and snowshoers are free to roam widely with little concern for trampling or erosion. But snow travel brings with it several different concerns, mostly related to wildlife and other recreationists. The following guidelines are useful wherever skiers and snowshoers find enough snow for their particular brand of play. For more information, see the section on Snow and Ice beginning on page 161.

◆ The main ethical consideration for backcountry travelers in winter should be to minimize disturbance to wildlife. Winter is a challenging season for most animals—food is scarce, weather can be severe, and cold saps strength and endurance. Human presence in the backcountry during this time can spook wildlife, robbing them of crucial energy stores and opportunities to rest and feed. Many studies, including several of the elk herds in Yellowstone National Park, indicate that people on skis and snowshoes cause as much or more stress to animals than motorized traffic. This is due, in part, to the fact that skiers and snowshoers typically leave roadways and penetrate otherwise secure backcountry regions. Avoid areas where wildlife are likely—feeding and resting grounds especially.

◆ In popular areas, stay on established ski tracks. When unofficial tracks proliferate, neophyte skiers can easily be led astray. To ski away from set tracks, kick snow to cover your tracks where they leave the official route, particularly if you're heading for difficult terrain.

◆ Snowshoers should avoid walking on or across set ski tracks. Leave tracks intact for skiers to enjoy.

◆ Always ski in control. Remember that skiers of different skill levels will travel at different rates of speed. In popular areas, watch for other skiers on the tracks. Yell out a friendly warning to avoid surprising others. When climbing on a single track, step off to the downhill side to let faster skiers by. Also step to the downhill side when descending skiers approach. Everyone in your group should stand on the same side of the track to give other skiers one clear side for evasive maneuvers. Also, step out of the tracks when resting or adjusting clothes or equipment. When skiing downhill in tracks, be prepared to stop, turn, or step out of the tracks when approaching or overtaking other skiers.

◆ When taking skis off in deep snow, stamp on the snow with both skis on to create a pad firm enough to stand on in boots. This prevents creating "post holes" in the snow with your legs when standing without skis on. Post holes adjacent to tracks can collapse when someone else skis across them or hits one with a pole plant, causing unexpected falls.

◆ Some skiers apparently delight in urinating directly on ski tracks. Not only is this unsightly, it can wreak havoc with the next skier's waxing. Look for a spot well off-trail when nature calls.

◆ Remember that sound carries better over a firm crust of snow on a clear day. Keep joyous whooping and hollering to a minimum.

◆ Where snow cover is thin, such as on wind-scoured ridges, or when the snowpack is melting off, use extra care in crossing open ground. Exposed soils and plants may be saturated with water or brittle from freezing and more vulnerable to trampling and erosion.

◆ Snow campers should dismantle snow shelters after use, unless planning to reuse them in the near future. Also backfill any large holes, particularly snow pits dug into skiable slopes.

MOTOR VEHICLES

This book is aimed primarily at backcountry visitors traveling under their own power or on packstock, but most of the techniques discussed here are appropriate for anyone camping out under the stars, regardless of how they got there. Nearly everyone goes car camping now and then, and millions of Americans enjoy backcountry motorbiking and ATV use. Snowmobiling is a popular pastime during winter in our northern climes.

Granted, motor vehicles can be a lot of fun and offer access to remote places for people who otherwise might not be able to enjoy the backcountry. But ATVs also have the potential to cause greater disturbance to the natural environment and to other people than any other form of travel. Used carelessly or in the wrong place, motor vehicles can cause erosion, disturb other people and wildlife, and damage plants. All the more reason to look at ways to reduce the impacts of motorized backcountry travel.

◆ The easiest and best way for all motorized travelers to reduce damage to the backcountry is to stay on designated roads and trails. Do not ride off trail.

◆ Ride only in areas open to motorized use, and stay on routes designated for your specific type of vehicle. Maps are available for all national forests, parks, and BLM lands, with designated motor routes and areas closed to motorized use clearly defined. When in doubt, ask the local land manager. Land managers strive to educate rather than penalize visitors, but bear in mind that disregard for trail restrictions and closures may result in stiff fines, and where abuse is widespread, area closures to all motorized use.

◆ Motor vehicles of any kind are prohibited in designated wilderness areas, some wildlife management areas, and off-road in most national parks. Honor all closures, gates, fences, and traffic signs. Stay off wet or muddy roads, trails, and soils. Avoid streambanks, lakeshores, and wet meadows. Preserve motorized access by preventing erosion and other damage.

◆ Be considerate of other recreationists, especially hikers, stock users, skiers, paddlers, and other non-motorized visitors. Keep noise to a minimum, especially around campsites.

◆ Cross streams at right angles and at slow speeds. Try to avoid stirring up silt and mud from the bottom, which can smother fish, spawning sites, and other aquatic life.

◆ Use mufflers and spark arresters. Noise is one of the main complaints given by other travelers when encountering motor vehicles in the backcountry. Spark arresters are required in most backcountry areas to reduce the risk of wildfire. During fire season, regulations may require you to carry a shovel, bucket, and other fire-fighting tools. Know and obey the regulations relevant to your particular mode of travel.

◆ Keep your vehicle in good working condition. Poorly running engines pollute more than those that are well-tuned and maintained. Inspect your machine before each ride to ensure that it's not leaking engine oil, coolant, transmission fluid, lubrication, or fuel. A spill in the backcountry can threaten the health of local plants, wildlife, and waterways. Also tighten any loose parts to avoid leaving a trail of nuts and bolts.

◆ Keep a respectful distance from all wildlife. In general, studies indicate that motor vehicles cause less disturbance—or at least no greater disturbance—than people traveling under their own power. Researchers theorize that animals grow accustomed to the presence and noise of machines and do not perceive them as a threat unless approached too closely. When in doubt, back off. Never chase wildlife.

◆ Give all other trail users right-of-way. When overtaking a slower traveler, slow down and make sure they see you. Wait to pass until they step off trail or the track widens enough to permit it. Always ride in control, and heed all traffic regulations, including speed limits. Be alert for other traffic—and people enjoying other types of recreation—especially on trails with limited-sight distance, over the crest of hills, and when weather limits visibility. Stop and shut off your engine when meeting packstock on the trail.

◆ Wear helmets and other safety gear. Land managers are more likely to support access for recreationists who take proper steps to minimize risks.

◆ Avoid skidding or spinning tires, especially on steep slopes or in muddy conditions.

◆ Snowmobilers should try not to ride over the set tracks of cross-country skiers. Skiers often prefer to ski in tracks because it saves energy; beginners also find tracks aid in keeping their balance. Snowmobiles often leave hillocks and divots in their wake, creating a challenging (and usually unwanted) obstacle course for skiers of all abilities. Also ride in control and watch for skiers when snowmobiling on shared trails.

CLIMBING AND SPELUNKING

Highly specialized sports tend to generate idiosyncratic concerns when it comes to leaving no trace. Climbing and spelunking (exploring caves) are no exception, and practitioners of both sports have developed some interesting solutions to some odd problems many backcountry travelers never encounter. Ever wonder where climbers put human waste during a three-day ascent of the sheer granite face of El Capitan? Or how spelunkers mark their route in the dark maze of a new cave? Read on.

Climbing

◆ Many access and exit routes to popular climbs have webs of unofficial trails created by climbers. Try to halt the spread of such trails—keep foot traffic to a minimum and use existing trails whenever possible. Tread lightly when standing on belay—look for a rock or other durable surface to stand on and keep your pack, ropes, and other equipment off of fragile areas. After completing a climb, either rappel back down (if it's safe to do so), or choose a gradual, switchbacking route back to the bottom. Avoid clambering down the fall line and be willing to go a little out of your way to stay off unstable slopes.

◆ Whenever possible, use removable protection (chocks or nuts, and cams). Placing pitons and bolts scars the rock, detracts from the area's pristine character, and takes away the sense of discovery and challenge for subsequent climbers. As of this writing, the Forest Service is considering banning fixed anchors in designated wilderness areas. According to John Twiss, Forest Service National Leader for Wilderness Management, the agency is looking to cooperate with climbing groups to identify alternate sites outside wilderness where fixed anchors would be allowed. The National Park Service is also concerned about fixed anchors, but so far is taking a less restrictive approach. Yosemite climbing ranger Gary Colliver notes that "nearly all of the climbs in Yosemite—including all of the routes on El Capitan—are within designated wilderness. If you prohibit the use of fixed anchors, you eliminate eighty percent of climbing in the park." Climbers should recognize, however, that damage from climbing is a genuine concern. Colliver says that climbers should regulate themselves, using fixed anchors judiciously and practicing no-trace techniques. "Ask yourself," he says, "to do this climb safely, will I cause a serious impact? If the answer is yes, then you shouldn't do the climb." When fixed anchors are needed, Colliver recommends using natural-colored bolts that blend in with the rock.

◆ Do your best to remove all ropes, slings, and other equipment from your route after the climb. If a sling must be left behind, use camouflaged webbing. Search the ground and undergrowth at the base of the route for any litter, gear, or other items that may have fallen during the climb. Never throw anything off a climb—not even wads of tape or tissue paper. Pack out everything.

◆ Leave the rock face intact and as you found it. Chipping, chiseling, or gluing to improve holds or cracks scars the route for other climbers. It is ok, however, to remove small rocks if they are loose or in danger of falling.

◆ Avoid "gardening" (cleaning) cracks and on ledges. Removing soil and plants is prohibited in all national parks and designated wilderness areas. "When you garden a crack," says Colliver, you're removing an ecosystem. The soil supports countless micro-organisms, insects, plants, and other life up to the size of birds and small lizards. Leave it be."

◆ Climb as quietly as possible. Hammering, drilling, and shouting between lead and belay should be kept to the minimum needed for safe climbing. The use of power drills is prohibited in designated wilderness areas and in national parks.

◆ Reduce or eliminate the use of chalk. Colliver estimates that "half of all chalk use is unnecessary. It's probably not needed on anything but the most difficult free climbs." In dry climates, chalk leaves highly visible stains on the rock that will linger until the next cleansing rain. If you must chalk up, use a natural-colored chalk or mix a colored chalk with the standard white in your chalk bag. Many climbing stores now sell a chalk mix that matches local rock. In wetter climates, where frequent rains wash the rock, a small amount of chalk is permissible; it's still a good idea to buy colored chalk to blend in with the rock. Enclosed chalk bags are also available; these reduce the amount of chalk used.

◆ Whenever possible, pack out all human waste. The staff at Yosemite National Park have developed a workable method for coping with human waste on multi-day wall climbs. "Carry some lunch-size paper bags and a hard plastic container," recommends Colliver. "A heavy-duty, wide-mouth plastic bottle works well, but some people make their own 'poop tube'

Poop tube.

out of four-inch diameter pvc plastic pipe with a glued-on cap on one end and a threaded adapter for a screw-on plug on the other." Cut the pipe to length as needed for the number of days you'll be in the backcountry; a two-foot section is enough for five to seven days for most folks. Climbers often duct tape a loop of webbing onto the screw-plug end so they can hang the cannister from their haul bag, keeping the waste isolated from food, clothing, and other gear. Defecate into a paper bag and then "sprinkle in a handful of kitty litter to reduce odors and absorb moisture," says Colliver. Shake the bag to distribute the kitty litter, then roll it up and put it into the plastic container. Used toilet paper can go in the container, too. At the end of the climb, empty the contents, paper bags and all, into a designated non-flush ("vault" or "pit") toilet.

According to Mark Butler, a staff researcher and avid climber, Yosemite is planning to provide designated dump stations for climbers using this method. For now, anyone packing out human waste should first ask a local land manager to suggest an appropriate deposit site. "The idea is to get the waste into the formal sewage management system. But you don't want to overload or plug the pumps used to clean out vault toilets," says Butler. Make sure you use unwaxed paper bags, which will decompose more quickly.

Colliver says day climbers should use the same system, even if there are places on the climb with enough soil to bury waste. "On popular routes, such sites tend to be over-used; you end up with more waste than soil."

Butler notes that Yosemite sees about four million visitors each year. "Overnight use has held steady, but day-use—and the associated impact—is on the rise. And day-use impacts are harder to control because they're more widespread." Day-use visitors should use trailhead toilets whenever possible. If they must defecate in the backcountry, they can easily pack out their waste. It's only one day's worth of waste; a dump station is usually readily available at the trailhead; and day-hikers generally carry far less weight than overnighters. Butler and Colliver advocate using the poop tube method whenever traveling in sensitive environments, especially in designated wilderness areas or where surface waters could easily be contaminated.

Extended mountaineering expeditions (a week or more) may require on-site waste disposal. Mount Rainier National Park provides plastic bags to all climbers, and has stationed large barrels near popular basecamps on the mountain. When a bag is filled, it goes into the barrel, and the contents are later trucked to Bellingham and incinerated. At Alaska's Denali National Park, where the average trip to the summit of Mount McKinley takes twenty-four days, J.D. Swed and other park rangers advise climbers to collect human waste—including urine—in plastic bags and drop it into deep glacial crevasses. Says Swed, "This at least keeps surface snow, which is melted and used for cooking by other climbers, relatively clean, and the glacier should have about ten thousand years to chew on the waste before spitting out what little is left."

◆ Pack out all trash, worn-out equipment, and excess food. Plan and pack carefully to reduce your pack weight on the way out.

◆ Be courteous to other climbers. Ask for consent before passing other climbers on the same route. Don't monopolize good resting or belay places. Always climb as though people were below—do not drop anything and strive to minimize rock falls.

Spelunking

◆ Caves, especially deep ones, are essentially closed systems compared to habitats in the daylight world. Nothing much enters the bowels of a cave, and little more ever exits. Darkness is constant; air exchange may be limited; humidity, temperature, and other factors are often fairly static. Natural features and processes (such as stalactite formation) and subterranean life forms develop in these conditions and are highly susceptible to harm when changes occur. The main concern of the conscientious spelunker, then, is to minimize change to the cave environment. Bring in as little as possible, leave nothing, and take nothing out.

◆ Leave natural features as you found them. Some surfaces, such as travertine, can be marred by touch.

◆ When people explore caves, they tend to follow the most obvious routes. Travel by subsequent spelunkers, then, is concentrated along the same corridors and chambers. For this reason, it is doubly important to pack out what you pack in.

◆ Use temporary route markers. In the past, cavers have relied on many methods, too many of them permanent, for marking their return route to the outside world. Today, cavers either trail a spool of twine as they go in, rewinding it on the return trip, or place reflective decals or swatches of tape along the route, to be removed on the way out. The decals work particularly well in dry caves and on longer routes where the length of twine needed would be prohibitive.

◆ On brief cave trips, refrain from eating while in the cave. Any food, even dropped crumbs, may upset the natural balance of nutrients and organisms that feed there.

◆ Carry out all human waste. Generally, it is best to exit the cave to defecate and urinate, but on extended underground expeditions or rescue operations this is not always possible. See the climbing section above for details on how to pack out waste.

Snorkeling and Scuba Diving

When we hear the word "wilderness," most of us conjure up images of craggy mountains and deep forests. Few people think of the realm beneath the waves, yet here is the last great unexplored region on our planet. And today's explorers don't have to plumb the ocean depths to find adventure—just pull on a diving mask and take a look beneath the surface of any coastal bay, inland lake, or river. Suddenly you're flying through a strange new world, seemingly far removed from civilization.

Underwater recreation now has devotees in every state. The warm waters of the Gulf Coast boast some of the finest snorkeling and diving in the world, with coral reefs, sunken ships, and a wide menagerie of sea life. In the Northeast, divers explore the depths of old marble quarries inundated by rain, runoff, and the local water table. In Montana, Idaho, and California, gold prospectors don wet suits, masks, and air tanks in search of nuggets lodged among streambed cobblestones. And across the country, many urban and state parks with lakes have added to their recreational offerings by sinking an old boat in the middle of the pond as a training tool and playground for divers.

Innovations in equipment design and the widespread availability of professional instruction have brought snorkeling and scuba diving into the reach of anyone who can swim. But by the same token, the underwater world is also now more accessible—and more liable to damage. Florida's John Pennekamp Coral Reef State Park, along Key Largo, is probably the most popular site in the United States for snorkeling and diving. The reefs here draw one million visitors each year, and park officer

Andrea Ash says that teaching reef etiquette is a full-time job. "We can't keep our brochures in print because we hand them out so quickly," she says, "so we rely on little plastic cards that cover the basics." Local boat rental businesses also preach reef etiquette to their clients, but damage still occurs. "We have a lot of groundings on the reefs," says Ash, "mostly due to lack of experience handling a boat, or lack of navigation skills. Some people approach the reefs too quickly or too closely, even though the shallows are posted with big warning signs with 'DANGER' spelled out in ten-inch high letters." Boaters who learn the hard way pay dearly for the lesson, notes Ash. "Coral is expensive—valued at $263 and spare change per square foot. When somebody runs a boat into it, we issue a criminal citation and a fine based on the extent of damage done to the coral. A $20,000 to $30,000 fine is not unusual for a twenty- to forty-foot boat. And that doesn't include the cost of repairs to the boat." It's far better to heed the following simple precautions.

♦ Coral is alive. Reefs provide habitat for thousands of different fish, crustaceans, invertebrates, and plants. Do not touch coral—neither with hands, tools, or swim fins. Do not break off pieces of coral from the reef. Leave coral intact and as you found it.

♦ Do not stand on coral or other aquatic organisms. Refrain from kicking up sand, which can smother coral. Reef Relief, an environmental education center in Key West, Florida, recommends wearing a float jacket when snorkeling so that you can adjust your equipment without standing on the reef or sea floor. Divers should wear only as much weight as needed and properly control buoyancy at all times.

♦ Display a diver's flag—a buoy marked with the international sign of a red rectangle cut by a white diagonal stripe.

♦ Use extra caution when boating in shallow areas. Carelessness has led to unnecessary propeller and keel scars on many coral reefs and the backs of dolphins, whales, and manatees. Many areas levy fines for damage done (not all as stiff as Pennekamp's, but costly nonetheless). Anchors also damage coral; use a reef mooring buoy or anchor on a sandy bottom away from reefs and seagrass beds. Watch for and steer clear of divers' flags.

♦ In waters without coral (inland lakes, cold coastal areas, and rivers), treat all aquatic plants and animals gently. Keep boats out of shallows and avoid handling aquatic life or walking on the bottom.

♦ Avoid conflicts among divers and anglers. Do not boat or swim near fishing lines; similarly, do not fish around snorkelers or divers. Move to another area.

♦ Collecting shells and other natural features is a popular hobby for many snorkelers and divers, and it is fast becoming too popular in some areas. Bottoms are picked clean of unbroken shells and sand dollars. In most national and local parks along Florida's coast and in the Caribbean, divers are prohibited from taking anything back to the surface with them. Queen conchs are a protected species and are illegal to collect. Ask beforehand about local regulations. In unregulated or less popular areas, it's still best to leave shells, rocks, and even human artifacts as you found them. Those who insist on a momento of their dive should invest in an underwater camera and take only photographs.

◆ Contrary to the common portrayal of divers frolicking with sea turtles, manta rays, eels, and whales, it's best to leave all underwater wildlife undisturbed. Do not feed them. These animals are under the same pressures to find food, fend off preda-tors, and conserve energy as are wildlife on land. They deserve the same considera-tion. Remember that it is illegal to approach or harass marine mammals, on land or in the water.

SAFETY

There is no such thing as pure pleasure;
some anxiety always goes with it.

—Ovid

A good scare is worth more than good advice.

—Ed Howe

Wild country is probably no more dangerous than our backyards, and certainly less so than the highways we drive to reach the trailhead. But there are a few hazards unique to the backcountry, and even mundane, garden-variety accidents and injuries can turn serious when they strike in a remote, unpeopled area. When trouble hits in the wilderness, there's no phone, no 911, no emergency room crew to turn to.

Of course, that's one of the attractions of wild country—the inherent risk and challenge, the opportunity to be self-reliant. In a society as specialized and interdependent as ours, it's a welcome change to head for the hills—for a day or a week—to play weather forecaster, botanist, wildlife biologist, sanitation engineer, navigator, mechanic, cook, doctor, and security guard all in one.

At the same time, each of us must know and heed our limits. No one can be an expert on every subject or always prepared to cope with every hazard. The best we can hope for is to reduce our risks by learning about backcountry hazards and how to avoid them. Bear in mind that it is impossible and probably undesirable to remove all elements of risk; there is simply no way to ensure your absolute safety from lightning, falling rocks, animal attack, or sudden illness. That's life, particularly life in a wild, wide open environment where human control is limited or absent. In his book, *Safety*, Alton Thygerson goes so far as to suggest that safety "should not be the main objective in life." His focus instead is on the rewards that safety offers: continued enjoyment of a potentially risky endeavor, personal growth, and an interesting, exciting life. Indeed, part of the fun of backcountry travel is gaining the skill and confidence to deal with the challenges, dangers, and emergencies that arise. Life is risky, Thygerson suggests; to cocoon ourselves in safety—in fear of injury or death—is to deny ourselves the opportunity to fully live.

But each of us must choose a level of risk that is acceptable to ourselves. What is risky to one person is safe to another. The key here is knowing and heeding *your own* limits. Each of us responds differently to any given situation, based on a lifetime of experiences and on our personal skills and abilities. Rather than comparing yourself to others or bowing to peer pressure, listen to your inner voice.

To guide that inner voice in a reasonable way, Thygerson poses three guidelines for assessing risk.

◆ Never risk more than you can afford to lose.
◆ Do not risk a lot to gain a little. Rely on reason—not emotion—to assess risk.
◆ Weigh the odds, and assess whether you—or circumstances—are in control.

In other words, *measure the risk*. Is injury probable? Will the injury likely be minor, severe, or fatal? Is the degree of risk acceptable? What is the worst that can happen? Do the rewards justify the risk? How do other members of the group feel? Remember that risk is relative and personal; never push anyone to go beyond what they think is reasonable.

Also bear in mind that certain human factors may increase risk. Fear, depression, or anger may interfere with a person's judgment and physical abilities. Lack of knowledge or skill, or inexperience with a given hazard, often leads to emotional stress—or an absence of stress when a dose of adrenalin might be in order. Fatigue or previous injury or illness may prevent a person from performing at a normal level. A lack of sleep, insufficient food, or simply being too hot or cold may reduce a person's stamina, strength, or coordination. Drugs—medicinal or otherwise—sometimes play a role. Statistically, alcohol is a big factor in accidental injuries and deaths. Be aware that some medicines may cause drowsiness, slow reaction time, and impaired judgment.

Perhaps the biggest human factor, as we've already hinted, is attitude. Know your own limits. Don't let desire or ego override good judgment and common sense. Have a back-up plan for when things go wrong and leave yourself an out. Learn from each experience, and don't be afraid to back away from a challenge if it seems too big. Live to try again when you're better prepared. Learn new skills on familiar terrain where the level of challenge and risk is small and controllable.

Not surprisingly, the first principle we listed in Chapter 2 works as well for safety as it does for leaving no trace: Plan ahead, prepare well, prevent problems before they occur.

Plan ahead. Know what to expect; learn about the area you plan to travel in, its weather, wildlife, and topography. Contact the local land managers for specific information and guidelines on safety concerns peculiar to the area or region. Scan maps to learn the general lay of the land and familiarize yourself with prominent landmarks and terrain features. Plan your route, complete with alternate routes and back-up camping destinations. Leave your itinerary with a friend and with local authorities.

Prepare well. Some preparation is long-term and begins well before any specific trip even reaches the planning stage. Your health and physical and mental fitness play an important role in coping with risks and hardship in the backcountry. To stay healthy, eat a proper diet high in complex carbohydrates, vitamins, and protein and low in fats, particularly saturated fats. Each day the average adult needs about sixty-five grams (2.3 ounces) of protein and from two thousand to six thousand calories, depending on the level of activity. Most of these calories should come from nutrition-packed foods such as potatoes and rice, cereals, whole grains, fruit, and vegetables.

Begin a regular exercise routine that includes at least twenty minutes of aerobic activity three or four times a week balanced with three to four strength workouts a week. Request a physical from your doctor before beginning any exercise program, and start out gradually. Even brisk walking can be good exercise. Choose workouts that simulate the type of exercise you will encounter in the backcountry: walking or running helps prepare for backpacking, and a stationary bike, ski, or rowing machine tones the right muscles for those respective sports. Make a year-round effort and you will enjoy the first trip of the new season as much as the last.

Also strive to continue learning about all aspects of wild country recreation—wildlife, botany, weather, health and first aid, travel and camping techniques, and leave-no-trace practices. Some subjects require regular practice or training to maintain proficiency. Take annual refresher courses in first aid, cardio-pulmonary resuscitation (CPR), avalanche safety, life-saving, and map and compass orienteering. Be aware that new information or ways of doing things are continually coming to the fore. Subscribe to magazines in your fields of interest and watch for news reports and special classes to update your skills and knowledge. Also try to learn from each new experience in the backcountry. "Education teaches you the basics, the rules," says the voice-over on the video *Avalanche Awareness*, "and experience teaches you the exceptions."

Prevent problems before they occur. Undoubtedly the easiest way to repair an injury, cure an illness, or survive a natural calamity or wildlife attack is to avoid the hazard in the first place. Careful planning and preparation serve that end well. And knowing what to expect and how best to fend off particular problems is the key to effective planning and preparation. That's what this chapter is all about—supplying the basic information about common (and a few not-so-common) hazards found in North America's diverse wild country.

If you do get into trouble in the backcountry stay calm and take charge of the situation, rather than letting circumstances control you. Repeat to yourself Teddy Roosevelt's all-purpose mantra: "Do what you can, with what you have, where you are." Remind yourself that even if help is hours away, it is not unreachable. Few corners of North America are now so remote that they are not covered by local search-and-rescue teams and life-flight helicopters. Realize, however, that *you alone are responsible for your safety*. Don't expect others to come to your aid. If a rescue is organized keep in mind that you may be held liable for the costs of rescue operations, including helicopter flight time. This may hold true even if the rescue was un-necessary—if, for example a search party was sent out because you didn't return to civilization at an appointed place or time. If you filed your itinerary as suggested (see page 76), somebody will know where you are and will eventually come looking for you.

In many cases, an injured or ill person cannot or should not travel or be moved. Attend to any life-threatening injuries and make the patient as comfortable as pos-sible, providing shelter, food and water (unless contraindicated), and emotional support. Have at least one person stay with the patient while one or two others go for help. Before they leave, make sure that the people going for help know the best route to the nearest vehicle, telephone, or road, and carry with them a map with the patient's location marked precisely. Send with them a written summary of the patient's injury. If awaiting help, try to make your location more visible. Build a small, smoky campfire and spread out any large, brightly colored clothes or equip-ment in a conspicuous manner to attract attention. The universal emergency signal is anything in groups of three. Make three large, parallel hatch marks by laying big branches or rows of stones next to each other in a clearing. Use bright colors and distinctly human markers when possible. Save your energy; do not shout or whis-tle unless you know rescuers are nearby, and then do so in bursts of three.

If a rescue helicopter arrives, stay at least 150 feet distant until the rotors stop or the pilot asks you to board. Protect your eyes and face (and the patient) from flying debris as the helicopter lands. Never approach a helicopter unless instructed to do so, and then only from the front, in sight of the pilot. Bend over to keep your head clear of the rotor blades. If the helicopter cannot land and a rope or cable is dropped, allow it to touch the ground before grabbing at it to avoid a static electri-cal shock. Never affix the rope to an immovable object—this could cause a crash.

BASIC FIRST AID

Ideally, everyone who ventures into wild country should first take a certified first aid training course, including cardio-pulmonary resuscitation (CPR). And then, because first aid is definitely one topic where a little education can be danger-ous, enroll in a refresher class each year. There's simply no other way to ingrain all of the skills and knowledge needed to cope with the wide variety of possible back-country injuries and illnesses.

First aid and CPR courses are offered in most communities through the American Red Cross, colleges and universities, and local hospitals. You can also improve your first aid skills by joining the local ski patrol or search-and-rescue association and partaking of their training programs, in turn contributing some of your time to help others in need.

The following section examines a number of common first-aid concerns, from assessing vital signs to patching a blister. But detailed instructions for critical emergency care (such as rescue breathing, CPR, and splinting broken bones) are beyond the scope of this book and are not provided. An excellent reference text, *Outdoor Emergency Care*, by Dr. Warren Bowman, president of the Wilderness Medical Society, is available for purchase through the National Ski Patrol office in Denver, Colorado (see Sources). These are vitally important topics, to be sure, but also complex ones. The proper performance of CPR, for example, cannot be learned by reading about it in a book and to try to do so would be dangerous. We have focused, instead, on special concerns that arise when emergency care is given in the backcountry, where "first" aid is likely to be the *only* aid until the patient can be evacuated. Considering CPR again as an example, it is a far different decision to begin CPR on a patient in a crowded downtown restaurant, where help is just a phone call away, than to do so on a remote, windswept ridge with a storm rolling in and no way to summon help until the next day. (See pages 80 and 81 for further discussion of this issue.)

Nonetheless, every wild country traveler should pursue basic first aid training with the awareness that someday soon, he or she will actually need it. The likelihood that you will need first aid training does not arise because injuries and illness are any more common in wild country, but because there usually isn't anyone else around to help. You, as a first responder, must know how to assess a patient's condition, perform needed life-saving measures, and keep the patient alive and as comfortable as possible until he or she can be evacuated.

Due to HIV/AIDS and other transmittable diseases, any first aid kit should include disposable rubber gloves (to protect hands from blood and other body fluids) and a plastic mouth shield or pocket mask (for rescue breathing and CPR).

The first rule of first aid is to NEVER MOVE A PATIENT UNLESS IT IS NECESSARY TO PROTECT THE PATIENT'S OR RESCUER'S LIFE. Assess the patient's condition and treat any serious injuries (including splinting broken bones) on the spot. But before you rush in to help, consider the risk of hazards such as rockfall, avalanche, lightning, hypothermia, or attacking wildlife. Approach carefully so as not to injure yourself or others or further harm the patient.

Always ask permission before beginning first aid care. Some people may refuse it. If injury or illness is serious, stay with the person—they may decide they need help after all. It helps to have a witness if the patient is unconscious or appears irrational and refuses care; you may decide to help anyway (in a life-threatening emergency).

When first examining the patient, always move the person as little and as gently as possible to prevent further injury or discomfort. Assume that there are head, neck, and spinal injuries until you can determine otherwise, especially if the person is unconscious. Also gather a "first impression" of the scene—position and general responsiveness of the patient; immediate circumstances that may need to be addressed while caring for the patient (wind, heat or cold, rain or snow, nightfall, etc.); and presence of a "smoking gun," a likely cause for the injury or illness. According to Dr. Bowman, the objectives of an assessment are to quickly detect and treat life-threatening injury and illness; to find out if anything else is wrong; and to miss nothing significant.

If the patient is alert and responsive, ask his or her name and the date, time, and place. Ask if the patient can move; ask where it hurts. Ask how the injury occurred. Ask if there's anything else you as the rescuer should know (relevant medical history, current medicines, allergies).

The ABCs of First Aid

Standard first aid practice is to first assess a patient's ABCs—Airway, Breathing, and Circulation. Bear in mind that you may have to pause during assessing a patient's vital signs to care for life-threatening conditions (obstructed airway, loss of breathing or pulse, serious bleeding). For an unconscious patient or a patient in obvious distress:

Check the Airway—make sure the person's airway is unobstructed. Open the mouth, lift up on the lower jaw or chin slightly to clear the tongue out of the airway, and look for any foreign object. If the person is not breathing and you do find an obstruction, sweep it out with a crooked finger, being careful not to shove the object in deeper. Do not attempt a finger sweep on a child or infant. Remove dentures only if they have fallen out of place and are in the way.

Check Breathing—watch the person's chest or place your hand on the sternum; does it rise and fall? Put your face close to the person's mouth and nose; can you feel any breath on your cheek or hear air going in and out? If the patient is breathing, move on to assess his or her circulation. If the patient is not breathing, begin rescue breathing (mouth-to-mouth resuscitation).

Check Circulation—check the patient's pulse by placing two fingers on the carotid artery, located on either side of the neck directly beneath the jaw and slightly behind the Adam's apple. You also can check the pulse on the inside of the wrist, about an inch below the base of the thumb. Feel the pulse for ten seconds, assessing whether it is weak or strong, slow or rapid. If a pulse is present, return to monitoring breathing and examining the patient for injuries. If no pulse is found, you may decide to begin CPR. Do NOT give CPR if any heart beat is present.

Before beginning CPR in a remote setting, weigh the possible outcomes. In a remote setting where help may be days away, it may be senseless to try and resuscitate a person suffering from massive or multiple severe injuries to vital organs. Remember too that CPR is exhausting labor—should the rescuer risk physical collapse, hypothermia, or heat exhaustion by attempting CPR for hours? In some cases, harsh reality says no.

Dr. Bowman suggests that CPR should NOT be started if:

◆ There is no heart beat due to major injury.
◆ There is no heart beat and help is more than an hour away, especially if the patient must be carried out.
◆ The chest cannot be compressed (due to freezing of tissues, massive chest injury, or rigor mortis).
◆ The patient drowned and has been immersed for more than an hour.
◆ Giving CPR would be dangerous to rescuers.
◆ The person appears dead—body is stiff, blood has pooled where body touches ground, rectal temperature is below sixty degrees F.

There are exceptions to the above list. DO start CPR if you suspect cardiac arrest is due to:

◆ lightning strike   ◆ avalanche burial
◆ hypothermia   ◆ cold-water immersion

If the chest can still be compressed on such patients, according to Bowman, "CPR should be given aggressively." Do not stop CPR until the patient's heart begins to beat on its own, or other rescuers arrive to take over CPR, or you are too exhausted to continue.

Finally, look for signs of head, neck, and chest injuries, and check for external bleeding. Also look and feel for signs of internal bleeding, especially around the abdomen and pelvis. Then examine the legs and feet, arms and hands, and finally the back, taking special care to look and feel for swelling, tenderness, or bruising along the spine, which may indicate a spinal cord injury. Do your best to find the cause of any significant symptoms (such as unconsciousness, an abnormal pulse, difficulty breathing, or pain) so that basic treatment can be given.

Heart Attacks

According to the National Safety Council, heart disease is still the number one killer in America. And due to the strenuous nature of most outdoor recreation, heart attacks are a not uncommon occurrence in the backcountry. Before undertaking any exercise, anyone unaccustomed to hard physical effort should be examined by a doctor before heading out for the backcountry. Ask your doctor to help you set up (and stick to) a year-round fitness routine that includes walking, jogging, aerobics, swimming, or other cardio-vascular workout and strength training for the major muscle groups. Also monitor your intake of fatty and high-cholesterol foods.

◆ Take it easy when starting out on any backcountry trip, and don't push the pace. Travel at a pace comfortable for the slowest member of the group, with that person at the head of the pack.

◆ Learn CPR and take an annual refresher course. CPR cannot be properly learned from a book, and it should never be practiced on another person. Enroll in a course that provides specially designed practice mannequins and a certified instructor.

◆ Know the signs of a heart attack: pain or tightness in chest that may radiate to the jaw, neck, left shoulder, and arm; person may clutch at chest; anxiety; weakness or sudden dizziness; shortness of breath; tingling or numbness in left arm, neck, or jaw; profuse sweating; pulse can be normal, slow, fast, weak, or strong; or no pulse; pale and cold skin; lips and extremities turn blue; unconsciousness; breathing stops.

◆ Keep the patient calm and comfortable. Send for help. Be prepared to give CPR. Watch for complications, including shock. Monitor vital signs.

Bleeding

The average human body contains about six quarts of blood. Even though each of us has our own private stash, most folks are highly impressed by the sight of blood, and this often leads to over-reaction and even panic when coping with external bleeding. Even minor wounds can get messy, particularly on the face or scalp. And severe hemorrhaging is legitimately frightening: if left unchecked, it can lead to irreversible shock and death in a matter of minutes. In either case, staying calm and acting quickly is the best response.

◆ **To treat minor bleeding,** clean the wound by rinsing with water and pick out any pieces of dirt with sterilized tweezers. If the bleeding does not stop on its own, apply firm pressure with a clean cloth (gauze pads or a bandanna) directly on the wound. Most minor wounds will stop bleeding in five to ten minutes. Pat the area dry and cover with a band-aid, gauze and tape, or other clean dressing. Keep lotions or ointments off of wounds, but a spritz of Bactine or other antibiotic is ok on minor scrapes and shallow cuts.

◆ **Puncture wounds** can be more serious, even though bleeding may not be profuse. Penetration into deeper tissue brings a greater risk of infection or damage to vital organs within. Most puncture wounds demand medical attention, including antibiotics and a tetanus shot if the person has not had a recent booster. Leave any impaled object in the wound and never remove anything imbedded in the eye. Trying to remove an object can further injure the patient, causing more serious bleeding or damage to nerves, tendons, muscles, or vital organs. Immediately evacuate anyone with an imbedded object—the risk of infection is serious and the wound should be treated by a doctor within eight hours. Clean the wound as well as possible and try to immobilize any protruding object. Cover deep or puncture wounds with a dry gauze dressing and leave the wound open so it can drain.

Swelling or spreading discoloration around the wound may indicate internal bleeding or infection.

◆ **Serious bleeding** must be stopped immediately. Loss of a quart of blood causes moderate shock, which can rapidly worsen (and turn life-threatening) if the bleeding is not stopped and shock symptoms reversed. Severed arteries tend to bleed more than veins and so are more serious. Arterial blood is bright red and typically comes out in spurts as the heart pumps away. Venous blood is a darker maroon and flows steadily. Direct pressure is the treatment of choice, combined with elevating the injury above the level of the heart. Do not apply a tourniquet unless properly trained to do so.

◆ **Internal hemorrhaging** can be difficult to diagnose and even harder to treat in the backcountry. Signs include increasing pain, swelling, and discoloration. Bleeding from internal organs may cause nausea; weakness; and blood in feces, urine, or vomitus.

For simple bruises, apply a cold compress—ice or snow in a bandanna. Elevate the injured part. Take acetaminophen or aspirin for the pain and rest. In the field little can be done to stop internal bleeding if it's more serious than simple bruising.

Keep the patient calm and quiet, and evacuate to the nearest hospital. If a body part is accidentally amputated, wrap it in a clean plastic bag, keep it cool (but not in direct contact with cold water, ice, or snow), and transport the part with the patient to a hospital. Use direct pressure to stop bleeding from the stump, and apply a tourniquet only if the patient would otherwise die from loss of blood.

◆ Prevent **nosebleeds** by protecting the nose from hard knocks and keeping the inner tissues moist. Several large blood vessels run near the surface inside both nostrils, and it is possible to lose a lot of blood in a hurry from a simple nosebleed. In dry or cold climates, a light coating of petroleum jelly in both nostrils will prevent cracking of the mucus membranes. Also don't blow your nose too hard, especially after exertion or at high elevation, and blow only one nostril at a time. Seal the other closed with a finger when you blow.

To stop a nosebleed, sit down, leaning forward slightly so the blood won't drain down the throat. Blow gently out of the injured nostril to clear out any clots. Press the nostril closed with a finger on one side of the nose and hold for five minutes. If that doesn't stop the bleeding, roll up a corner of a clean bandanna or other cloth and put it under your upper lip. Press firmly against the upper lip to restrict blood flow in the arteries that supply the nose. Hold the compress in place for five to ten minutes, longer if needed. For minor bleeding, breathe in gently through the nose and out through the mouth. Air helps clot the blood. For heavier bleeding, place a rolled up gauze pad in the opening of the nostril (do not push it up the nose) and gently hold the nostril shut with one hand while also pressing on the upper lip. An ice pack may also help.

Shock

Anticipate **shock** in patients with any serious injury, especially when accompanied by spinal cord damage, heart failure, or severe bleeding. The patient often exhibits anxiety, a sense of impending doom, nausea (maybe vomiting), and weakness or dizziness. As shock progresses, the skin turns pale or bluish, cold, and clammy; the patient may feel cold; and the eyes go dull. The pulse will become rapid and weak, and rapid breathing becomes labored, then gasping. Sweating and dilated pupils are characteristic.

Shock is a life-threatening emergency, and in later stages it cannot be adequately treated in the backcountry. Do your best to stop its progress and treat the injury that is causing the shock. Encourage the patient to lie on his or her back and elevate the feet about twelve inches off the ground. If breathing is difficult, allow patient to sit in a reclining position with knees bent slightly. Monitor the patient's airway, breathing, and circulation, and give rescue breathing as needed.

Look for and treat injuries. Control bleeding, splint broken bones or dislocated joints (this helps control bleeding and pain). Cover the patient to prevent chilling but do not over warm. Do not give food or fluids unless the patient is in shock from dehydration or is hypothermic but responsive. Check vital signs every ten minutes. Send for help and evacuate to a hospital as soon as possible.

Broken Bones

Proper backcountry emergency care for broken bones requires a high degree of training and hands-on experience under expert guidance. Some fractures pose risks to blood vessels, nerves, or other vital tissues, and open wounds with exposed bone are especially susceptible to infection. Learn the appropriate care in an advanced first aid course, and practice splinting various body parts until you become proficient.

While tending to a fracture also assess the patient's airway, breathing, and circulation. Try to figure out what caused the fracture; examine the site of the break and any other areas of pain indicated by the patient. Look for other injuries, particularly if the patient has problems with breathing or circulation.

The idea behind a splint is to immobilize the *joints* above and below the fracture. This prevents the movement of other body parts from jostling the break. Splinting also helps reduce swelling, pain, and bleeding, and hence reduces the likelihood of shock. It's also much easier and safer to move and evacuate the patient once the fracture is splinted. Regardless of where or why a splint is applied, do not bind it on too tightly. Check frequently to ensure that the splint and straps do not interfere with circulation or nerve function.

You may need to re-align a broken arm or leg before splinting. DO NOT RE-ALIGN FRACTURES OF OR NEAR THE SPINE, KNEE, WRIST, ELBOW, OR SHOULDER. Because important nerves and blood vessels could be injured in these areas, splint these injuries in the position in which they were found. A break of the thigh bone, or femur, should also be splinted as it was found because of danger to the femoral artery (unless you are a trained emergency care provider and experienced in applying traction splints).

Since most people don't carry specially designed splints into the backcountry (though several models of collapsible or inflatable splints are available), some way to immobilize the injured body part must be improvised. This is easier than it might seem, even with nothing more than the common contents of a hiker's pack. Excellent splints can be fashioned by wrapping and strapping a sleeping pad around the injured leg or arm. Or use clothes to pad a branch, paddle, bicycle pump, ice axe, tent or ski pole and lash it to the injured part. Padded hipbelts and shoulder straps also work well. You can also strap an injured leg to the good leg, or a broken upper arm to the side of the chest.

It is impractical in most backcountry situations to improvise a backboard or other splint to immobilize injuries to the spine. The best option is to immobilize the patient on the ground with sleeping bags, packs, and rolled up clothes. Pay particular attention to protecting the neck and limiting its range of motion. Also make sure the patient is well insulated from the ground and sheltered from weather. Set up camp around the patient, monitor vital signs, provide basic life support and emotional support, and send for help.

Burns

Burns are ranked by severity, determined by how deep the burn is and whether the tissue is reddened, blistered, or charred.

A *first degree* burn is superficial. The skin is red, tender or painful, and may be swollen. No blisters form.

A *second degree* burn involves deeper layers of skin. The victim suffers intense pain, swelling, and blisters.

A *third degree* burn penetrates through the skin and into deeper tissues. The skin turns dry, leathery, and charred or discolored. Muscle and bone may also be burned. There are no blisters, and the skin is numb due to destruction of nerves. Surrounding tissues may bear second degree burns and be quite painful.

Burns are life-threatening and should be treated as critical when:

◆ Third degree burns cover ten percent or more of body surface, or second degree burns cover twenty percent or more of body surface.

◆ Hands, feet, face, or genitals are burned to the second or third degree.

◆ Nostrils, mouth, throat, or lungs are burned, even if only to the first degree.

◆ Burns occur in combination with other serious injuries such as severe bleeding, broken bones, or nerve damage.

Undoubtedly the most common type of burn suffered by backcountry travelers is **sunburn**. Though most cases are mild and require little treatment short of getting out of the sun and applying cold compresses, sunburn can be serious and debilitating. In addition, exposure to the sun's ultraviolet rays should be limited to prevent eye and skin damage and the possible, eventual onset of skin cancer. Severe sunburn should be treated by a doctor, especially if it is extensive or if blisters form.

Remember that sunburn is a year-round hazard: winter snows may reflect seventy to ninety percent of the sun's UV rays, and solar radiation is more intense at higher elevations. Prevent sunburn by covering all exposed skin. Wear long-sleeved shirts and long pants and a hat with a wide brim, or desert-rat style with a neck coverlet. Don't neglect to cover the back of your neck, ears, nose and cheeks, backs of hands, and tops of feet. Be aware that ultraviolet light can penetrate wet or sweat-soaked cotton t-shirts, burning the skin beneath.

Use a sunscreen with a sun protection factor (SPF) of at least fifteen. Brands are now available that are water and sweat proof, and won't run into your eyes. It's best to apply sunscreen an hour or two before exposure to the sun; reapply as needed. For extreme conditions (at high altitudes, on snow or ice, on water), or for those with extra sensitive skin, use a sun block containing zinc oxide or titanium dioxide.

The other main sources of burns in the backcountry are cookstoves, campfires, and hot water. Always follow the manufacturer's instructions when fueling, priming, and operating cookstoves. Keep sparks and other ignition sources away from stoves and fuel stores. Most campfire burns happen when someone falls asleep too near the flames or embers, or when a fire rages out of control due to wind or tinder-dry grasses and other fuels surrounding the fire. Do not build a fire in dry or windy conditions. Pitch tents well away from the fire, preferably up wind. Keep combustibles a safe distance from the fire, and do not let clothes or hair drape near the flames. It is more comfortable and safer to cozy up to a small fire than a large one; embers can also be more easily contained should the wind pick up.

Remember that water transmits cold and heat more quickly than air of the same temperature. Water need not be boiling to cause burns. Third degree burns (the most severe) can occur after just five minutes immersion in 120 degree F. water. Use extra caution when soaking in natural hot springs or using stove-heated water for bathing or washing dishes.

If a person's clothing does catch on fire, get them to *stop, drop, and roll*. Extinguish any flames or smoldering clothes on the victim. Move the person to safety, away from any flames or smoke. Gently apply cold water to the burn. This halts the penetration of heat into deeper tissues and eases the pain. Do not chill the patient.

Assess the patient's airway, breathing, and circulation. Estimate the extent and severity of the burn while removing rings, watches, bracelets from burned areas if possible. Look for other injuries and treat as needed.

To bandage any burn, use only sterile dressings; burned skin is sterile. Leave blisters intact. Do NOT apply any oil (including butter or margarine), ointment, lotion, or antiseptic cream to a burn. If fingers or toes are burned, put sterile gauze between the digits. Apply a cold dry compress if available (ice or snow in a plastic bag wrapped in a towel works well). Immobilize any arm or leg with second or third degree burns. Anticipate shock and treat as needed; evacuate immediately to a hospital.

Blisters

Blisters on the hands and feet are one of the more common backcountry ailments. Though painful, they are rarely serious unless an infection takes over. And then things can go downhill in a hurry.

◆ Prevent foot blisters by wearing comfortable, broken-in shoes. Keep the laces snug and adjust them as needed while hiking. Try different lacing patterns—such as a half-hitch above and below a sore spot, with laces loosened slightly between hitches—to alleviate pressure. Also trim your toenails before each trip.

◆ Your choice of socks should be based on what works best for your feet. Some people find that acrylic socks wick moisture away from the skin better than cotton socks and are more durable. Others swear by cotton or wool. For heavy-duty walking, try a thin liner sock with a thicker wool oversock. Change socks when wet. Avoid soaking your feet until end of day. But do air out your feet—and socks and shoes—during lunch or long rest stops.

◆ Wear gloves when hands might be exposed to friction, such as when holding reins, ski poles, or paddles and oars.

◆ Some people ward off blisters by putting athletic tape over known trouble spots or at the first hint of warmth. Use a blister doughnut pad cut from moleskin for real trouble spots (as a preventive measure) or after the blister has formed. Leave skin over blisters intact to prevent infection.

Eyecare

Vision is perhaps the most important sense for wild country travel. Without eyesight, an acre of unfamiliar terrain would be as incomprehensible as the dark side of the moon. Yet our eyes too often go unprotected, vulnerable to spraying dirt, protruding branches, flying insects, and the full bore of the sun's radiation.

Good sunglasses are the first line of defense for eyes that brave the wilds. Wear sunglasses designed and certified to block the sun's ultraviolet (UV) A and B light waves. Darker lenses help cut glare, but the darker the lens, the wider your pupils dilate. If UV light isn't filtered while the pupils are wide open, the retinal damage may be worse than wearing no sunglasses at all. Also look for a high UV rating (one hundred percent) when buying ski goggles or sunglasses to be worn at high elevations or while traveling on snow, water, or sand. Some sunglasses include leather shields around the nose and sides to block reflected light. A hat with a dark visor also helps.

Sunglasses also help protect eyes from flying insects and debris. Shatterproof polycarbonate lenses are best for activities where flying objects or falls are likely such as mountain biking, skiing, and climbing. If you do get a hair or grit in your eye, a small metal mirror or a partner with a steady hand makes removal easier. Wash your hands first to prevent infection. Sometimes it's easiest to rinse the object away with a gentle stream of clean water. Always rinse with your head tilted sideways and the affected eye held lowest to the ground to prevent the object from being washed into the other eye. If rinsing doesn't work, avoid touching the eyeball directly. Use the corner of a clean tissue or try to maneuver the object onto the lower lid where it can be picked off.

Never try to remove any object imbedded in eye or impaling the sclera, iris, or pupil. Serious damage and blindness can result. Pad the eye with a sterile dressing, then cover with a paper cup taped in place. Patch the other eye to keep both eyes from moving (which can further harm the injured eye). Seek medical help immediately.

Constipation and Diarrhea

Digestive irregularities are unpleasant at best, but constipation or diarrhea in the backcountry is a sure recipe for misery, and sometimes worse. The pain of intestinal cramps can immobilize a person, and diarrhea, if left unchecked, can lead to severe dehydration, exhaustion, and potentially fatal complications.

◆ Most backcountry intestinal problems stem from a change of diet. Avoid freeze-dried foods, which are high in starch and can plug up the most reliable plumbing. If you are prone to constipation, try eating fruit (especially a few pitted prunes or raisins) each day and be sure to drink plenty of non-caffeine, non-alcoholic fluids.

◆ To prevent diarrhea, try to match the diet you are accustomed to at home. Stay away from excess fats (common in nuts, cookies, and many canned meats and stews). Treat all drinking water by boiling or filtering, and clean your hands thoroughly after dealing with human waste and before handling food (see page 45 for details).

◆ If a bout of the runs does strike, watch what you eat. For severe cases, lay off solid foods until your condition improves. But keep fluid intake up to prevent dehydration. Drink only clear, non-caffeinated liquids such as water, mineral water, and weak soup broth. With improvement, you can ease into solid foods with toast, crackers, bananas, applesauce, and hardboiled eggs. Avoid milk products, alcoholic drinks, spicy foods, citrus fruits and juices, and aspirin until the diarrhea subsides.

♦ Although you can buy over-the-counter drugs to help control diarrhea, few work as well as advertised. And if the diarrhea is caused by certain bacterial infections, the drugs may actually prolong or worsen the symptoms. Also, anti-diarrhea drugs should never be given to infants or children unless directed by a physician.

♦ If diarrhea persists for more than forty-eight hours, or if it is accompanied by fever, repeated vomiting, bloody stools, or swelling of the abdomen, the patient should be evacuated immediately and taken to a doctor.

Common Illnesses

One aspect of emergency care that's often overlooked is illness. Dr. Warren Bowman stresses that it is important to "learn how to cope with illness in the backcountry, how to provide emergency care for flu, pneumonia, and gastroenteritis." He notes that without antibiotics and other prescription drugs or the proper medical training to administer them, proper diagnosis and emergency care become all the more crucial in the backcountry. Even minor infections or respiratory conditions can turn serious when help is far away, and many illnesses require specific medicines or treatment unavailable outside a hospital. Here, the rescuer's primary goal is to keep the patient comfortable, prevent worsening of the condition, and evacuate the patient as soon as possible to the nearest hospital.

Streptococci, staphylococci, and other **bacterial infections** may affect the skin, eyes, mouth, throat, ears, sinuses, and internal organs. Symptoms may at first resemble a common cold or the flu, with fever, chills, irritated eyes, a sore throat, an ear ache, or stomach upset. On the surface, the affected area may appear red or swollen, and it may itch. Strep and staph infections persist long after lesser germs are defeated by your body's defenses, though you may feel temporarily better only to relapse a few days later. Untreated bacterial infections can lead to chronic illness and irreversible damage to vital organs, including the heart and brain. Acute cases may cause collapse, coma, and even death. Cancel the trip and see a doctor if a bad cold refuses to go away, gets worse, or gets better then worse. Also play it safe with any pain in the ears, sinuses, or throat and chest when accompanied by fever.

The **influenza virus,** or flu for short, is a serious respiratory illness that annually kills thousands of people in the United States alone. Though the very young, the elderly, and the infirm are most at risk from complications, a case of the flu could also turn ugly in anyone exposed to the elements or increased stress while traveling in wild country. Symptoms begin with a sudden high fever and chills, sore throat and cough, weakness, muscle and joint aches, headache, and loss of appetite. Sometimes nausea and vomiting or diarrhea accompany the flu. If these symptoms appear at home, cancel your trip. If they strike while deep in the backcountry, set up camp and hunker down for three to four days of rest. Drink plenty of fluids and take acetaminophen to control the fever. Keep warm and dry, changing out of sweat-soaked clothes as needed. If the patient's condition does not improve within three days, evacuate to the nearest hospital or send for help.

Pneumonia is an infection of the lungs that can deteriorate rapidly and may prove fatal if untreated. Symptoms include fever and violent chills, coughing, wheezing, shortness of breath or difficulty breathing, a tightness or pain in the chest (frequently aggravated by breathing or coughing), and the production of yellow, green, or brown phlegm. A patient may develop pneumonia as a complication of the flu or bronchitis, or it may arise on its own. Also suspect pneumonia in near-drowning victims who may have inhaled even small amounts of water into the lungs. Antibiotics and supplemental oxygen are the only effective treatment, so immediate evacuation is called for.

Also know how to recognize **appendicitis**, or inflammation of the appendix. Appendicitis usually begins with pain or discomfort, not always severe, around the belly button. Pain may come and go at first. Then it moves to the lower right side and becomes constant. Other signs to watch for include fever, loss of appetite, nausea and vomiting, possible diarrhea or constipation, and tenderness upon pressing on the abdomen or right side. All or only one of these symptoms may be present. Surgery is the only cure. Evacuate the patient immediately to the nearest hospital. Do NOT give laxatives, enemas, drugs, or any food or liquids including water.

Acute Mountain Sickness and Related Illnesses

With every step gained in elevation, the backcountry traveler takes one step further into a world to which most humans are not well-adapted. As elevation is gained the air grows colder, barometric pressure decreases, radiation from the sun is more intense, and oxygen is less available. On a gradual climb, most of these changes are subtle and barely noticeable. But climb too quickly and the symptoms of Acute Mountain Sickness (AMS) can strike with a vengeance.

At elevations greater than 7,000 feet, there is a significant decrease in the amount of oxygen absorbed through respiration by the blood. This, coupled with decreased air pressure, can damage blood cells and blood vessels in the lungs and brain. Exposure to cold, fatigue, and dehydration may also contribute to the problem, but the main culprit is almost always ascending too rapidly. To prevent AMS, climb gradually, avoid flying in to high elevations from near sea level, and schedule frequent rest days during prolonged ascents. Drink plenty of fluids and eat well to ward off fatigue.

Early symptoms of AMS are headache; dizziness; irregular breathing, especially at rest and while sleeping; fast, bounding pulse at rest; difficulty sleeping; lack of appetite, nausea, and vomiting; puffy hands and face; decreased urine output (urine may appear darker); and weakness and muscle aches. These difficulties quickly improve or go away as soon as the patient returns to lower elevations. The symptoms also usually disappear—more gradually—if the patient stays at the same elevation for several days to acclimate. Rest, drink plenty of fluids, try to relax your breathing, and take aspirin for headaches.

If the ascent is too rapid, however, or to an elevation of 12,000 feet or higher, the symptoms may worsen. The danger then is that the patient will develop a potentially fatal form of high-altitude sickness: High Altitude Pulmonary Edema (HAPE), or High Altitude Cerebral Edema (HACE). *Edema* is swelling caused when fluids leak from cells and blood vessels into surrounding tissues. *Pulmonary edema* is swelling in the lungs; *cerebral edema* is swelling in and around the brain. Because vital organs are affected in either case, and the condition often progresses very rapidly, both HAPE and HACE should be recognized as life-threatening emergencies requiring immediate treatment.

In a patient with HAPE, the symptoms of AMS worsen and the patient develops a dry cough, which soon turns watery, sometimes producing pink sputum. Breathing grows more labored and fluid build-up in the lungs causes a gurgling noise. The pulse becomes rapid, greater than 120 beats per minute. As HAPE progresses, the patient becomes disoriented, incoherent, and may hallucinate. If the condition is untreated, the patient will lapse into a coma and die.

A patient with HACE will progress beyond the symptoms of AMS, developing a persistent and often severe headache; disorientation, confusion, and possibly hallucinations; a loss of coordination and balance; the inability or unwillingness to sit, stand, eat, or urinate; and profound apathy. The patient may fall into a coma within twelve to twenty-four hours; if untreated, death soon follows.

To treat progressive AMS, or any sign of HAPE or HACE, descend immediately, while the patient is still able to walk. Watch for a decline in coordination or balance, a rapid pulse or rate of breathing that doesn't subside during a rest stop, nausea or vomiting that lasts for more than a few hours, severe headaches, or gurgly sounds coming from the chest. At the first hint of trouble, DESCEND! Drop at least 2,000 feet in elevation, preferably to below 10,000 feet. Carry the patient down if he or she can no longer walk.

Monitor the patient's condition during descent, paying particular attention to breathing, pulse, and responsiveness. Provide oxygen, if available, and rescue breathing if necessary. Breathing difficulties may be worse at night; work in shifts to monitor the patient, and never let a person with AMS, HAPE, or HACE symptoms descend alone.

Remember that altitude sickness is unpredictable. AMS, HAPE, and HACE can strike anyone, even the young, healthy, physically fit, and those who have previously had no difficulty at the same or higher altitudes. Mild AMS has been reported at elevations as low as 5,000 feet. Any form of altitude sickness can strike even after a person has apparently acclimated to altitude, though most cases occur within ninety-six hours at a given elevation. Delayed cases are sometimes caused by added stress, such as immersion in cold water, hypothermia, a respiratory infection, or even a hard fall.

Acute Mountain Sickness	
Symptoms	*Treatment*
Headache.	Try to breathe deeply and evenly.
Dizziness.	Rest. If traveling, slow your pace and your ascent.
Irregular breathing, especially at rest and while sleeping.	Drink plenty of fluids.
Fast, bounding pulse at rest.	Take aspirin for minor headaches.
Difficulty sleeping.	
Lack of appetite or nausea.	
Vomiting.	
Puffy hands and face.	
Decreased urine output; urine may appear darker.	
Weakness and muscle aches.	

The symptoms may go away after a few days at elevation. If the symptoms persist, or if any one symptom is serious enough to cause distress (such as a severe headache, vomiting, or difficulty breathing), descend immediately.

High Altitude Pulmonary Edema (HAPE)	High Altitude Cerebral Edema (HACE)
Symptoms	*Symptoms*
Headache.	Headache.
Nausea, lack of appetite.	Disorientation, confusion.
Dizziness.	Hallucinations.
Weakness and fatigue.	Loss of coordination and balance.
Dry cough, turning productive with watery, sometimes pink sputum.	Inability or unwillingness to sit or stand.
Difficulty breathing.	Lack of appetite.
Fluid build-up in lungs causes gurgling when breathing.	Apathy.
Rapid pulse, greater than 120 beats per minute.	Coma within twelve to twenty-four hours.
As HAPE progresses, patient becomes dis- oriented, incoherent, and may hallucinate.	Death.
If untreated, coma and death.	
Treatment	

Descend at first signs of HAPE or HACE.

If necessary, carry the patient to lower elevation.

Supplemental oxygen, a hyperbaric chamber (Gamow Bag), and advanced first-aid care are stop-gap measures only. Immediate descent is the only effective treatment.

Monitor breathing during descent, especially at night. Be prepared to assist breathing as needed.

ACCIDENTS

The National Safety Council reports that accidents are the fourth most common cause of death. Within the accident category, motor vehicle wrecks account for the greatest number of fatalities, but also high on the list are falls, drowning, burns, choking, poisoning, and accidental discharge of guns. Far too many of these mishaps occur in the backcountry.

But accidents are a part of life, and, as John Lennon noted, "Life is what happens when you're busy making other plans." If you know what to expect—what sorts of accidents to anticipate in wild country—you can at least ward off the worst mishaps and minimize the damage from the remainder.

Slips and Falls

One of the most common causes of injuries, at home or in the boondocks, is falling down. The National Safety Council reports that half of all falls from a height of at least eleven feet are fatal. Nearly all falls from sixty feet or higher are fatal.

Gravity gets us all in the long run, but many falls can be prevented. Here's how.

◆ Wear shoes with good traction. The best shoes for all-around backcountry use are light-weight hiking boots with a tacky, matt-finish rubber outer sole and a fairly shallow tread. See page 27 for a list of features found on such boots.

◆ Carry only as much weight as you can safely handle. Overloaded packs only make balancing (and recovery from a near-fall) more difficult and increase the chance for injury in a fall. Use a stick or ski pole for added stability.

◆ Watch where you step. Feet accustomed to sidewalks and manicured lawns forget how to walk on rough, uneven ground. Scan the ground ahead for obstacles and stop when you want to enjoy the scenery. Be alert for loose rocks, holes, exposed roots, mud, and ice. When wet, rocks and logs (including water bars across trails) can be incredibly slick.

◆ On steep terrain, move slowly and deliberately. Avoid loose rock and soil and stay away from cliff edges. Look for hand holds if necessary. Know your limits. If your stomach knots at the thought of forging ahead back off. When crossing scree, talus, or other loose rock spread the group out on a gentle contour so no one hikes directly below another person. Avoid steep-sided gullies and convex slopes. Seek out routes on bedrock or talus imbedded in soil.

◆ Wading through a stream is much safer than crossing on a log or stepping stones. Wet logs and rocks are especially slick; carrying a pack adds to the risk of falling. Regardless of how you cross a stream, test each step for steadiness and slipperiness before committing all your weight to it. If the footing is unsafe look for another way across. See page 143.

◆ Wear protective clothing and equipment when needed. A helmet is essential to the safe pursuit of some sports; make it a habit to wear a brain bucket when climbing, mountain biking, kayaking, or riding any off-road motor vehicle. Safety glasses also are worth wearing.

◆ Avoid travel at night. It's surprisingly easy to walk off a cliff in the pitch black. And even moving around camp can be risky. Allow your eyes to adjust to low-light before moving (it takes at least fifteen minutes), or use a small flashlight.

◆ If you do happen to lose your balance or step off a cliff, don't panic. In a short fall on the level (tripping over a root in the trail, for example) try rolling onto your pack, letting it absorb most of the impact with the ground. Thrusting a hand or arm out to break your fall may only break your wrist instead. For longer falls, if you have time to react, try to land feet first, preferably on the balls of your feet. Success in avoiding injuries will depend on the height from which you fell and the cushioning effect of the landing surface, but even two broken legs are better than one smashed skull.

Falling Objects

Gravity is constantly at work on everything around us as well, so it's wise to keep an eye on things perched in precarious circumstances.

◆ Camp well away from dead trees. Look around before pitching the tent to make sure you are out of range of any standing deadwood, including overhanging dead branches. Whole trees can come down, apparently on a whim, even on windless nights.

◆ On mountainsides and in canyons, scan the terrain above and overhead for rocks, overhangs, and loose or sluffing soil. Camp well away from the base of cliffs, and do not linger where falling rocks could land. Reduce your risk by reducing the amount of time you are exposed to danger.

◆ Wear helmets when the risk of falling objects is high and cannot be avoided, such as when rock climbing or caving.

◆ On snow, stay away from avalanche paths. See page 105 for information about traveling in avalanche terrain.

Equipment Mishaps

As we noted at the head of this chapter—and despite this chapter's litany of potential woes—the backcountry really isn't all that dangerous a place if you take a few simple precautions. Not surprisingly then, the source of many injuries and unpleasant lessons learned isn't what you find waiting, but what you bring with you. Nearly every veteran camper has at least one horror story about a piece of balky equipment—the axe with an eye for toes and fingers, the cookstove turned nuclear reactor, the high-strung canoe, the quick-release mountain bike wheel that released a little too quickly.

Some equipment mishaps are unavoidable—things break, parts are lost, and sometimes weather or wilderness conditions simply overwhelm our technological gadgetry. But the vast majority of mishaps are the result of human error or carelessness, which can be prevented in most cases.

♦ Know how to use your tools and equipment. Take the time at home to practice setting up tents, lighting cookstoves and lanterns, and using a compass. Gain confidence both in your abilities and the equipment's performance in the relative safety of your backyard.

♦ Maintain your equipment well. Follow manufacturers' instructions. Clean off trail dust and any other dirt after each trip. Store equipment properly—for most gear it's best to avoid exposure to temperature extremes, direct sunlight, and hungry insects or rodents. Also store it out of reach of children and pets. Keep essential spare parts on hand. After each trip, and again beforehand if the equipment hasn't been used for a while, check for wear and tear, rust, and loose or missing parts.

♦ Use an appropriate tool for the job; know the equipment's limits. A knife blade used as a screwdriver or pry bar may break, spraying shrapnel. Rocks and hatchets make poor hammers.

♦ Do not use a cookstove inside a tent or other enclosure. Any cookstove can generate dangerous levels of carbon monoxide in five minutes or less, even with partial ventilation. The progressive signs of monoxide poisoning are headaches, fatigue, dizziness, nausea, vomiting, cyanosis (lips and fingernails turn blue), sleepiness, unconsciousness, and death.

♦ Never store gasoline in a glass jar. If the glass were to break, not only would it make a smelly, combustible mess, but the pent up vapors are highly volatile and could explode if any ignition source happened to be near. Use aluminum bottles with threaded, leakproof stoppers designed to hold volatile fuel.

♦ Keep all guns unloaded, locked, and stored separately from ammunition when not in use. In the field, leave the safety on until ready to shoot, and carry all firearms with the barrel pointing away from all people, either straight up (as with a shoulder sling) or down toward the ground. If you need to put your gun down, check the safety and lay the weapon flat; a leaning gun is just waiting to fall and perhaps discharge.

♦ Archers should wait to nock each arrow only when ready to aim. Sheath all arrowheads, especially broadheads, when not in use.

♦ Knives, axes, and saws should be kept sharp so they do their job efficiently, with a minimum of force required. Wear gloves when sharpening a blade and use a leaf or wood shaving (rather than a finger) to test sharpness. Put a sheath over any blade when not in use.

WEATHER

Remarking on the vagaries of New England's spring skies, Mark Twain—never one to exaggerate—once wrote, "I have counted one hundred and thirty-six different kinds of weather inside of four-and-twenty hours." In fact, such prodigious variety is a hallmark of North American weather in all seasons of the year no matter where you roam. "If you don't like the weather," the locals confide, "just wait five minutes."

For the backcountry traveler, this means carrying—on every trip—clothing and gear appropriate for *all kinds* of weather. Expect the unexpected. If the forecast calls for rain, then certainly pack raingear, but don't forget the sunglasses, sunscreen, and a hat for shade. Snow in July? It's possible, particularly in the far north and at higher elevations. At a minimum, always carry a rain coat, a hat, and a sweater or pile top for insulation. These essentials belong on every outing, even a one-hour day hike, particularly in the mountains. But even during summer in our warmest climes, a dousing rain, wind, and plummeting temperatures can spell misery for the under-equipped traveler. Carry a sleeping bag and tent or tarp for shelter whenever an overnight stay is anticipated.

Also be alert for severe weather—thunderstorms, wind, flooding, heavy snowfall, and temperature extremes. Check the forecast before hitting the trail, and keep one eye on the horizon for incoming weather. When visiting an unfamiliar region, ask locally about seasonal weather patterns and likely conditions.

Cold Injuries

The human animal is not particularly well-adapted to cold environs. These near-hairless bodies are better able to shed heat than retain it, thanks to a number of adaptations—a high ratio of skin area to body volume, sweating, and a vast network of blood vessels running near the surface. Our physiological responses to cold are no less ingenious, but they tend to be short term or even short sighted. We shiver, the metabolism burns a few extra calories, and blood flow to the extremities is reduced.

That's great if the cold spell only lasts for an hour or two. But what happens after the second hour, if the cold spell in this case lasts for days and has a name— say, February? Unless we take immediate steps to insulate ourselves from the cold or build a fire, the shivering stops, the metabolic rate falls, and those bloodless extremities grow stiff, clumsy, and vulnerable to freezing. Just when you need them the most, those ten wonderful fingers can't strike a match to save your life. Then the feet and legs seize up, like pistons without oil. Without outside help, there's no way to stop the lethal slide into hypothermia.

Hypothermia

Hypothermia occurs when a person loses body heat faster than he or she can generate it, resulting in a decline in core body temperature. Common causes are exposure to cold, physical exhaustion, and too little food intake. Contributing factors may include exposure to wind, rain, or snow; dehydration; wearing damp or wet clothing; or prolonged inactivity.

Temperatures need not be below freezing for hypothermia to be a threat; most cases occur at temperatures between 40 and 50 degrees Fahrenheit, often coupled with windy or wet conditions. Even at 70 degrees F., prolonged exposure to the elements can lead to hypothermia. Wind hastens the chilling process by a factor of five, and immersion in cold water draws away body heat twenty-five times faster than exposure to air of the same temperature.

◆ The best treatment for hypothermia is prevention. Wear layers of clothes as dictated by the weather and your level of exertion. Add layers to keep cold out; strip off layers before breaking a sweat. Most importantly, wear a warm hat—fifty to seventy percent of your body heat can be lost through an uncovered head.
◆ Change insulating layers when damp, before you get chilled. Wool and synthetic pile wick moisture away from the body and retain much of their insulating capacity even when wet. Avoid cotton, which is a poor insulator that is even worse when wet. Down-filled clothes are unsurpassed as insulators against extreme cold in dry conditions, but down is useless when wet. Put on raingear before your clothes get wet. Wrap your dry clothes and sleeping bag in a waterproof stuffsack or plastic bag to keep them dry regardless of rain or river dunkings.
◆ Snack throughout the day on high-calorie foods such as fruit, granola, trail mix, soup, and sandwiches. Drink plenty of fluids to prevent dehydration.

Shivering marks the first stage of hypothermia, when it can be easily treated. Stop, change into dry clothing (even if clothes are only slightly damp from sweat), seek shelter from wind and rain, and drink lots of warm liquids. Build a fire if convenient, or start a stove and prepare hot drinks and food. Also eat high-energy foods. Stay away from alcoholic beverages, as these only increase heat loss. With proper care, the shivering should soon stop as your body's furnace revs up again.

In advanced stages, the body stops shivering, but only because it's too tired to keep it up. The patient often feels sluggish, drowsy, and cold. Look for signs of fatigue, clumsiness with the hands, stumbling, slurred speech, and impaired judgment. Keep the person awake and get them into shelter. Strip off their clothes, dry them off if needed, and place them in a dry sleeping bag with another person, also naked. Skin to skin contact is the best way to rewarm the patient, but do not rub the skin. Use an extra sleeping bag on top if one is available and an insulated pad beneath to prevent heat loss to the ground. Fill water bottles with hot water, cap tightly, and place in sleeping bag (use care not to scald the patient). Gradually give warm drinks.

If the patient is unconscious, try zipping two bags together and have two helpers lay with the patient, one on either side. Do not give liquids to a person who is unconscious. Also handle the patient gently—jostling and jolting or moving the person can cause heart complications or failure. If possible, evacuate and seek medical help immediately.

Make sure all other members of the group stay warm and dry, eat well, and drink fluids to prevent dehydration.

Hypothermia		
Stage	*Symptoms*	*Treatment*
I	Shivering	Find shelter Change into dry clothes Drink warm liquids (no alcohol) Eat high-energy foods—fruits, candy bars
II	Fatigue Sluggishness Drowsiness Shivering stops Slurred speech Impaired judgement	Find shelter Strip off clothes, put a dry, warm hat on victim Place in dry sleeping bag on insulated pad Have 1 or 2 naked helpers lie next to victim, skin to skin Use extra sleeping bag on top for added warmth As victim warms up, dress in dry clothes Give warm fluids—tea with sugar, hot chocolate Feed high-energy foods
III	Uncooperative behavior Unconsciousness	Place victim in sleeping bag with 1 or 2 helpers Do <u>NOT</u> give fluids until victim improves to stage II Do <u>NOT</u> try to walk victim around—jostling or activity can cause heart complications or failure Do <u>NOT</u> rub victim's arms, legs, or skin Evacuate if possible; send for help Monitor pulse, be ready to give CPR if needed
IV	Apparent Death	Give CPR Continue rewarming efforts

Frostbite

Frostbite is the freezing of living tissue. Exposed skin is particularly vulnerable, as are the extremities. Most cases of frostbite involve fingers, toes, ears, noses, and cheeks. These parts are more often exposed to cold, and blood flow to them may be reduced as a person's body struggles to keep its internal vital organs warm.

In the first stage of frostbite, the skin turns red and may itch, tingle, or feel raw. As frostbite progresses, the skin turns a waxy gray or white, goes numb, and feels stiff or hard to the touch. In severe cases, the frozen tissue may blister and crack. Thawing is excruciatingly painful, and the victim is at high risk of tissue loss, including gangrene. Often, a doctor's only recourse for treating severe frostbite is to amputate the damaged appendage.

◆ To prevent frostbite, do not venture out when temperatures or windchills drop below −20 degrees F. Remember that your first defense is to keep your entire body warm so that extremities receive their share of blood circulation. Eat high-calorie foods and carry extra food with you. Always dress in loose-fitting, insulating layers, and carry spare clothes to change into when the first set becomes damp. An extra hat, socks, and mittens are particularly important. When exposure to severe cold is unavoidable, wear an insulated face mask that covers the nose, and boots and mittens specifically designed for Arctic conditions.

◆ Stay alert for the early signs of frostbite. Mentally check your hands, feet, nose, ears, and cheeks for tingling or itchiness. Members of the group can repeatedly scan each other's noses and cheeks for reddening or graying of those areas.

◆ In the early stage, mild frostbite can be treated in the field by gently rewarming the affected area. For fingers, breathe on them or tuck them into your armpits or crotch inside your clothes. Rewarm nose and cheeks by cupping your gloves over your face and breathing. To treat frostbitten toes, or if other areas do not stay warm after treatment, seek shelter. Often, the wisest course is to change into dry clothes, cover any exposed skin, eat a high-energy snack, and head for home.

◆ Do not rub or massage frostbitten skin. Do not slap frostbitten hands or feet. These actions will only add injury to already damaged skin cells.

◆ In cases of severe frostbite, evacuate the patient as soon as possible. Do not thaw the affected tissue unless you can ensure that it will not refreeze. Thawing can be extremely painful and will likely rob the patient of any use of the affected parts. Refreezing greatly increases the amount of damage done to the affected tissue. In remote areas, it is often best to forego rewarming and focus on keeping the patient's core temperature and other vital signs stable until you can evacuate. Also do not try to rewarm frostbitten appendages of someone suffering hypothermia until their core body temperature has returned to normal.

◆ If frozen tissue begins to thaw on its own (as you hike down to a warmer zone on a mountain, for example), be prepared for an agonizing trek out. Allow the tissue to thaw gradually, and treat the patient for shock. Provide painkillers, such as acetaminophen or aspirin, if the person is conscious. Seek medical attention immediately.

Mild to Moderate Frostbite

Symptoms - Skin reddens and itches, tingles, or feels raw. Untreated, skin turns a waxy gray or white, goes numb, and feels stiff or hard to the touch.

Treatment - Gently rewarm the affected area. Breathe on fingers or tuck them into your armpits or crotch inside your clothes. Rewarm nose and cheeks by cupping your gloves over your face and breathing. To treat frostbitten toes, or if other areas do not stay warm after treatment, seek shelter. Change into dry clothes, cover any exposed skin, eat a high-energy snack, and head for home. Do not rub or massage frostbitten skin. Do not slap frostbitten hands or feet. These actions will only add injury to already damaged skin cells.

Air temperature (°F.)	Wind speed in miles per hour								
	0	5	10	15	20	25	30	35	40
	Equivalent wind chill temperatures								
35	35	32	22	16	12	8	6	4	3
30	30	27	16	9	4	1	–2	–4	–5
25	25	22	10	2	–3	–7	–10	–12	–13
20	20	16	3	–5	–10	–15	–18	–20	–21
15	15	11	–3	–11	–17	–22	–25	–27	–29
10	10	6	–9	–18	–24	–29	–33	–35	–37
5	5	0	–15	–25	–31	–36	–41	–43	–45
0	0	–5	–22	–31	–39	–44	–49	–52	–53
–5	–5	–10	–27	–38	–46	–51	–56	–58	–60
–10	–10	–15	–34	–45	–53	–59	–64	–67	–69
–15	–15	–21	–40	–51	–60	–66	–71	–74	–76
–20	–20	–26	–46	–58	–67	–74	–79	–82	–84
–25	–25	–31	–52	–65	–74	–81	–86	–89	–92

National Weather Service

Shaded area indicates high risk of cold-related injuries.

Severe Frostbite

Symptoms - Frozen tissue may blister and crack. Thawing is excruciatingly painful.

Treatment - Do not thaw unless you can ensure that it will not refreeze. Evacuate and seek immediate medical attention.

Heat-related Illness

Exposure to hot ambient air temperatures, when combined with too much sun and/or strenuous exercise, will lead to an elevated body temperature. The human body responds by increasing blood flow near the surface of the skin and by sweating, both of which help to dissipate heat. But, if the heat is severe or the exertion too harsh, you may not be able to shed heat as fast as it is gained. Also, fluid intake may not keep pace with fluid loss from sweating. The result, if unchecked, is heat exhaustion or its more severe relative, heat stroke. Treat any sign of heat stress as a warning to slow down, increase fluid intake, and get out of the sun. Don't push through muscle cramps, fatigue, and light-headedness. Remember: heat stroke is a killer.

Prevention:

Water intake is the most important factor in preventing heat-related illnesses. The human body doesn't signal that it's thirsty until it's too late. An adult may need 1.5 gallons of water a day when exercising in hot weather.

♦ Drink plenty of water *before* you get thirsty, and drink frequently. Plain water is best, though electrolyte replacement drinks are effective in extremely hot weather or during strenuous activity. DO NOT take salt tablets.
♦ Avoid exercise (including travel) during the heat of the day. Early morning hours are coolest; mid to late afternoon, the hottest.
♦ If exercise can't be avoided, work up to it gradually. Seek shade and cool breezes when possible and increase water intake.
♦ Wear light-colored, loose-fitting clothes that breathe. A white hat with good ventilation, a high crown (with air space between the hat and scalp), and a wide brim will help shade the head and ward off heat from the sun.
♦ A wet bandanna draped over the head or back of the neck adds evaporative cooling to your body's own cooling efforts.

Heat Exhaustion	
Signs	*Treatment*
Pale skin	Sit or lie in cool, shady spot.
Sweating, usually heavy	Sip water (electrolyte beverages are ok)
Skin temperature normal	
Nausea	Rest until symptoms are gone.
Weakness	
Dizziness	Take patient's temperature if you have a thermometer.
Thirst	
Headache	
Muscle cramps	

Heat Stroke	
Signs	*Treatment*
Skin is pale, damp, and cool	Reduce body temperature as quickly as possible.
OR skin is red, dry, and hot	
Person acts confused, dazed, or angry	Remove or loosen tight clothing.
Weakness	Put patient in cool, shady spot.
Dizziness	Bathe patient with cool cloths and water, especially on the head, neck, armpits, and groin.
Headache	
Unconsciousness	Fan the patient to speed cooling.
	Give water in sips if patient is conscious.
	Seek medical help immediately.

Big Winds, Tornadoes, and Hurricanes

Wind is an often-overlooked element...until a hell-bent gust knocks you to your knees or sends the tent kiting away to the next drainage over. Strong gusts can blow trees down and carry debris that may strike a person (or stock animals or tents) with surprising force. In cold weather, or if you're wet, windchill speeds the loss of body heat, heightening the risk of hypothermia and frostbite. Wind can also load ridges, gullies, and cornices with snow, increasing the avalanche hazard. Be especially wary of wind on open bodies of water—large waves may be whipped up on short notice.

Know the seasonal wind patterns of the area you plan to visit. Consider how local terrain may reduce or heighten the effects of wind; windspeed usually rises around peaks, ridges, and narrow valleys. Check the weather forecast before leaving.

Tornadoes are the most intense form of weather, and the United States bears the dubious distinction of spawning more twisters than any place else on Earth. Each year an average of 630 twisters touch down in the United States, and about half of them occur in Tornado Alley—a swath running from northern Texas through Oklahoma and Kansas to Missouri. Lest the rest of us grow complacent, it should be noted that tornadoes have occurred in all fifty states, and in all seasons of the year. The Midwest and Plains states, from the Gulf of Mexico as far north as Minnesota and the Dakotas, see the greatest tornado activity, but other trouble spots include southern Florida, central Georgia and Alabama, and southern New England.

Tornado activity peaks in the East in March and April, in the West in April and May. According to the National Oceanic and Atmospheric Administration, eighty-two percent of all tornadoes strike between noon and midnight, with the highest concentration falling between 4 p.m. and 6 p.m. These times correspond with peak thunderstorm activity; tornadoes typically form within squall lines of severe storms. A single storm may spawn more than one tornado. A twister's average lifespan is fifteen minutes, though some monster tornadoes have lasted for more than two hours, traveling hundreds of miles. The vortex may sit still over one spot or rush over the ground at speeds up to seventy miles per hour. Nearly all tornadoes travel on a northeasterly track, though variations are possible due to local terrain and general wind direction.

Waterspouts, most common in the Gulf of Mexico, are less powerful than tornadoes. Windspeeds rarely exceed fifty miles per hour, and the spout usually dissipates when it hits land. But a strong spout can upset small boats and uproot trees where it meets the shore.

◆ Watch the weather, particularly during spring and summer in the central United States. The clash of warm humid air from the south with cooler air from the west or north often presages tornadoes. Check the forecast and consider carrying a radio to monitor weather broadcasts and tornado warnings. Also keep an eye on the clouds and local wind directions when a severe thunderstorm approaches. Towering thunderheads with bumpy or lobe-shaped bottom clouds, swirling winds, and funnels forming at the base of clouds are all warnings of a potential tornado.

◆ If you are caught outdoors when a tornado develops, seek shelter immediately. In the open, lie down and cover your face, neck, and head as well as possible. Huddle against the side of a hill. If the tornado forms at a distance of a mile or more, try to get out of its way by moving perpendicular to its path.

◆ Heavy rain, hail, and frequent lightning often accompany tornadoes. Golf-ball sized hail can break bones; larger stones can kill (the largest hailstone on record landed near Coffeyville, Kansas, and weighed 1.6 pounds). Seek shelter and do not leave until the storm passes.

Hurricanes are large, spiraling storm systems with winds of seventy-four mph or higher. High winds, heavy rains, and storm surges (a sudden rise in the sea's level, often twenty feet or more above normal high tide) cause widespread damage, primarily along coasts. Hurricane season on the Atlantic and Gulf coasts runs from June through November. Strong storms may penetrate far inland without weakening significantly.

Today's hurricane forecast and tracking system allows most backcountry travelers (including those in coastal areas) to anticipate the storm's arrival and leave the area or return to civilization to hunker down in a safe location.

If a hurricane warning is announced:

◆ Evacuate the area at first notice. Move to high ground well inland from the coast. Go to an established emergency shelter if other safe options are not available.

◆ Anticipate heavy rains and flooding, even far inland. Stay out of valleys and runoff drainages.

Lightning

According to the National Oceanic and Atmospheric Association, about three hundred people in the United States die each year from lightning strikes. Many more are injured, some permanently. Though there's no way to be absolutely safe from lightning, understanding how lightning works and following a few simple precautions will greatly reduce your risk of being struck.

Cloud-to-ground bolts are the most familiar form of lightning, though not necessarily the most dangerous to recreationists. Cloud-to-ground lightning is actually composed of two types of electrical discharge. First, a *leader* zig zags down from the cloud, blazing a path of ions through the air. As it nears the ground, a return stroke flashes back up to the cloud at about 422 million feet per second. The average lightning strike includes one leader stroke and four return strokes.

A more dangerous form of lightning is called a *ground discharge*. Ground discharges typically occur after a bolt from the sky has hit nearby, temporarily giving the ground a positive charge. Electrical currents then pass through the ground, returning it to its normal negative charge. Ground lightning often covers a wide area, flashing between objects (such as trees and people), and zapping anyone within a one hundred-foot radius.

Of course, no one *wants* to be struck by lightning, but how many of us have been lulled into a false sense of "it won't happen to me" simply because it hasn't happened *yet*? And some folks lean toward John Muir's almost fatalistic attitude. During storms, Muir was fond of climbing to the top of a tall tree, to cling there as the boughs whipped back and forth in the wind and lightning cracked all around. This is not recommended. Instead, try the following.

◆ Watch the weather. Spring and summer are the busiest seasons for lightning, though discharges can occur any time of the year, even during snowstorms. Most lightning storms occur in mid to late afternoon, though in the Great Plains the frequency of lightning strikes peaks at night. Storms are usually preceded by wind and the approach of dark, towering clouds. Lightning may travel far ahead of the storm. Take cover well before the storm hits.

◆ Seek shelter away from open ground or exposed ridges. Even dropping a few yards off a ridge top will reduce your risk somewhat. In a forest, stay away from single, tall trees. Look for a cluster of smaller trees. Avoid gullies or small basins with water in the bottom. On open ground, find a low spot free of standing water.

◆ During a lightning storm, assume a low crouch with only your feet touching the ground. Put a sleeping pad or pack (be sure it has no frame or other metal in it) beneath your feet for added insulation against shock. Do not huddle together; members of a group should stay at least thirty feet apart. Then, if someone is hit, the others can give first aid.

◆ In a tent, get in the crouch position. Stay in your sleeping bag and keep your feet on a sleeping pad.

◆ Watch for signs of an imminent lightning strike: hair standing on end; an itchy feeling—one hiker described it as "bugs crawling all over"—on your skin; an acrid, "hot metal" smell; and buzzing or crackling noises in the air. Tuck into a crouch immediately if any of these signs are present.

◆ Stay out of shallow caves, crevasses, or overhangs. Ground discharges may leap across the openings. Dry, deep caves offer better protection, but it's still best to crouch and do not touch the walls.

◆ Boaters should get to shore before a storm hits. After securing the boat, move at least one hundred feet inland. On larger boats, if landing is not possible, move to a central low spot in the boat.

◆ If someone in your group is hit by lightning, be prepared to give CPR and first aid for burns and shock. Many victims survive, even from direct hits, especially if help is nearby and CPR is continued. Check the person's breathing and pulse and look for burns or other injuries. There is no danger of electrocution or shock from touching someone who has been struck by lightning.

Floods

Spring runoff can turn a mountain rivulet into a stone-crushing torrent; a desert thunderstorm can send a wall of water surging down a once bone-dry arroyo; and prolonged rains can force dam operators to open the gates, abruptly raising water levels for miles downstream. In developed areas, flooding often presages disaster— property damage, economic and social disruption, and possible loss of life. For the backcountry traveler, the disaster may be readily avoided by careful route and campsite selection, and by practicing humility in the face of nature on the rampage.

◆ When flooding is forecast or likely, stay away from affected watercourses and low-lying areas. Plan alternate routes that do not require water crossings. Camp only on high, safe sites.
◆ The most common mistake made by flood victims is entering or trying to cross flood waters. Currents are usually stronger than they look, and dirty or turbulent water often hides deep holes, snags, and other dangers. Floods also tend to rearrange the floodplain, sculpting surprises into once-familiar stream crossings. Never wade or ride into flood waters.
◆ Especially in the desert, avoid arroyos and narrow canyons when rain is imminent. Watch for rain in headwater areas; a distant storm may send a flood down the canyon. Look for silt lines and debris piles on canyon walls to determine local flood stages.
◆ In the mountains, hot sunny days can add snowmelt to streams and rivers. A snow or glacier-fed stream can be an easy knee-deep ford in the morning, but the same stream may swell to a chest-high flood after a warm day.

Avalanche

Anyone who ventures into the hills or mountains when snow blankets the ground should first read *The Avalanche Book* by Betsy Armstrong and Knox Williams (1986, Fulcrum Publishing, Inc., 350 Indiana St. #350, Golden, Colorado, 80401, ph: 800-992-9208). The authors are veterans of avalanche research and education, and the book drives home its lessons with riveting narratives about real-life avalanches and their victims. At the very least, the book will motivate anyone who sets out for the snowy hills to first enroll in an avalanche safety course. The only way to travel safely in avalanche terrain is to learn firsthand from experts how to evaluate the risk.

Armstrong and Williams estimate that, in the United States, some 100,000 avalanches occur every year. On average, one hundred of these cause injury, death, or destruction to property. About 140 people a year (again, looking at averages) are caught in avalanches; 17 of them are killed. Canada averages seven avalanche fatalities a year. In the United States since 1950, fully seventy-five percent of avalanche fatalities were recreationists. Undoubtedly, as more people head for the hills during avalanche season, the number of fatalities will increase.

Avalanche Anatomy

An avalanche has three body parts: a starting zone, a track, and a runout. The *starting zone* is a slope, bowl, or basin, often above timberline, where snow is deposited by storms and wind. The *track* is the path an avalanche takes as it moves downhill. The track may be dictated by topography (a narrow V-shaped gully), or shaped more by the avalanche itself (a broad slope scoured of trees and vegetation). The *runout* is where the avalanche stops, depositing its load of snow and debris. Though many avalanche areas are obvious—even to the untrained eye—some avalanches occur on innocent-looking terrain.

The recipe for avalanche is simple: snow and slope. Slides can happen on any slope but are most common on slopes of between thirty to fifty degrees. Exceptions can be deadly. According to Armstrong and Williams, one wet-snow slide in Japan released on a beginners slope at a ski area, killing seven people. The slope angle was only ten degrees.

To better evaluate avalanche risk, it helps to understand how snowflakes behave when they gang up together. As snow falls, it accumulates on the ground in layers, collectively called the *snowpack*. Some layers are made up of loose, sugary snow; other layers, composed of rounded and tightly packed crystals, are more solid and cohesive. Sun, wind, and surface thawing and freezing add hard or brittle crusts to the snowpack's profile. Some layers are thick, some thin.

Temperature plays an important role in a developing snowpack. The snowpack is usually warmest near the ground, and coldest just beneath the surface of the snow. This difference in temperature is called the *temperature gradient* (TG, in the lingo). A wide spread of temperatures (a high temperature gradient) causes TG crystals or depth hoar to form. TG crystals bond together poorly. Grab a handful of TG crystals and the stuff drains between your fingers like coarse sugar. A TG layer often forms at the base of a snowpack, acting like a sheet of ball bearings for the layers above. A low temperature gradient allows snow crystals to bond together, forming a stronger, cohesive layer. This layer, or slab, on top of a TG layer means a higher risk of avalanche.

Generally, the snowpack changes very slowly in sustained sub-zero cold. But from 20 degrees F. to near freezing, the snowpack settles rapidly and bonds will form between grains of snow. At temperatures warmer than freezing (32 degrees F.), the snowpack settles densely onto itself and begins to thaw. A thaw, particularly in the spring, produces wet-snow avalanches and is the second most common cause of avalanches.

Avalanches come in two forms: loose and slab. A loose slide typically starts at a single point and fans out as it travels downhill. Loose slides usually involve fairly dry snow near the surface of the snowpack. A slab avalanche occurs when a strongly bonded layer (usually resting atop a weaker layer) breaks all at once across a wide area, and the entire layer or slab slides downhill. Dangerous slabs can form due to wind or sun crusts, thawing and consolidation of a surface layer, or when relatively warm, dense snow settles on a weak, loose layer.

Tools

For any outing into avalanche terrain, always pack along a few essential tools of the trade.

◆ Carry a shovel. Several lightweight, compact models are available with telescoping handles or folding blades. The shovel must be stiff, strong, and durable. New snow is easy to dig through, but when an avalanche stops, its load of snow sets up like concrete. You can also use the shovel to dig snow analysis pits and shelters.

◆ Skiers should use special ski poles that thread together end to end to make a single long pole for probing the snow when searching for an avalanche victim.

◆ Rescue beacons or transceivers are proven time—and life—savers when searching for buried avalanche victims. These small radio transmitters and receivers send a signal, allowing survivors (wearing transceivers) to home in on the victim. They are standard equipment now for all ski patrollers. Transceivers are costly (around $225 apiece), and require training and regular practice. You must have at least two—one to receive the other's signal—and ideally everyone in the group should wear a transceiver.

◆ Some skiers advocate using an avalanche cord, a long string that trails out behind the skier in hopes that it will remain on the surface if a slide strikes. Rescuers can follow it to the victim. But Armstrong and Williams cast doubt on the cord's effectiveness: it may not stay on the surface, and it may twist and dive on its trail to the victim, requiring a long hard stint of fruitless digging. Transceivers are more reliable, but avalanche cords are better than nothing.

Evaluating Avalanche Risk

Perhaps the most important fact to remember when weighing avalanche risk is that *eighty percent of all avalanches occur during or just after fresh snowfall.* The hazard is highest when snow accumulates at a rate of an inch per hour or more. And large slides—big enough to kill—are most likely when a foot or more of snow is added to the snowpack...the more snow, the bigger the potential slide. Wind generally increases the avalanche risk. Wind-deposited snow is more dense and heavier than fresh snow, and when loaded onto leeward slopes it adds weight and stress to the snowpack. Armstrong and Williams warn that "wind can turn a one-foot snowfall into a three-foot drift in a starting zone."

With this said, the first step everyone should take before heading into the hills is obvious: look out the window at the weather and check the forecast. Also consider the effect on the snowpack of recent weather—last week's snowfall, yesterday's winds, and temperature patterns through the winter. Call the avalanche report for the area you plan to visit; look in the phone book under U.S. Government—USDA Forest Service. Heed their advice.

As you travel across the snow, stay alert for signs of avalanche danger. Look for evidence of recent slides. Think about the snow you're traveling on. Is there an obvious crust or slab? Is it strong ("will it support my weight"), or weak ("do I break through now and then")? Watch for cracks radiating out from your skis or snowmobile. Listen for hollow noises underfoot. Does the snow settle all at once in a wide area as you travel on it? All these factors indicate a dangerous slab.

Also consider the layers beneath the surface. You can take a rough survey of layers within the snowpack by poking a ski pole down through the snow, feeling for crusts, air pockets, and dense or loose layers. But the best way to test the snowpack is to dig a quick snow pit. Once again, a course in avalanche safety is invaluable. You can learn the basics of how to dig a snowpit from a book, but only hands-on experience—with an avalanche expert explaining each step—will teach you how to interpret the nuances of the snowpack revealed in the wall of the pit.

Select a safe place to dig the pit. It should be on or near the slope you intend to cross, facing the same compass direction, and subject to the same winds. The pit should also be near a likely point of fracture or release but safely removed from any obvious avalanche track.

With a shovel, dig a pit all the way to the ground, if possible. Dig so that the uphill wall is fairly vertical or perpendicular to the slope. Look at the layers of snow. Poke each layer with a finger to test its density. Brush the wall of the pit with your glove to reveal soft

rime (magnified)

and hard layers. Grab a fistful of snow at various depths to see whether the grains run through your fingers (TG) or mold together well.

A simple shear test will disclose any weak bonds between layers. Use the tail of a ski to saw down through the pit wall once and then again about a shovel's width over. Push the shovel's blade into the snow about ten inches behind the pit wall between the two cuts. Tug toward you: watch for cohesion between layers, and where the snowpack breaks. Continue to push the shovel down and pull toward you all the way to the bottom. The easier a layer shears, the more likely it could fail and cause an avalanche.

Remember that snow pits are not fool proof; interpreting the clues of a pit requires intuition built on years of experience. Dig a pit whenever you get the chance—start acquiring

TG crystals
(magnified)

that experience. It also helps to dig more than one pit (in another part of the slope) to compare findings. If the evidence is unclear, avoid the slope and live to try it again some other day. And regardless of what the pit indicates, stay alert to other signs of avalanche risk.

Also look carefully at the terrain. Steep bowls and gullies are obvious slide zones. Look for suspicious clearings between trees, or trees stripped of branches on one side, leaning downhill. Stay off slopes of thirty degrees or more. Dangle a ski pole like a plumb line to eye the angle of a slope.

A slope does not have to be long or broad to slide. Even small pitches can slide. And previous ski or snowmobile tracks do not indicate a safe slope. The snow may slide on the second person to cross it, or the third, or fifteenth

Remember that even slopes covered with trees can avalanche. If the trees are spaced widely enough to allow downhill skiing, then they do not provide enough of an anchor to prevent a slide.

To find a route around an avalanche track, either stay above the starting zone or below and far away from runouts. Generally the best route is on windward sides near tops of ridges. Avoid cornices. Even road cuts can be dangerous; a slide may start on the slope above and careen onto anyone skiing or snowmobiling below. Consider the risks: What's the worst that could happen? Are there safe havens or possible escape routes? Where would I end up if this slope slides?

Choose campsites well away from starting zones, tracks, and runouts. Also don't travel alone in avalanche terrain.

When traversing suspect terrain, loosen your pack straps, put on a hat, gloves, and goggles, and zip up your jacket—anything to seal out snow and cold. Remove ski straps. Turn your transceiver on if wearing one. Expose only one person at a time to risk. Others in the group should remain in the shelter of trees or well above or to the sides of the slope. Watch each traveler until he or she is safe—if the slope does slide, you'll have a better idea of where to look for the victim. Don't pause in the middle of an avalanche slope; minimize the amount of time you are exposed to risk.

If you are caught in an avalanche:

◆ Try to reach the side of the slide; kick skis off or jump away from your snowmobile. Try to swim toward the surface. As the slide slows, swim with all your effort toward the top, bring your hands in front of your face, and try to create breathing room around your head and chest before the snow stops and sets up. Then relax. Try to remain calm, breathing slowly. Conserve oxygen. Yell only if you hear rescuers approaching. Try to wiggle anything free that might be near or above the surface to attract attention. It's nearly impossible to dig yourself out, even if buried only one foot deep. One avalanche survivor likened it to being encased in a giant body cast. Buried more than two feet deep, you've got a fifty-fifty chance of survival. The deeper you are, the worse are your chances. Only half the victims buried for longer than thirty minutes survive. In the backcountry, when additional help is far away, it's up to your companions to dig you out...soon.

◆ Rescuers looking for a buried person should consider the risk of another slide before rushing to help. Post a sentry if another slide is possible and you can spare the manpower. Then, if it's safe to do so, mark the spot where the person was last seen. If you're wearing transceivers, make sure everyone switches to receive. Search the fall line below the last-seen mark for clues—clothing, equipment, a foot or hand poking out of the snow, even a smear of blood—anything to lead to the person. Look for likely pockets where a person might have hung up—near trees, boulders, in snow-filled hollows. Armstrong and Williams report that many victims are found right at the toe of the debris in the runout zone. Use ski poles or a probe pole to feel for a body or gear. Kick at the surface with your boots to dislodge chunks of snow. Keep looking. Remember, each passing minute reduces the person's chance of survival.

◆ If you find the victim, check breathing and pulse. Look for a plug of snow in the mouth and nose and remove it. Check for bleeding, broken bones, internal injuries. Treat for shock and hypothermia as needed.

◆ Finally, heed the advice of Armstrong and Williams. "Avoiding avalanches is easier than surviving them."

WILDLIFE

According to the Center for Wildlife Information, more than 42 million people visit public lands in the United States each year, and the numbers are increasing. Many of these folks undoubtedly come to see wildlife—to hunt, fish, photograph, or simply observe animals in their natural surroundings. But as more and more people trek into the backcountry, two unfortunate outcomes are likely: more animals will be disturbed or displaced by human activity, and more people will be injured or killed by wild animals.

The vast majority of confrontations between wildlife and people occur because the people were unaware of the animal's presence, did not understand the risk, or were purposefully harassing the animal. Instances of truly unprovoked attacks by wild animals, even by insects, are extremely rare. A few such attacks involve predation and most are likely the result of disease or injury. Suspect rabies whenever a wild animal behaves oddly or approaches without fear.

◆ Stay alert. Remember that you are a visitor—a guest—in the wilderness. To wildlife, this is home. Keep a respectful distance, avoid surprising or cornering animals, and back off before an encounter turns ugly. When photographing or watching wildlife use a telephoto lens or high-powered binoculars.

◆ Avoid travel or camping in areas likely to be used by wildlife. Stay away from nests, dens, birthing grounds, feeding areas, food caches, and resting places.

◆ Keep an eye on children. Do not let them wander ahead or lag behind. High-pitched voices or screams and squeals may attract predators. In recent years several children have been mauled or killed by cougars and black bears.

◆ Do not feed wild animals. Minimize any opportunity for an animal to move close, bite, kick, or scratch. Many diseases can be transferred from animal to human with just a nip or scratch. Feeding also harms the animal, replacing its natural diet, which is typically more nutritious, and habituating the animal to people. The next person to come along may not be so friendly. Large animals that lose their fear of people become a nuisance or a danger and often must be relocated or destroyed.

Bears

Bears loom large in the imaginations of many backcountry travelers. We've all heard horrific bear stories that are at once gruesome and intriguing, and few people have camped in bear country without at least once waking in the dark heart of the night to listen as a large animal—a bear?—shuffles and sniffs its way through camp.

But these are the bears of our dreams (and nightmares). What about the genuine article? Truth is, bears are rarely seen by backcountry travelers, and actual encounters or confrontations are rarer still. Even then, coming face to face with a real bear is almost always less frightening than what most people imagine. Unfortunately, the exceptions—those extremely rare instances where someone is mauled or killed by a bear—are what stick in our minds. Let's unstick those horror stories and replace them with a more accurate picture. Consider the following facts.

Your chances of simply seeing a bear in the backcountry range from essentially zero throughout most of the East, Midwest, and South, to a high of one bear sighting for every seven backcountry visitors at Yosemite National Park. Bear sightings are relatively common in certain pockets of wilderness and in national parks within the lower forty-eight, and in many areas of Alaska and northern Canada. What do we mean by "relatively common?" Glacier National Park in Montana provides a good example, where some 160,000 people hit the trails in an average year and roughly one out of every forty-eight backcountry visitors sees a bear.

Even if you do see a bear, the risk of injury is extremely low. Let's look again at

Glacier National Park, which has a widespread (and perhaps undeserved) reputation for ornery bears. According to research ecologist Kate Kendall, an average of 2,368 bear sightings occurred each year over the last ten years. For the same period, an average of 2.8 people a year were mauled by bears in the park. In other words, of all reported bear sightings, 0.12 percent (on average) resulted in injury.

More people are injured or killed by other wildlife, even by moose and deer, than by bears. On average, two or three people are killed by bears each year in North America. Poisonous snakes kill fifteen to twenty people each year; bees are perhaps the most worrisome North American wildlife, accounting for some forty fatalities a year.

Grizzly bears are often cited as more aggressive than black bears, but black bears—because they are more numerous and live in closer proximity to humans—injure more people. In all of North America, an average of one person a year is killed by a grizzly bear.

Remember too that the typical slice of North American backcountry doesn't house as many bears as Glacier (or Yosemite), and most people are lucky to see more than two or three bears in the wild throughout their lifetimes.

Nevertheless, there are a number of good reasons to take special precautions when traveling and camping wherever bears live:

◆ *For peace of mind.* Your trip will be more relaxing and enjoyable because you know you've done everything you can to minimize the risk of running into or attracting a bear.

◆ *For your safety.* If a bear is nearby, you're less likely to encounter it. If you do encounter it, you're less likely to be attacked. If it does attack, you can try to minimize your injuries.

◆ *For the bear's well-being.* In many cases, the bear ultimately loses in an encounter with a person. Problem bears may be relocated, forcing them to adjust to unfamiliar habitat and to compete with resident bears. And bears that actually attack a person are often tracked down and destroyed by authorities. Though such action may assuage our fears, it's not a sustainable solution.

Think of it this way: we enter their home, uninvited as far as the bears are concerned, and when they respond to our trespassing with normal bear behavior, they are sent packing to new territory, or shot. Such a beautiful, intelligent animal, symbol of everything wild, deserves a place to live and thrive. If we choose to visit its home, we must heed certain precautions and courtesies.

The Bear Necessities

Anyone planning to spend much time in bear country should first acquaint themselves with bear behavior. For general information, read *Bears: Their Life and Behavior* by William Ashworth and Art Wolfe and *Bears of the World* by Terry

Domico. Both offer detailed, accurate observations of bear behavior, with photographs and engaging text. *Bear Attacks: Their Causes and Avoidance*, by bear biologist Stephen Herrero, also comes highly recommended. *Bear Attacks* presents detailed accounts of encounters between bears and people, with Herrero's solid analysis guiding the way through the intricacies of bear behavior and suggested human responses.

Backcountry travelers should also learn to identify North America's three species of bear: black, grizzly, and polar bear. The polar bear's distinctive white coat and remote home range readily set it apart from other bears. But

Grizzly bear and tracks

where the ranges of grizzlies and black bears overlap, distinguishing between the two is not always easy. Fur color is not definitive; both species come in shades of black, brown, cinnamon, and blonde. Identification is based on other characteristic features.

Grizzlies have a muscular hump where the neck joins the shoulders; black bears do not. The grizzly has a slightly dished or concave profile to its face, whereas a black bear's is straight. At close range, the grizzly's longer, light-colored claws and teeth may be readily visible; a black bear's claws are usually fairly blunt and dark colored.

Tracks also differ between the two species. Though the hind feet leave similar tracks, the front paws are distinctive. The black bear's toe prints form an arc following the curve of the foot pad; the grizzly's line up fairly straight next to one another. Poke marks from the black bear's fore claws are again just ahead of the toes, but a grizzly's fore claws are long, rarely less than 1.75 inches. The tips of the claws create a row of holes well in front of the toes. On firm ground, a black bear's claws may not show, but a if a grizzly print is visible its claws almost always leave marks.

Black bear and tracks

All bears are powerful, intelligent, and unpredictable animals. They have an excellent sense of smell and their hearing and eyesight is at least as good as a human's. Bears are also quick to learn and are great opportunists, scavenging widely and taking advantage of any food source available. A bear raiding a front-country camp in Yellowstone once used a claw to pop a hole in each can of a six pack, then knocked the cans over and lapped up the brew.

How to Read a Bear's Intentions

Upon seeing their first bear in the wild, most people are so excited or frightened that they notice few, if any, details about the bear's appearance or behavior. This book won't make an expert out of anyone, but knowing what to look for will help you respond appropriately during an encounter.

Bears (particularly grizzlies) will rear up on their hind legs to better smell, hear, and see an intruder. This is not an aggressive posture. A bear on all fours may act agitated, swaying its head from side to side, making huffing sounds, or chomping its teeth together noisily. The bear may circle, sometimes at a run, around an intruder to get downwind for a better smell. Alone, these actions indicate curiosity, and at worst, anxiety on the part of the bear. A truly aggressive bear would probably have charged the intruder by now.

Bears sometimes charge, even repeatedly, but stop short of actually attacking. "The seriousness of a grizzly's charge," writes Herrero, "is usually indicated by the position of its ears. Like wolves and dogs, grizzly and black bears use the position of their ears as an indication of aggressive intent. Generally speaking, the farther back the ears are, and the more they are flattened to the neck, the more the grizzly is aroused."

Doug Peacock, self-appointed patron saint of bears and author of *Grizzly Years*, offers some advice for reading a grizzly's frame of mind. He writes, "A grizzly with its head lowered near or across a forepaw and looking off to the side is indicating a willingness to move on peacefully if you do." On the other hand, notes Peacock, "If the grizzly opens and closes its jaw, and slobbers, it's time to leave."

In certain situations, bears may be more aggressive toward intruders. Females with cubs (especially grizzlies) are highly protective and more likely to charge. Bears feeding on or guarding a kill also are more dangerous. And as with all wildlife, an animal with an obvious injury (limping or trailing blood) may behave more aggressively.

Remember that bears (and most other predators) can sense fear. If you are anxious about bears learn more about them and consider teaming up with people who are experienced bear-country travelers.

Bear Country—General Guidelines

Be cautious and alert. Never hike alone in bear country. Travel in groups of two or more and stay together. In his survey of 143 bear encounter reports, Herrero could find no record of a bear attacking any group of six or more people. Some experts recommend traveling in groups of four or six in grizzly country, but there is no guarantee of safety in numbers. Conversely, many people have hiked without incident through grizzly habitat in pairs and even (though this is not recommended!) solo.

Avoid places where bear activity is likely. Bears often travel on ridges, across mountain saddles, and along game trails and streams or lakeshores—the same places favored by people. In the heat of the day, they may bed down to rest in streamside thickets or in dense, shady stands of trees. Bears are often active at night and may use hiking trails then, especially in dense timber. During spring and early summer, bears favor valley bottoms and lower-elevation meadows. They sniff out winter-kill carcasses, forage on young grasses, and may try fishing, particularly where spawning trout or salmon run. In midsummer, bears move to high ridges, avalanche slopes, and alpine meadows, digging for roots and ground squirrels or marmots. As berry crops ripen (usually beginning at lower elevations and progressing uphill), bears return to familiar harvesting grounds. By late summer and fall, bears concentrate on late-ripening berries, roots, and pine nuts, where available. They are especially fond of whitebark pine nuts; learn to recognize this tree of the higher ridges.

Watch for bear sign and be extra careful if you find any. Signs of bear activity include tracks, scat, worn bear trails, diggings for roots or rodents, torn apart logs and ant hills, overturned rocks, partially eaten or buried animal carcasses, and flattened grass used for day beds.

Report all bear incidents to local authorities. It is extremely important to report any instance of a bear coming into camp or otherwise showing that it has lost its fear of people. Be especially wary of bears with ear tags. Bears are often ear-tagged for scientific research, but problem bears may also be ear-tagged when they are relocated. Don't give a bear the opportunity to reveal the reason for its tag. Also, leave your dog at home; it may be "man's best friend" at home but not in the wilderness where it could attract a bear.

There are important differences between meeting a bear while hiking versus finding a bear in your camp. Most encounters with bears on the trail or traveling cross-country are accidental—neither the bear nor the person wants to be there. But a bear that wanders into camp has learned through previous experience that food can be found with people. And in rare cases, a few rogue bears have pursued people as prey.

While Traveling

To avoid a bear encounter on the trail stay with your group and hike during midday, avoiding travel during early morning and late evening. Also make noise while traveling to help warn bears of your approach. Most bears will quickly leave the area. Bells were once the noise-makers of choice and still are for some folks. Hung from packs or tied to shoelaces they signal every step, and the metallic jingling is distinctively human. Bells are also a "fix-it-and-forget-it" solution, though not without trade-offs. Their constant noise is always there when it's needed, and that may save an inattentive or inexperienced hiker from a bear encounter. But by the same token, bells can encourage complacency or a false sense of security. Hikers relying on their bells may fail to notice tracks, scat, or more subtle bear signs, or may choose to ignore them and blunder, heedless of danger, down the trail. The jingling can also drown out other important sounds—the whoof of a surprised bear, for instance. Bells are also indiscriminate. They scare off other (otherwise watchable) wildlife, and may annoy other trail users. Finally, a bell's noise level is fixed—the volume can't be turned up when wind or rushing water threatens to overwhelm it. Nonetheless, many park rangers and bear experts recommend wearing bells when traveling in bear country

So what are the alternatives? Most experts recommend clapping, talking loudly, singing, or shouting ("Hey Bear!" is a traditional favorite). Clapping has the added benefit of mimicking a gun shot, and singing and shouting help drain off some of the adrenalin rush that comes with the territory. Any of these methods can be used selectively: travel quietly in open country where any bear would be seen at a distance, and make noise where sight distance is limited, when traveling into the wind, or when environmental noises may drown out the sounds of your approach. Be sure to make lots of noise when traveling through dense trees or underbrush, along a noisy stream, or whenever a bear's presence is suspected. You can also raise the volume as needed; don't be shy about making extra noise any way you can when circumstances warrant it.

The only drawbacks to clapping or auditioning for the lead soprano in Aida as you hike are two-fold: you can wear out the noise-makers (especially your vocal chords), and you have to remember to make noise. The two concerns are related. Make noise too often and you'll be hoarse before you've gone a mile. But forget to shout hello before entering a willow thicket and you may get to shake hands with one of Smokey's nastier cousins.

If you see a bear at a distance make a wide detour around it on its upwind side so that it can get your scent. If a detour is not possible slowly back down the trail until out of the bear's sight. Then wait (if no other route is available) for the bear to leave. The bear should be gone when you get back to your earlier observation point. If the bear is still there and you can't safely get around it abandon your route. Save your destination for another day and savor the good fortune of seeing a bear in the wild.

Remember that most bears will try to avoid contact with humans, so if you meet a bear along the trail the odds are good that it will turn and flee. If the bear lingers, however, or is cornered or surprised at close quarters, the best course of action is to talk in a firm, unexcited voice to the bear while slowly backing away. Sometimes dropping a hat, bandanna, or other non-food item will distract the bear long enough for you to leave the area.

Running from the bear is almost certain to provoke a chase, and all bears can easily outrun the fastest person. With a top speed near forty miles per hour, a grizzly can cover rough ground two to three times as fast as a person on foot. Also avoid screaming or abrupt movements, as these too can provoke an attack.

Climb a tree only if a suitable one is nearby, and you have enough time to climb at least ten feet (which is usually not the case). Climbing a tree tends to provoke a bear's instinct to pursue prey just as running does. Contrary to conventional wisdom, all bears can climb trees; some are just better at it than others. Black bears are excellent climbers and if determined will pursue a person up a tree. Most grizzlies are less adept climbers because of their long claws and heftier weight. But they make up for this with a higher reach and by using momentum from their charge to carry them into the lower branches.

If a bear charges, you must make a quick (and often irrevocable) choice among several options:

◆ Stand your ground, but try to appear non-threatening. Turn sideways and avoid eye contact. Do not turn your back on the bear or crouch down. Bears often "bluff charge," stopping short or running past. Never turn your back or run—this invites attack. Try to back slowly away.

◆ Move behind a tree or boulder, not to climb it but to use it as a shield.

◆ As a last resort, play dead. Curl into a ball face-down and cover your neck and stomach. Try to remain quiet and passive, rolling onto your stomach to protect vital organs. Do not scream. This takes courage, to say the least, but it's preferable to facing such an overwhelming opponent head-on.

◆ In extremely rare cases, bears treat people as food and playing dead will not work. The bad news is that fighting back is almost always a hopeless cause. Remember that struggling against a bear defending its food, cubs, or itself will only prolong (and probably intensify) the attack. If you are sure that the bear intends to eat you fight back with any weapon at hand.

◆ Trying to shoot a charging bear is not recommended. The bear, now injured and enraged, almost always reaches the shooter and lives long enough to severely maul the person. Guns are also prohibited in national parks and some other areas.

Immediately after a bear attack:

◆ Don't move until certain the bear has left the area. Most bears leave within a few minutes after a sudden encounter, once they're sure you are not a threat.

◆ Cautiously look around, moving only your head to do so. If the bear is nearby, remain still.

◆ Once the bear is gone, assess your (or your companion's) injuries and begin first aid. If the wounds are life-threatening, treat them where you are; according to Herrero, bears rarely return to the scene of the attack. If the patient is stable but cannot be evacuated, send for help. Otherwise, leave the area at once and take all injured persons to a doctor immediately.

In Camp

Don't camp in a site obviously frequented by bears. If you see a bear or fresh signs where you intended to camp, pick another campsite. Where bears are plentiful, look for bear sign in a wide circle around any potential campsites before setting up camp. Pitch tents at least one hundred feet from hiking trails and one hundred yards from any game trails. If a bear trail runs near the area, camp elsewhere. If possible, camp near tall trees that can easily be climbed.

Sleep upwind (usually uphill) and at least one hundred yards from your cooking and eating area. This way, any food odors will drift away from the sleeping area. Locate your kitchen on high ground or at the edge of a clearing so that any approaching bears can be seen before they get too close. Also refrain from eating or preparing food in places that would be likely campsites for subsequent backcountry travelers.

Keep food odors off clothes, tents, and sleeping bags. It may be wise to wash tents and sleeping bags (with unscented detergent) before traveling in grizzly country. Do not enter tents or sleeping bags while carrying food or wearing food-soiled clothes. Clothes readily absorb odors, especially from the vapors of cooking food or when messy hands are wiped on them. After dinner, change out of the clothes you wore while cooking or eating and hang them with the food bag. Clean your hands and face after eating or cooking.

Avoid fresh, perishable, or smelly foods such as bacon, lunch meat, sardines, and tuna fish. To reduce food odors, some experienced bear-country travelers eat only foods that do not require cooking. This is not as big a sacrifice as it may sound, particularly on short outings of a night or two. Try cheese, nuts, dried fruit, whole-grain breads, carrots, and protein-fortified drinks. These foods allow convenient snacking throughout the day and require remarkably little preparation or clean up at meal times.

Be careful with food and garbage. Keep a clean camp. Try not to spill food or waste water, and promptly clean up any messes. Put all garbage in a double plastic bag and store it with the food in a bear resistant manner.

In bear country, always store your food, garbage, toiletries (including toothpaste), medicines, horse feed, pet food, and any other scented or flavored items in bear resistant containers (see page 122) or in a sturdy bag hung well out of a bear's reach. Never leave food or garbage unattended unless it is properly stored. The food cache should be at least one hundred yards downwind from camp. Use a cache pole or steel cable where provided (mostly in national parks). Where suitable trees are available, hang all food and garbage at least twelve feet above the ground and six feet from the nearest tree trunk. The bag should also be at least four feet below the supporting branch so a bear cannot reach it from above. If suitable branches cannot be found, tie a line between two trees at least sixteen feet above the ground. Toss a second rope over the line and hoist the bag, again at least twelve feet high. Carry thirty to fifty feet of rope for hanging food; five millimeter nylon climbing rope works well.

If you choose to build a fire (and regulations and natural conditions allow it) completely burn combustible trash (including fish entrails) in a hot fire. Burn cans

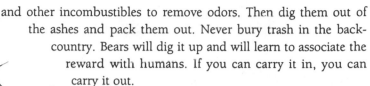

and other incombustibles to remove odors. Then dig them out of the ashes and pack them out. Never bury trash in the backcountry. Bears will dig it up and will learn to associate the reward with humans. If you can carry it in, you can carry it out.

Most cosmetics, shampoos, hair sprays, deodorants, sunscreens, and body lotions are scented. Evidence suggests that bears may be attracted and even infuriated by these scents. Use only unscented products or, better yet, do without them while in bear country. Toothpaste, chapstick, soap, chewing gum, throat lozenges and other medicines, and other scented or flavored non-food items should be stored with food out of a bear's reach. Do not leave these items in your pack and never bring them into the tent.

Hanging food in bear country.

Before going to bed for the night, check camp for any food, garbage, or dishes left out. Double check your pockets for food or other scented items. Take a flashlight to bed with you in case you need to investigate noises in the night.

When a bear comes into camp despite all your precautions, the situation is completely different from meeting a bear on the trail. A bear in camp has chosen to approach humans and must be considered highly dangerous. Though some bears are simply curious and will move on if no food is found, others are predisposed to cause trouble. If conditioned to human food or garbage, the bear "expects" a meal and may not leave if it finds nothing edible in camp. In very rare cases, bears have been known to enter camp to prey on people directly.

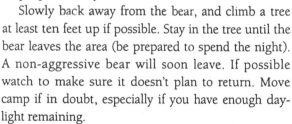

Slowly back away from the bear, and climb a tree at least ten feet up if possible. Stay in the tree until the bear leaves the area (be prepared to spend the night). A non-aggressive bear will soon leave. If possible watch to make sure it doesn't plan to return. Move camp if in doubt, especially if you have enough daylight remaining.

If a bear attacks you, particularly while you are in a tent or sleeping bag, fight back with all your might. Use any available weapon, even rocks and large sticks. Spray the bear with bear repellant if you have it (see page 122). Punch and slap the bear's face if he is upon you, or gouge at the eyes.

Pushing fingers in the bear's nose and ripping at the nostrils has proven effective in some cases. Aim the strobe light and flash on your camera at the bear's eyes. Try to escape the bear's grasp to climb a tree. Do not scream and DO NOT PLAY DEAD in this situation. The bear has chosen to attack and is treating you as prey.

Once the bear is gone, whether or not anyone was physically attacked, leave the area immediately. A bear habituated to humans will likely return and may act more aggressively the next time. Seek medical help as needed, and report the incident immediately to the local land manager or wildlife agency.

Women in Bear Country

Some people recommend women stay out of bear country during menstrual periods. But to date there is no evidence that bears are attracted to menstrual odors more than any other odor, and no known attacks have been traced to menstruation as the cause. The simple fact that bears have a keen sense of smell does, however, suggest that women should take a few common sense precautions when traveling in bear country.

Keep yourself as clean and odor free as possible. Use pre-moistened, unscented cleaning towelettes. Use tampons instead of pads.

Do not bury used tampons or pads. A bear could smell them and dig them up. Used tampons or pads will provide a small food "reward." Place all used tampons, pads, and towelettes in double zip-lock bags and store them with other garbage—in a bear resistant container or hung ten feet off the ground.

Tampons can be burned in a campfire, but the fire must be very hot. Remove any charred remains from the ashes and store them with other garbage.

Fishing and Hunting in Grizzly Country

Hunters and anglers can protect themselves and avoid confrontations with bears by adhering to the following guidelines:

◆ Hunt with a buddy. Avoid traveling alone. People traveling with horses generally have less trouble with bears.
◆ Make noise when driving game through thick brush or dense trees.
◆ If you see or smell a carcass or gut pile, do not investigate. Leave the area.
◆ If your hunt is successful, gut and remove the carcass as soon as possible. Never leave the gut pile near a trail or where other people are likely to travel.
◆ Do not drag a carcass to camp; a bear may follow the scent trail.
◆ If a carcass or other game meat is left unattended, it should be hung in the same manner as other food—twelve feet above the ground and six feet from the nearest tree. Cut the meat into smaller pieces if necessary. The cache must be at least one hundred yards from any campsites, trails, or other recreation site. These actions are required on some national forests with resident grizzly bears.
◆ A carcass left on the ground should be put in an open area where a scavenging bear can be seen at a distance upon your return. Approach it from upwind, making

lots of noise from a safe distance. Scan the area with binoculars. A bear may have dragged the carcass or partially buried it in your absence, in which case the bear is likely nearby. In grizzly country, abandon the kill if a bear has claimed it. Do not harass or shoot the bear.

◆ When fishing, remember that bears also like to catch fish, particularly during spawning runs. Bears also travel along streams and lakeshores. Make lots of noise, especially where visibility is limited or rushing water drowns out other sounds.

◆ Watch for partially eaten fish and other signs of bear activity.

◆ Gut and clean fish where they were caught. The Interagency Grizzly Bear Committee recommends puncturing the air bladder and tossing the entrails as far out into the current or deep water as possible. Do not leave entrails in small streams, in camp, or near shore on larger streams and lakes. After cooking and eating fish, burn all residue completely and pack out any remains with other garbage. DO NOT bury fish remains.

◆ Try to avoid getting fish odors on your clothes. Wash your hands thoroughly after handling fish.

◆ When camping at popular fishing sites scout around the area for fish scraps or entrails left by previous campers. Sift through the fire pit for any traces of partially burned fish or food scraps. If you see bear sign find another campsite.

Keep in mind these are merely general rules. They're the best available, but generalizations have a way of falling short when you most need advice. Certainly, there is no concrete formula for avoiding confrontations or for what to do when confronted. Dr. Charles Jonkel, a wildlife biologist and one of the nation's leading experts on grizzlies, suggests trying to evaluate each individual situation based on these general rules. And by all means, Jonkel emphasizes, "try to avoid an encounter." It is far easier to avoid a bear encounter than to get out of one.

Having said so much about the dark side of bear behavior, we should remind ourselves that bears are mere animals, after all, and not evil incarnate just waiting for a human thigh bone to gnaw on. In *Bears of the World*, Terry Domico tells of a close encounter with an Alaskan brown bear and her two cubs. He and a companion rounded a bend in the trail to find themselves face to face with the bear family sitting not forty feet away. After a few tense moments, the mother bear stood and led her cubs down a short hill to a riverbank, keeping her back to the intruders. The hikers quietly walked by while the bears splashed in the water. Looking back down the trail, Domico saw the great bear and her cubs lumber back onto the trail and resume their resting place.

Recalls, Domico, "This was the first time I had ever encountered a wild animal that displayed a sense of discretion. Most of my fear of bears had suddenly been replaced by a great deal of respect."

Pepper Sprays

Pepper-based bear repellant sprays are now widely available and have shown promise in neutralizing aggressive bears. The sprays contain capsicum, a resin that causes burning and irritation to eyes and mucous membranes. Though few thorough studies have been done, reports of success in actual encounters keep trickling in. Bear repellants are no substitute for careful behavior, but they do offer a last line of defense when a close encounter turns ugly.

Kate Kendall, a research ecologist at Glacier National Park, Montana, recently offered the following testimonial. "Glacier had two incidents during the fall of 1993 where pepper sprays were used. The first was a mauling on Flattop Mountain involving two hikers. The bear was on top of one hiker after a surprise encounter. His partner sprayed the can off to one side—he was afraid he'd hit his friend if he aimed it directly at the bear. Apparently the sound distracted the bear. It moved toward him, came in contact with the spray, and then left the scene."

"In the second incident, a sow and a cub charged a party of two on Ahern Pass. One hiker was kneeling, the other standing, when they both released the spray at the two bears. The hiker knew the sow got a good dose, because the spray painted one side of her face orange. Both bears slammed on the brakes and ran the other way. Who knows...maybe it was only a bluff charge to begin with. But at least we know that the spray didn't enrage the bear."

Kendall stresses that every situation is different. The spray may not always work; there are too many variables. "One ranger tried spraying a roadside bear with an outdated canister," she reports, "and it just fizzed, spraying a thin stream." Weather also makes a difference, notes Kendall. "Rain diminishes the spray's effect, and wind can misdirect it. The Ahern Pass incident was on a windy day, but it must have been blowing in the right direction."

The high-pressure cans also pose a risk of their own. "We've had a number of accidental firings inside tents and cabins, usually it's because the safety has fallen off or been removed to be ready in an emergency," Kendall says. When park staff carry the spray in vehicles, the can goes inside a PVC pipe, tightly capped at both ends. This is particularly important when flying in a plane or helicopter.

Recreationists can buy the sprays at sporting good stores; cost ranges from $7 to $40 depending on the brand and canister volume. Most canisters come with a handy belt holster for ready access on the trail.

Bear Resistant Food Containers

Travelers in the Arctic or alpine zones once faced a difficult dilemma when it came to protecting their food supplies from marauding bears—there were no trees (or none large enough) in which to hang the food out of a bear's reach. What to do?

One recent answer to this problem is the bear-resistant food container (BRFC for short), a hard plastic cylinder with a lockable lid. BRFCs were used early on and met with some success against Yosemite's persistent black bears. Today they are gaining widespread acceptance in parks and wildlands where few other options exist.

Denali National Park, for example, issues BRFCs to everyone who obtains a permit to stay overnight in the park's backcountry. The containers are made from ABS plastic with a locking lid built to withstand a prolonged encounter with bruin curiosity. Sandy Kogl, a Denali backcountry ranger, emphasizes that the cylinders are "bear resistant, not bear proof." If crammed too full of food, the lid·may pop off during investigation by a bear, and a few BRFCs have been opened because the locks weren't fastened properly. For the most part, though, BRFCs discourage all but the most determined bear.

The cylinders come in two sizes, and the smaller fits easily in a hiker's backpack, measuring eight inches in diameter by twelve inches long, and weighing in at 2.9 pounds, empty. "An astute, experienced backpacker," Kogl says, "can fit four to five days worth of food into the smaller BRFC." Canned goods, she warns, make packing the cylinder difficult. For larger hiking parties or extended trips, a "base camp" model is available, measuring eight inches in diameter and eighteen inches long. It weighs a hefty five pounds empty.

In open country, Denali rangers recommend caching food in a BRFC at least one hundred yards from tents. Kogl suggests laying out camp in a triangle, with tents at one point, kitchen downwind one hundred yards at another point, and the food cache at the third point, one hundred yards from both kitchen and tents. It helps to locate the kitchen and food cache on a hill or rise with a good vantage where approaching bears can be seen at a distance. And, as always in bear country, if bears or signs of bear activity are present, find another place to camp.

For more information, write to the Forest Service, Region 1, P.O. Box 7669, Missoula, MT 59807 for a copy of *Living with Grizzly Bears—Structures that Work.*

(Editor's note: In areas with trees suitable for hanging food securely, authorities are less inclined to endorse BRFCs as a storage method. As of this writing, the use of BRFCs alone does not meet the food storage requirements spelled out in Yellowstone National Park's backcountry regulations.)

Bison

Each year, millions of tourists jam the roads and leave their cars to look at bison in Yellowstone, Elk Island, and the National Bison Range (among other places), and each year somebody is bumped, trampled, or gored. In nearly every case, the person got too close and then couldn't retreat when the bison charged. There's a reason for this: bison look docile, ponderous, even slow and imperturbable...until provoked.

An adult bull can weigh up to one ton and stand six feet at the shoulder. But even at this heft, a bison can run thirty-two miles per hour—faster than an Olympic sprinter. And they go from zero to thirty in an awful hurry—bison are incredibly agile, with explosive power in their legs and neck muscles. They can spin, lunge, and hook with their horns. Despite their usual calm demeanor, bison are wild animals who do not like being approached by humans. The wood buffalo (a subspecies) of Canada tend to be more skittish than the plains variety in the States.

◆ In the backcountry, keep at least one hundred yards from bison. Walk around a herd rather than through it, and never step between a calf and an adult (both sexes have horns, and both protect calves). Keep a watchful eye on the animals; charges sometimes come without apparent provocation or warning.
◆ Bison are more active during early morning and late evening. During the heat of the day, watch for bison bedded in tall grass, gullies, and low wallows. Avoid camping in areas where bison tracks, scat, and wallows are present.
◆ If a bison acts agitated—turning to face you, pawing at the ground, raising its tail—back away immediately. If charged, your only hope is to run for cover—into a dense stand of trees or onto a pile of rocks.

Other Hoofed and Horned Animals

Moose, elk, and deer can be surprisingly dangerous, especially during mating season when a fresh dose of hormones kicks in. Bulls and bucks respond to this boost with increased aggressiveness, which may override their natural fear of humans. All ungulates, when cornered or surprised, will rake with antlers, slash with hooves, headbutt, and stomp. Bighorn sheep and mountain goats may butt, kick, or bite. Moose tend to be more ornery than elk or deer and can be especially dangerous, and not only during the rut. Bull moose may charge during any season of the year, and cows with calves are equally aggressive. Never underestimate the speed and power of any animal; even deer have killed people by goring with antlers or kicking with hooves.

◆ Keep at least 150 feet from all wildlife, farther back if the animal changes its behavior because of your presence. Many animals will flee or attack if approached to within two hundred yards.
◆ Never walk between adult and young, or between any members of a herd or family group.
◆ Avoid traveling through or camping near feeding, calving, or resting grounds. Watch for tracks, scat, and day beds.

Cougar

Cougars are found throughout the West, in desert, chaparral, forest, and even high mountain regions. Remnant populations are also scattered in pockets across southern Texas, Louisiana, Alabama, Tennessee, and the southern tip of Florida. Rare sightings are reported in New England, upstate New York, and Canada's Maritime Provinces. Generally, cougars are found where deer and other large prey are plentiful.

An adult male cougar can reach 8 feet long and weigh 150 pounds. They are capable of leaping twenty feet and can outrun a deer over short distances. Cougars are most active between dusk and dawn. They hunt by stalking their prey, then lunging or rushing from behind. The kill is made with a bite to the back of the neck or base of the skull. A cougar feeding on a kill may aggressively defend itself against all intruders.

When traveling or camping in cougar country:
◆ Make lots of noise when traveling, especially around dawn and dusk when cougars are likely to be more active. Travel in groups of two or more.
◆ Cougars may view children as prey because of their small size. Closely supervise children and do not let them roam out of sight. Also instruct them that running and high-pitched noises may attract a cougar and provoke an attack. Dogs are also an attractive prey for hungry cats; it's best to leave the dog at home.
◆ Frequently check on packstock, particularly at night if horses seem nervous and spooked.

Sightings of cougars are rare, and even when a large cat is seen it's usually just a glimpse of disappearing fur and tail. Yet reports of cougar attacks are on the rise, particularly in California, Colorado, and Montana. Many of the recent attacks occurred near homes or rural residential areas and most of the victims were small children. Experts blame this trend on residential sprawl overtaking cougar habitat and an increase in the cougar population. As young cougars are forced into new territory, they more often come into contact with people. Attacks in the backcountry are still relatively rare.

If you do happen to meet a cougar, heed the following guidelines (*adapted from the Colorado Division of Wildlife*):
◆ Do not approach a cougar, especially one that is feeding, appears injured, or has kittens in tow. Most big cats will flee on sight; give them room to escape.
◆ Stay calm, talking firmly in a monotone. Stand still or move slowly. Face the cat and remain standing. Do all you can to appear taller and larger—open a coat, raise your arms above your head. Pick up and hold small children so they won't run. Back away slowly if it seems safe to do so.
◆ Running triggers a cougar's instinct to attack and any cat can easily outrun a person. Teach everyone in your group, and especially children, to stand still if a cougar is encountered.
◆ If a cougar lingers or acts aggressively, throw stones or branches at it. Do not turn your back on the cat. Continue to speak firmly and keep your arms outstretched. Try to convince the cougar that you are not prey and may in fact be a danger to the cat.
◆ If a cougar actually attacks, fight back with all your might. DO NOT play dead. Hit with rocks, branches, or walking sticks; punch and kick at the cat's face, neck,

and belly. People have successfully fended off cougars with their bare hands. Try to remain standing and facing the cat at all times.

Small Mammals and Rodents

Two forms of wildlife that backcountry travelers encounter on almost every trip is small mammals and rodents. Depending on where you travel, you are likely to see squirrels, ground squirrels, chipmunks, rats, mice, voles, pikas, lemmings, marmots, raccoons, skunks, opossums, hares, and rabbits. Though most of these animals rarely pose a threat themselves, all can carry serious diseases, and all will bite or scratch in self defense.

Otters, badgers, and wolverines are more elusive and rarely cause problems unless cornered. Badgers and wolverines are particularly dangerous when surprised or cornered—give them both a wide berth.

The two main concerns regarding small mammals and rodents are safeguarding your food and protecting yourself from transmission of disease. Food should be stored as described in the bear country section on page 118 whenever it is unattended, day or night. Keep an eye on food while preparing meals and seal all containers to ward off curious squirrels, chipmunks, and mice (and also crows, ravens, gulls, and gray jays—all notorious camp robbers). Clean up food spills immediately and never feed wild animals.

Wild mammals and rodents are often hosts to various diseases, which can be transmitted by direct contact with the animal or its body fluids or feces, or by the bites of fleas that have recently fed from an infected host. In North America the most severe diseases so transmitted are rabies, bubonic plague, and hantavirus. All are deadly.

Rabies is carried in an infected animal's saliva and can be transmitted when the animal bites or if it licks a break in your skin. Any contact with saliva is risky. A girl in Massachusetts contracted rabies after a rabid animal nibbled on food left out. Some saliva dribbled on the food, which the girl later ate. A wide variety of mammals can carry rabies—a hunter in Virginia was once attacked by a rabid bobcat. Cavers are at risk because bats are frequent carriers. Suspect rabies in any wild animal that approaches too closely or behaves strangely. Whenever contact with a wild animal results in a bite or scratch, wash the wound vigorously with soap and water and apply an antiseptic (iodine or Bactine) if available. Seek medical attention; rabies is fatal if untreated. A doctor can determine whether a bite is high-risk or not and whether to give a rabies inoculation. If the animal is captured or dead, bring it with you for rabies testing. But do not risk further injury by pursuing or trying to kill the animal.

When most people hear of **bubonic plague** they think of the Black Death that swept across Europe in mid-fourteenth century. But reservoirs of the disease still exist today around the globe, including North America where squirrels, rats, and

126

mice are the major carriers. The United States sees about twenty cases of bubonic plague each year, mostly in the West during summer months. The plague is usually transmitted by flea bite, and victims often include children playing around rodent nests or burrows or handling dead rodents. Occasionally a hunter or trapper is exposed to plague when dressing or skinning out an infected animal; recent cases have been traced to pronghorn antelope and bobcat.

To reduce the risk of catching plague, avoid close contact with all rodents and their nests or burrows. Especially do not camp where rodents or fleas are plentiful, and keep a clean camp so scavengers won't be attracted. Do not pick up or closely examine dead animals. Hunters should use care when dressing kills—work slowly to prevent cuts and wear disposable rubber gloves if hands are cut or chapped. If symptoms develop (fever; chills; swollen lymph glands in the neck, groin, and armpits; headache; collapse; delirium; vomiting; diarrhea; reddish-purple spots on the skin), seek medical help immediately; treatment is effective if the disease is caught early.

From May 1993 through January 1994, there were fifty-four confirmed cases of a once rare (in North America) respiratory disease called **hantavirus**. Thirty-one people died, and although New Mexico and Arizona bore the brunt of the disease, twelve other states saw fatalities. Prior to a case in Pennsylvania in the mid-1980s, hantavirus had not been detected in the Western Hemisphere. But the disease, which is carried by deer mice and possibly other rodents, has apparently spread rapidly across the country. Hantavirus is spread by inhaling airborne particles of blood, urine, saliva, and droppings of deer mice. Early symptoms resemble the flu—fever, chills, fatigue, muscle aches, coughing, abdominal and lower back pain, headaches, and vomiting. But unlike the flu, which usually eases after two or three days, the person's condition deteriorates. The patient soon has difficulty breathing as the lungs begin to fill with fluid. If not treated in the early stages, the result is coma, respiratory failure, and death.

Scientists are still scrambling for specific answers to the hantavirus puzzle. Researchers have traced many cases to mice inside homes, sheds, or abandoned buildings. But the Centers for Disease Control and Prevention (CDC) also recommends taking extra precautions when recreating in the outdoors. Do not sleep on open ground where small mammals or rodents are plentiful or where hantavirus is known to occur. Use a tent with a sewn-in floor and mesh-covered, zippered doors and windows. Promptly patch all holes in tent floor or walls. Keep food out of tents.

Backcountry cabins and shelters are havens for mice and pack rats; make an extra effort to keep the area clean and store all food in rodent-proof tins. Traps are preferable to poison for eradicating pests (a poisoned animals often crawls off to die and the decaying carcass may attract other small carnivores, continuing the cycle). If traps are set, use extreme care when handling a dead animal. Wear rubber gloves and a dust mask, douse the carcass with Lysol or bleach before moving it, and dispose of the carcass by burying it far from human habitation or burning it in a hot fire.

In the outdoors, do not move or handle dead rodents. Also leave all nests undisturbed. Stay out of abandoned buildings. If you develop flu-like symptoms after contact with rodents or their nest sites, get to a doctor immediately.

Poisonous Snakes and Gila Monsters

Each year, between fifteen and twenty thousand people are bitten by poisonous snakes in the United States. But fatalities from snakebite are remarkably low, averaging six to fifteen a year. Rattlesnakes account for most of the deaths; the Mojave rattler injects a particularly potent venom, and other rattlers make up in volume for what they may lack in toxicity. The wide discrepancy between the number of bites and fatalities is due to a combination of factors. Snake venom is relatively slow-acting, allowing the victim in most cases to reach medical care. In up to twenty percent of bites from poisonous snakes, little or no venom is injected. And effective antivenins are now available at most hospitals across the country.

The two types of poisonous snakes native to North America are pit vipers and coral snakes. The pit vipers, which include six species of rattlesnake, the cotton mouth, and the copperhead, account for nearly all bites that occur in the backcountry. All pit vipers have triangular or arrowhead-shaped heads and vertically-slit pupils. Harmless snakes have slender, tube-shaped heads and round pupils. Pit vipers also show a small dent or pit on each side of their head, midway between the eye and nostril. In general, they tend to be thicker and heavier for their length compared to harmless snakes. Rattlesnakes have a rattle on the tip of their tail, though sometimes this is missing due to injury. They usually—but not always—rattle before striking. All pit vipers also have hollow fangs through which they inject venom. Their bite leaves two (or more) deep holes in the skin, while a harmless snakebite leaves two rows of shallow indentations and no substantial holes.

Pit viper

Coral snakes are related to cobras. They live in Florida and Arizona, favoring brushy areas and underground burrows. The coral snake has bright black, yellow, and red bands ringing its body, resembling the color scheme of the harmless scarlet king snake. Coral snakes have black heads, and yellow bands at each end of the longer red bands. Scarlet king snakes usually have red heads and narrow black bands on either end of the red bands. Think of "red on yellow, kill a fellow; red on black, venom lack" to remember how to distinguish the two species.

Non-poisonous

Preventing most snakebites is relatively easy. Most bites occur in the South and Southwest, primarily between April and October, when both people and snakes are out in the same habitat. Watch where you step or sit down to rest, and always look carefully before putting a hand into a cleft or notch or under a log. Wear high leather boots and long pants in snake habitat, and avoid hiking at night. Anticipate snakes around rodent burrows (especially ground squirrel and prairie dog towns), and consider their daily rhythms. Snakes generally hole up in the shade during the heat of the day, then bask on sun-warmed rocks or sand when air temperatures cool in the evening. Snakes hunt primarily at night, so it's best to sleep in tents with sewn-in floors and zippered doors. Finally, a third of all bites happen when snakes are picked up and handled; leave such stunts to paid and well-insured herpetologists.

Emergency care in the backcountry for pit viper bites and coral snake bites differs slightly because the venoms are different and cause distinct types of symptoms and tissue damage. In either case, however, the primary goal is to do no harm and to get the patient to a hospital as soon as possible.

A pit viper bite causes burning and local swelling within five minutes, which then spreads up the limb toward the torso. Swelling is often accompanied by bruising and blood-filled blisters. In severe cases, the patient suffers nausea, vomiting, profuse sweating, weakness, fainting, muscle spasms, blood in vomitus and urine, and difficulty breathing. Complete collapse may occur six to twelve hours after the bite, sooner in small children.

To treat a pit viper bite:
◆ Get the victim and all others out of range of the snake. Do not try to kill or precisely identify the snake—this only risks further bites. Also, do not handle a dead snake or its severed head; a reflex bite can be delivered even hours after it is dead.
◆ Remove all watches, rings, bracelets, and constricting clothing from the bitten arm or leg.
◆ Use of commercial snake venom extractors is helpful if done within three minutes of the bite and if the manufacturer's instructions are precisely followed. DO NOT make incisions with a knife or try to suck poison out with your mouth; these actions are rarely effective and often lead to infection.
◆ Also DO NOT apply tourniquets, cold water, or ice packs. All may worsen the symptoms; ice heightens the risk of gangrene.
◆ Splint the injured arm or leg. Any muscular motion tends to hasten the venom's absorption. Check the splint frequently to make sure that swelling is not interfering with circulation.
◆ With a pen, mark the limit of swelling every fifteen minutes on the patient's skin. Write the time next to each mark so the attending doctor can judge how rapidly the swelling has progressed.
◆ To slow the venom's action, it's best if the patient does not run or walk. Carry the patient to the nearest trailhead and vehicle. If help is limited and you are twenty minutes or less from the trailhead, the patient can walk slowly, resting frequently. If bitten while traveling alone, walk out for help.

◆ While the patient is conscious, give water, broth, or fruit juices to replace fluids lost from bleeding and to help prevent shock.
◆ Take the patient to the nearest hospital or emergency room. Call ahead if possible so that antivenin can be ready.
◆ Anticipate and treat for shock as needed.

The bite of a coral snake produces far less burning, swelling, bruising, and blistering than those of pit vipers. Generally, effects on the nervous system begin to show in an hour or so. The bitten arm or leg becomes numb and weak. Then the patient may grow dizzy and anxious, and feel a prickliness all over the skin. Later symptoms include double vision, twitching, increased salivation, and drooling. Within several hours, the patient may have difficulty talking and swallowing and will die of respiratory or heart failure if untreated.

To treat a coral snake bite:
◆ Get out of striking range of the snake.
◆ Flush the bite thoroughly with clean water to wash away as much of the venom as possible.
◆ Place sterile gauze or other dressing on the wound.
◆ If an elastic bandage is available, wrap it loosely around the bitten arm or leg. Start near the bite and wrap toward the body. The bandage should be loose enough to allow a finger to slide between it and the skin and should not pinch or reduce circulation. Wrapping helps slow absorption of the venom.
◆ Splint the bitten arm or leg. Check frequently to make sure that swelling is not interfering with circulation.
◆ DO NOT make incisions, try to suck out the poison, or apply tourniquets, cold water, or ice packs.
◆ Carry the patient to the nearest vehicle and transport to a hospital as soon as possible. Treat for shock and basic life support as needed.

The Gila monster (*Heloderma suspectum*) is an endangered lizard of southwestern deserts, found today mostly in southern Arizona and southwestern California, and in Mexico. This two-foot-long lizard may bite if provoked, and is notorious for hanging on like a pit bull. Gila monsters produce a venom that is carried in the saliva. The venom may be delivered during a bite, causing burning pain, skin discoloration, overall weakness, and profuse sweating. Poisoning is most likely if the lizard does not relinquish its grip, or if a tooth breaks off in the wound.

To avoid an encounter with a Gila monster, follow the guidelines given for traveling in snake country. To treat a Gila bite, it may be necessary to pry the lizard's mouth off of the patient, or to break its jaw to release its grip. Thoroughly wash out the wound with clean water, removing any teeth or tooth fragments, and wrap a loose, dry dressing over the bite. Seek medical help immediately.

Alligators

The American alligator is a formidable hunter, weighing up to five hundred pounds and measuring fifteen feet from snout to tip of tail. *Alligator mississippiensis* favors warm waters of southern rivers and swamps, ranging from the Carolinas, Georgia, and Florida, west through Mississippi, Louisiana, and Texas to the Rio Grande. Gators avoid people when possible and do not as a rule hunt humans. Pets and small children are fair game, however, and even an adult is in trouble if a gator is surprised or cornered.

◆ Do not swim in muddy or tannin-stained water where visibility is limited. Where alligators are more common, stay alert when near water, especially at night.
◆ Stay out of water during mating season (April and May), when alligators are more aggressive. Also avoid nests, made of rotting leaves and debris; a female may charge to protect its eggs.
◆ Keep children in sight at all times and do not let them wade or swim alone where alligators may be present.
◆ Alligators attack by biting with their mouths and slashing with their tails. They can move with great speed and strength and are powerful swimmers. Get out of the water immediately if an alligator is present (they kill by clamping on with their teeth and pulling the victim under water). On land, run or climb a tree. One source recommends running in a zig-zag pattern, though this is often not feasible in heavy underbrush.

Jellyfish, Skates, and Other Sea Life

It's possible to suffer a sting while swimming, wading, or even by stepping on a beached jellyfish. Sea anemones, coral, and hydra can also sting. While on the beach or in the water, be alert for these animals. Jellyfish may be more numerous near the shore during certain seasons or after a storm.

◆ If stung, get out of the water. Rinse the area well with sea water (if stinging organs remain on the skin, fresh water may cause them to rupture or further discharge). Remove any large strands or tentacles with tweezers. Then rinse the area again, this time with vinegar or rubbing alcohol.
◆ If the sting is severe, apply shaving lotion and shave the affected area. Then soak it in vinegar or rubbing alcohol.
◆ Watch for an allergic reaction. Signs include increased redness, swelling, possible hives, dizziness, and difficulty breathing. Treat as anaphylactic shock—see page 134.

Skates and stingrays are armed with a sharp spine on the tops of their tails. Catfish, stonefish, scorpion fish, and sea urchins also bear sharp spines that release toxins upon penetrating the skin. Swimmers, snorkelers, and waders should watch their step and wear water shoes as needed. Also do not handle tidepool or beached animals that bear spines.

◆ If pierced by a spine, get out of the water. Rinse the area well with hot, fresh water, the hotter the better (up to 113 degrees F.) for thirty minutes.

◆ While rinsing, remove any spines or fragments with tweezers. If spines do not readily come out, are deeply imbedded, or are broken in the wound, seek medical attention. A tetanus shot may be warranted.

◆ Watch for an allergic reaction. Signs include increased redness, swelling, possible hives, dizziness, and difficulty breathing. Treat as anaphylactic shock—see page 134.

INSECTS AND THEIR KIN

Of all the known animal species on Earth, roughly eighty-five percent are Arthropods—spiders, flies, ants, mites, ticks, fleas...bugs, in short. There are more than forty thousand different species of weevils alone. All told, there may be one to two million species of bugs, most of which are as yet undiscovered. Some folks don't want to know about all those unknown bugs. The ones we do know about, they reason, give us trouble enough. Here's a North American sampler of insects and their kin that are best left alone.

Bees, Wasps, Hornets, Yellowjackets, and Fire Ants

The stings of these insects are cause for concern for two reasons. First, if a person is stung many times at once, he or she may develop a toxic reaction—the cumulative dose of venom may be too much for the body to handle. Multiple stings, most common when an entire swarm attacks, can be fatal. Second, some people (whether or not they know it) are allergic to insect stings. And anyone can develop an allergy, usually by being stung repeatedly, even over a period of years. Allergic reactions range from mild to severe, and can also be fatal. In the United States, about forty people die each year from bee stings.

Despite wide differences in behavior, habitat, and aggressiveness among bees and their cousins, one set of safety precautions and treatments applies equally well for dealing with any of these critters in the wild. For brevity's sake, we'll use the generic term "bee" unless a special concern warrants naming the specific culprit. Africanized honeybees (misnamed "killer bees") have immigrated from South America into Texas and Arizona. These bees may be more aggressive around their hives or when swarming. Their venom is no stronger than other honeybees, but the likelihood of multiple stings (and hence more severe reactions) is greater than with other types of honeybees.

Prevention:
◆ Be alert for nests or hives, and for large concentrations of bees. Nests are built in hollow trees, hanging from branches, under logs, in the ground, and sometimes in the mud or dirt banks of streams or even deeply cut trails. Fire ants nest in the ground or under rocks. Bees may congregate around flowers, overripe fruit, and on

clothes, pack straps, boots, or other sweat-soaked items. Yellowjackets especially are drawn to sweat, raw meat, sugar drinks, and exposed garbage.

◆ Bees are attracted by bright colors. Where bees are numerous (or if you're allergic), wear white or earth-tone clothes. Also avoid flowery or fruity smelling soaps, shampoos, perfumes, lotions, or other fragrances.

◆ Bees are attracted and excited by movement. Stay calm when bees come near; don't flail your arms at them, and do not run unless a swarm attacks, and then dash for shelter (a nearby tent with sewn-in floor and zippered door, a body of water to submerge in, or—at the trailhead—a vehicle).

◆ Protect your face, head, and neck if attacked by bees. Stings in these areas can cause serious pain and swelling, which may interfere with breathing, vision, or swallowing.

Treatment:

◆ If a stinger remains in the skin, carefully scrape it off with a knife blade. Do not pinch the stinger with fingers or tweezers; this only releases more venom into the skin.

◆ Apply a paste made from water and an unseasoned meat tenderizer containing papain (a papaya enzyme). This enzyme neutralizes the protein in bee venom. The traditional baking soda paste is largely ineffective.

◆ Apply ice packs or cold compresses to the sting.

◆ Watch for signs of a toxic (if there are multiple stings) or allergic reaction. An allergic reaction may strike suddenly within minutes or be delayed until hours later. The reaction may also be local (limited to swelling, pain, and itching around the sting site) or general (producing anaphylactic shock).

Toxic reaction	
Extensive swelling.	Rapid heart rate.
Nausea, possibly vomiting.	Unconsciousness.
Anxiety.	Death.
Shortness of breath or difficulty breathing.	

Allergic reaction (including anaphylactic shock)	
May occur from a single sting	Swelling of face or tongue.
Swelling larger than a half-dollar around the sting site (in a severe reaction swelling may be extensive).	Weakness.
	Cramps.
	Possible nausea and vomiting; diarrhea.
Hives (often around waist regardless of sting site).	Unconsciousness.
Itching or prickly skin.	Convulsions.
Light-headedness, anxiety.	Death.
Tightness of chest and throat; wheezing.	
Shortness of breath, difficulty breathing.	

◆ Carry an over-the-counter anti-histamine. Doctors frequently recommend diphenhydramine (Benadryl). This drug helps to control mild reactions.
◆ People with a known allergy should always carry a bee-sting kit (or two) with a syringe of epinephrine (available by prescription only; see your doctor). Follow the instructions in the kit. Carry the kit with you every waking moment (it doesn't do any good if left back in basecamp), and make sure other members of your group know where it's stashed so they can reach it if you are disabled. An anti-histamine can be given with the epinephrine.

Spiders, Scorpions, Centipedes

Only two spiders in North America pack a bite that's dangerous to people—the black widow and brown recluse. The black widow is all black with a red hourglass mark on its belly. The brown recluse is a pale tan or yellow, often with a violin-shaped mark on its head. Both are found most often in basements, garages and other outbuildings, and woodpiles. The black widow spins a web, sometimes under the seat of an outhouse, and may bite if the web is disturbed.

The widow's bite is usually painless, but symptoms soon follow, including severe muscle cramps, tightness of the chest, difficulty breathing, dizziness, nausea, vomiting, and acute stomach pain. The abdominal muscles often go rigid. Apply an ice pack to the bite and seek medical care immediately; an antivenin is available.

A brown recluse's bite is painful and quickly turns into a red, crusty, open sore that continues to spread and deepen for several weeks. The wound will heal very slowly. Apply ice packs to the bite and seek medical care.

Of the thirty or so **scorpion** species in North America (one species ranges as far north as Alberta, Canada), only one wields a dangerously poi-

134

sonous tail. The venom of the Arizona scorpion (*Centruroides exilicauda*) causes muscle cramps, convulsions, shock, and heart irregularities. The venom is particularly potent to children and the elderly. Apply ice packs to the sting and seek medical care immediately; an antivenin is available. Be prepared to provide CPR and to cope with convulsions en route. All scorpions should be avoided—most will sting in self-defense, and the results (pain, redness, and swelling) are unpleasant enough. Scorpions are nocturnal and hide during the day in burrows, under rocks or pieces of bark, and in dark crevices.

All **centipedes** have poison glands, but thankfully the mouths of many species are too small to readily bite through human skin. Throughout the southern United States, however, lives the genus *Scolopendra*, which boasts at least one species that grows up to six inches long. Its bite is very painful and slow to heal. Short of ice packs and a visit to the doctor, little can be done to ease the pain or speed the healing. Better to not handle any centipede—they can also pinch with their hind-most legs.

◆ Shake out your shoes and clothes before putting them on. Also shake out your sleeping bag before cozying in for the night. Look before poking your fingers into nooks and crannies.
◆ Use a tent with sewn-in floor and mosquito netting on doors and windows.
◆ Don't walk barefoot in scorpion and centipede country, particularly at night. And watch where you sit.

Ticks

Ticks are widespread throughout North America, thriving in grassy, brushy, or wooded areas. Ticks themselves are harmless, but not so for the diseases they carry. Lyme disease, Colorado tick fever, and Rocky Mountain spotted fever all produce serious symptoms, the latter two sometimes resulting in death if not properly treated. The incubation period for these diseases is generally two weeks or more, time enough that most backcountry travelers don't realize they've been infected until they're back home. After traveling in tick country, watch for symptoms of tick-borne disease, including a high fever, arthritic-like pain in the bones and joints, or a rash.

During tick season (spring and summer), stay out of tall grass or brushy areas, and inspect yourself and clothing after each outing. When camping, look for ticks nightly before going to bed. Carefully inspect legs, groin, armpits, ears, and scalp for attached ticks.

Ticks fasten on with their mouths, sucking blood from the host. Sometimes they will dig in for a better meal. If undetected, a tick may gorge on blood, swelling to several times its original size. To remove a loose tick, flick it off with a finger nail. If the tick is firmly imbedded, encourage it to back out by holding a hot (but extinguished) matchhead to its back. If the tick does not let go, use tweezers to pinch a small area around the tick's mouth and pull it out (you may have to remove a tiny chunk of skin to get all of the tick). Try not to squeeze the tick's body as this increases the risk of infection. Clean the wound with an antiseptic.

Flies and Mosquitoes

In many tropical countries, flies are the prime vector of disease. Africa's tsetse fly is infamous for the untold misery it has caused in transmitting the deadly sleeping sickness. Although the incidence of fly-borne illnesses is low in North America, the list of diseases carried by our New World flies is a long one. Even the common horse and house flies may transmit anthrax, tuberculosis, tularemia, tetanus, typhoid, dysentery, and cholera. A more macabre role is played out by the screwworm fly (*Cochliomyia hominivorax*), a widespread pest similar in appearance to a housefly but larger and with a shiny, metallic-looking abdomen. Screwworm flies are attracted to open sores and the nostrils of animals, where they lay their eggs. The eggs hatch within hours and the larvae then feed on the flesh of the host animal before dropping to the ground, causing infection and sometimes death in the process. Flies may lay eggs in the nose of a person sleeping in the open; removal of the larvae (which grow to 0.75 inch long) usually requires surgery.

To prevent disease or injury from flies, avoid travel during peak fly seasons, which vary widely by region. Wear insect repellant and cover all exposed skin. Wear a long-sleeved shirt and long pants. Also keep a clean camp—burn or bag all garbage as it is generated and do not leave food uncovered. Locate cat holes and latrines at least one hundred yards from camp and quickly cover any human waste. Where surface waste disposal is recommended (see page 47), sprinkle a handful of sand over the feces to discourage flies. Sleep in an enclosed tent with zippered, mesh windows and doors.

Unlike in more tropical climes, **mosquitoes** in North America are more a nuisance than a hazard. Contrary to popular belief, however, mosquito-borne malaria does occur in the United States, though rarely. The culprit is the Anopheles mosquito, a carrier for the protozoan *Plasmodium*, which causes malaria. Anopheles thrives along the Mississippi Valley as far north as Canada and east to Atlantic. Mosquitoes may also transmit a form of encephalitis, which is potentially fatal, especially to young children. This disease is most prevalent in southern Florida, though isolated cases have been reported in the East and in the Rocky Mountains.

The best way to avoid mosquito-borne diseases is to avoid being bitten. Ah, if only there were an effective repellant. Those with N, N-diethyl-3-methylbenzamide (commonly called DEET) seem to work best. Also wear long pants, a long-sleeved shirt, ankle-high shoes, and a cap that covers the ears. In serious mosquito country, wear a head net and gloves. In some places you can avoid the worst of the feeding frenzy by taking shelter during peak times. Mosquitoes generally won't fly during the heat of the day or if winds rise above ten miles per hour. The hordes usually appear during cooler periods around dawn and dusk, or at night. Try not to camp near stagnant water or fields of damp or dew-laden grass.

A few other bugs are also best avoided. Saddleback, puss, and gypsy moth caterpillars are armed with bristles that can cause an unpleasant rash if touched. Blister beetles (there are more than two hundred species in the United States, found mostly in the East and South), release cantharidin, a skin irritant. Blisters may form on contact with this chemical, particularly if the beetle is squashed on the skin. Treat as you would a second-degree burn. Also watch for leeches and worms, particularly in drinking water sources (another reason to filter or boil all water first). Remove any leeches clinging to your skin, and douse the wounds with an antiseptic. Bleeding is usually minor but may be difficult to stop—leeches produce an enzyme that inhibits clotting.

POISONOUS AND TROUBLESOME PLANTS

When most people think of poisonous plants they picture a smorgasbord of deadly inedibles: mushrooms, nightshade, dumb cane, may apple, and death camas. Indeed, many plants are wholly poisonous or bear toxic parts. Eat only plants that you can positively identify. Stay with familiar favorites: huckleberries and thimbleberries, for instance. The most dangerous plants are look-a-likes: Is it wild carrot or poison hemlock? Wild onion or death camas? Wild grape or moonseed? Delectable morrel or false morrel?

In fact, the majority of plant poisonings can be traced to just a few different species. Water hemlock (genus *Cicuta*) is probably the most commonly ingested poisonous wild plant. A single bite of water hemlock is often enough to kill a full-grown adult. The toxin is a fast-acting aliphatic alcohol that causes nausea, vomiting, lockjaw, and convulsions within fifteen minutes to one hour. Death quickly follows. Leave water hemlock to the mallards, which seem to be immune to the toxin. Most plant toxins act more slowly than hemlock, with a delay of four hours or more before the onset of symptoms. The effect of some toxic mushrooms may be delayed even longer—up to twelve hours—before symptoms arise.

Wild onion or death camas

The best protection against plant poisonings is prevention and prompt care.

Blue camas

♦ Never eat wild plants or mushrooms unless they have been positively identified as an edible species by an expert.

◆ Keep a watchful eye on children; a child who won't touch a salad at home may graze contentedly on unknown wild greens. And a toddler's sense of taste is poorly developed—a one-year old may be heedless to bitter or unpleasant flavors that warn of a plant's toxicity.

◆ If a poisonous plant is ingested, the person may vomit much of the material. If vomiting is not spontaneous, it can be induced (only if the patient is conscious and able to swallow) with syrup of ipecac given in the usual dose recommended on the bottle. Other symptoms—including sweating, headache, numbness or tingling, weakness, stomach cramps, diarrhea, difficulty breathing, and convulsions—may be present. Plant poisoning often goes unsuspected until such symptoms appear. By then, the only recourse is to evacuate the patient to the nearest hospital, providing rescue breathing and other care as needed. Bring along a specimen of the suspect plant if it is readily available, or write down a detailed description, including which parts of the plant were eaten and when.

Though plant poisonings do occur every year, most folks wisely defer from putting strange leaves, fruits, stalks, and seeds in their mouths. It's far more difficult, however, to avoid brushing up against any one of many plants that bear toxic resins and oils, sharp spines or thorns, or irritating hairs or bristles. The results range from minor itching and lacerations to serious puncture wounds, debilitating rashes, and even potentially lethal allergic reactions.

According to the *American Medical Association's Handbook of Poisonous and Injurious Plants*, poison ivy, poison oak, and poison sumac account for the lion's

Poison ivy

share of all "contact dermatitis," causing more cases of skin irritation than all other plants, and household and industrial chemicals, combined. Resins produced by these plants cause redness, itching, blisters, and possible headache and fever. The severity of the reaction varies from person to person and typically worsens with repeated exposures. Onset of itching and a rash occurs with twelve to forty-eight hours, and fluid-filled blisters soon form (this fluid cannot spread the rash). A bad case of poison ivy/oak/sumac will run its course in about ten days.

Avoid all contact with these plants by learning to identify poison ivy, oak, and sumac on sight. Remember: "Leaves of three, let it be." Poison ivy and

Poison sumac

138

poison oak are found in almost every habitat across North America. They both sprout leaflets in groups of three on woody, sometimes rust-colored stems. Leaves are shiny or dull green, turning red, orange, or brown in the fall. The leaves of poison oak are often heavily lobed around the edges, more so in western varieties. Both plants produce berries, which are also toxic. Poison sumac favors wetlands and swamps and is found only in North America. This shrub or bush grows to twelve feet tall, with smooth, dark green leaves growing in pairs (alternate, pinnately compound) from brown or reddish twigs.

Poison oak

◆ Wear ankle-high boots and long pants when traveling through brushy habitat. Watch for patches of three-leaved plants.
◆ Use care in choosing cat hole sites—rashes and blisters on the genitals can be particularly uncomfortable and debilitating.
◆ If you come in contact with poison ivy/oak/sumac, rinsing the area with water (do not use soap) within the first ten minutes may prevent a reaction. Soap may wash away protective skin oils, leaving skin more vulnerable to the toxin. Remove contaminated clothes and seal them in a plastic bag until they can be machine washed.
◆ If a rash develops, apply calamine lotion to reduce itching. See a doctor if the rash is on your face or genitals, or if more than one-quarter of your body is affected.

Another motley batch of plants contain saps that cause skin irritation (and blindness if the sap is rubbed in the eyes) upon contact with crushed leaves and stems. Crown-of-thorns, pencil cactus, and the century plant are common culprits in this category, but even the seemingly innocuous pasque flower and buttercup contain caustic sap. Reason enough to live and let live—don't pick the flowers.

Plants with thorns, spines, or irritant hairs are generally easier to avoid. Cacti are the most obvious spiny threats. But many cacti, not content to grow simple spines, expend the extra effort to add tiny barbs to each spine. Step on one, or brush up against it, and the spine easily penetrates your skin. Try to pull the spine back out, however, and the barbs dig in.

Devils club

Puncture by cactus spines can lead to infection and serious tissue damage—deeply imbedded spines should be removed only by a doctor.

Dumbcane, devil's club, nettles, and at least one species of lupine (among others) bear irritant hairs or needles that release chemicals or excite the body's defenses, resulting in itching, rashes, and sometimes more general illness. Removing the imbedded needles helps alleviate the symptoms. Lightly apply adhesive tape to the affected area and gently pull it away to remove the offending needles.

Drinking Water and Perishable Foods

Gone are the days when you can cup your hand in any mountain stream and drink your fill of cold, clean water. Even the most remote freshets in pristine country must now be considered likely homes for any number of disease-causing bacteria, protozoans, and viruses, chief among them the protozoan *Giardia lamblia*. Until an outbreak in Colorado in 1970, no one had ever reported a case of water-borne giardiasis in the United States. But by the mid-1980s, giardia had become the most common intestinal parasite in this country, infecting some sixteen million Americans at any one time.

Giardia thrives in cold, clear streams and lakes and has become widespread throughout North America, carried in the intestines and feces of beaver, muskrats, voles, moose, and other water-loving mammals. But humans, perhaps more than any other host, have spread giardia to far flung waters by careless or improper disposal of human waste. Because giardia spends a fair piece of its life cycle as a hardcased, microscopic cyst, it survives and endures in harsh environments (including cold water) and is easily ingested. A single drop of water may contain thousands of giardia cysts. Once inside a host animal, the bug feeds and reproduces. Cysts are shed in the feces, ready to repopulate another host. Runoff, erosion, or a wayward foot may carry the cysts to water, repeating the cycle.

A person with giardiasis may not feel the effects for days or even weeks after ingesting the cysts. (Some people are carriers without showing any symptoms.) If you develop foul-smelling gas, bloating, stomach cramps, loss of appetite and explosive diarrhea after drinking water in the backcountry, see a doctor. Symptoms may progress to include nausea, vomiting, headache, and low-grade fever. Giardiasis runs its course in one to three weeks, but may recur or become chronic. Untreated, the disease may cause marked weight loss, dehydration, and damage to internal organs.

Other intestinal critters also thrive in seemingly clean water sources. Cases of *campylobactor* and *E. coli* infection, and type A hepatitis, have been traced to drinking untreated water in North America's backcountry. There are only three reliable methods for protecting yourself from contaminated drinking water.

Carry treated water from home. On day trips and short outings, it may be possible and preferable to carry tap water from home in plastic bottles and jugs. Keep containers tightly sealed and do not immerse them in streams or lakes for cold storage.

Boil water for at least five minutes. Giardia cysts are killed in water heated to 140 to 160 degrees F. Other bacteria and viruses are even more vulnerable to heat. Boil water for the allotted time before adding foods, powders, or flavorings to ensure sterilization. For drinking, boiled water tends to taste flat because the oxygen has been bubbled out of it. Make it palatable again by pouring it back and forth repeatedly between two clean containers.

Filter water through an approved purifying device. A number of effective water filters are now available for backcountry use, ranging in price from $30 to $300. Pocket filters tend to cost less and suffice for short backpack trips and parties of two or three people. Mid-range filters can clean a greater amount of water at a faster rate, and some boast ceramic filters that screen out a wider assortment of pathogens and inorganic compounds. Base camp models are also available to purify large amounts of water for groups of six or more people. Always follow the manufacturer's instructions and keep water containers clean and free of contaminated water.

Other water treatment methods, such as disinfecting with iodine, Halazone, or chlorine, are less reliable and pose hazards of their own. These are not recommended.

Spoiled food is also a concern for most backcountry travelers because refrigeration is not available. Salmonella, staph infestation, and molds are the most common problems.

Salmonella grows in a wide range of foods, notably in poultry and dairy products. If foods cannot be kept chilled (below forty-five degrees), leave them at home. Symptoms of salmonella illness include diarrhea, nausea, stomach cramps, and vomiting. Severe cases can lead to dehydration, shock, and poor kidney function if diarrhea and vomiting persist. Give fluids as soon as the patient can tolerate them. Small children and the elderly may suffer life-threatening complications. Evacuate the patient and seek medical attention.

Staphylococci (staph germs) readily grow in bland, creamy foods left out at room temperature. The staph germs produce a toxin that causes violent vomiting, diarrhea, and cramps. Reheating the food may kill the staph, but it does not destroy the toxin. Do not eat any perishable foods that have been stored at temperatures above forty-five degrees for more than an hour.

Molds grow in warm, moist environments and show a special affinity for breads and cheese. Though some—such as penicillin—can be put to beneficial use, many others can cause illness when eaten in the raw. Diarrhea and vomiting may result, and some molds are more toxic, even deadly. Few of us are expert mycologists (students of molds and fungi), but we're all familiar with the green fuzz or blue splotch that spreads across food left in the fridge too long. That's proof enough that the food is inedible. Many people don't realize that a single patch of mold will lace an entire chunk of bread or cheese with microscopic strands to start new fuzz colonies elsewhere. Don't pare off the moldy piece and eat the rest—it could make you sick.

Remember: In the backcountry, eating questionable food isn't worth the risk of illness.

◆ In warm weather, pack mostly non-perishable foods. Carry dried rather than fresh fruits, and cereals or dried grains (rice and bulgur) rather than bread.

◆ Eat whatever perishables you do bring early in the trip, before they spoil. To keep cheese fresh, dip it in melted paraffin, set it aside to cool, and then wrap it in aluminum foil.

Another concern arises from food collected in the wild. Some shellfish are periodically contaminated by certain plankton and protozoans that produce a powerful toxin. If eaten, the toxin-laced shellfish cause Paralytic Shellfish Poisoning (PSP), which can be fatal. The most common culprits are oysters, clams, and mussels. Symptoms of PSP strike within minutes and include numbness and tingling in and around the mouth, lightheadedness, weakness, headache, thirst, clumsiness, and incoherence. The patient may begin to drool and suffer difficulty swallowing, diarrhea, stomach pain, blurred vision, sweating, and rapid heartbeat. Paralysis follows, with the danger that the patient will quit breathing.

Many areas prohibit shellfish harvesting during certain months—ask locally before gathering or eating any shellfish. If in doubt, abstain. If symptoms appear after eating shellfish, rush the patient to the nearest hospital; provide rescue breathing as needed en route.

WATER HAZARDS

Water is a giver and taker of life. We drink it, or perish in just a few days, but we also confront it in the wild as an elemental force. Waves, currents, tides, and the sheer quantity of water can each pose hazards for the backcountry traveler.

According to the National Safety Council, half of all drownings occur when the water is calm and 65 degrees F. or warmer, and when skies are clear. Most drownings occur when people are swimming, wading, or playing near water. Boating accidents account for only seven percent of drownings. Capsizing and standing up in a boat and falling overboard are the main causes of boat-related drownings.

Even with proper rescue breathing, half of all drowning victims die if they're not breathing after four minutes. After six minutes, ninety percent do not recover. It's important to know this—care must be given immediately. But don't give up or forego a rescue attempt just because a few minutes have passed. Also, be aware that near-drowning victims can die due to complications—including pneumonia—up to four days later. Always seek follow-up medical attention, even if the person appears healthy and normal.

When recreating on or near water, a few basic precautions can greatly reduce the risk of accident.

◆ Learn how to swim, and know how to conserve energy while floating to await a rescue. Wear a U.S. Coast Guard approved life vest or other personal flotation device.

◆ Learn CPR and take an annual refresher course. People who frequently work or play around water should also consider a life-saving class to learn different water rescue techniques.

◆ Know your limits—keep exposure to cold water to a minimum, and don't swim far from shore. Never swim alone.

◆ Alcohol and water don't mix. Abstain from drinking while boating or swimming.

◆ Keep a close eye on children and non-swimmers around water.

Crossing Streams

Crossing a stream or river can be the biggest challenge faced by backcountry travelers. Most of us have grown accustomed to trails with bridges—single-log foot bridges or stout cantilevered spans—across every brook and chasm. Coming to the banks of an unbridged stream, we are forced to solve a sometimes complex, and often dangerous, puzzle: how to reach the other side. Depth, strength of current, width, and water temperature and clarity all influence our choices of how, where, and even when to cross.

◆ In general, cross only where the water is waist deep or less on the shortest member of your group. Look for shallows where the stream widens, at the heads and tails of islands, and on the insides of bends.

◆ Watch for strong currents. Well-developed waves or rushing vees of water indicate fast, powerful flows that can easily knock you down. If the current seems too fast as you wade in, retreat: the current is almost always faster in mid stream. Also avoid the strong currents on the outsides of bends.

◆ Cross only where the stream is narrow enough for a person on one bank to visually scout its depth and currents all the way across. Be particularly wary of risking a difficult ford to an island, only to discover an impossible ford on the opposite channel.

◆ Most of North America's streams and rivers are fairly cold—some are outright icy. Reduce the risk of hypothermia: keep your wading time to a minimum (but don't rush across, risking a fall), carry a change of dry clothes in a waterproof bag, and, if needed, take a rest break after crossing for a hot drink and some food. When repeated cold-water crossings are unavoidable carry a pair of neoprene booties or waders.

◆ Murky or turbid water requires extra care. The beds of such streams are usually muddy—either bottomless and clutching, or greasy and difficult to stand on. Use a stick to probe ahead for holes, and feel with your feet for submerged obstacles.

◆ Anticipate stream crossings. Pack sleeping bags, dry clothes, and food in water-proof plastic bags inside your pack.

◆ For better traction and to protect your feet wear wading shoes or remove your socks and put your boots back on.

◆ Loosen packstraps and unhook the waistbelt so the pack can be shrugged off if you fall. A wet pack can easily anchor even the strongest adult to the bottom.

◆ Cross facing sideways to the current, hips angled slightly toward the shore. Don't face downstream; this only allows the force of the current to push against the back of your legs, and they may buckle. Walk diagonally across the current, following a riffle or shallow bar and angling downstream if possible.

◆ Take one step at a time and test the footing before committing all your weight to it. Keep one foot secure before lifting the other. Shuffle across, always leading with the upstream leg; avoid scissoring your legs.

◆ Use a hiking staff or big stick, held on the upstream side, to aid in balancing. Or have two or more people cross together, forearms interlocked with the strongest person on the upstream side.

◆ If you do lose your footing and are carried downstreamj slide out of your pack-straps and try to float downstream feet first in an upright, sitting position. Use your feet to fend off rocks or logs, and swim across the current toward shore.

◆ Remember that the volume of a river can change dramatically over just a few hours. Glacially fed streams tend to be low in the morning, then swell as afternoon heat melts ice and snow upstream. A ford that's knee-deep and easy in the morning may be chest high and surging with power by late afternoon. Plan your return routes and crossing times carefully.

Cold Water

Cold water conducts body heat much faster than air of the same temperature. The average person can survive for about two hours when immersed in 60-degree F. water before suffering severe hypothermia. But with the water temperature at 50 degrees, survival time is cut in half, to one hour. At 40 degrees, a person will last thirty minutes; and at 32 degrees it's all over in fifteen minutes.

Of course, other complications can arise before simple hypothermia sets in. Muscles cramp as the body pools blood in the torso and vital organs. Without functioning arms and legs, swimming is impossible and even wading may become difficult. Heart failure is also a possibility, even during very brief exposure to cold water. Finally, the larynx (or voicebox) may spasm and shut tightly if a person is suddenly immersed in cold water. Scientists call this the "mammalian diving reflex" and believe that it is a carryover from our days as primordial sea creatures. Unfortunately, clamping your larynx shut also cuts off the only airway to your lungs. Many cold water drowning victims die without a drop of water in their lungs, but no oxygen either.

◆ Never underestimate cold water's capacity for sapping heat and strength from your body. People have drowned trying to swim a mere fifty feet from shore to shore in cold mountain lakes.

◆ When immersion in cold water is likely, such as when boating or fishing in mountain streams and lakes, or in cold seas, always wear a neoprene wetsuit or a dry suit with adequate insulating layers underneath. Wear an approved life jacket designed for the type of water you're in and the sport you're pursuing. Use the buddy system—never enter cold water alone.

◆ Carry a dry change of clothes in a waterproof container.

Surf and Current

When traveling along a beach, keep an eye and ear tuned to the surf. A singular big wave—a "sneaker" much bigger and more powerful than the regular sets coming in—can suddenly load the beach with turbulent water and dancing driftwood. Surf may surge two hundred feet or more inland, much farther than other waves. Such a freak wave can occur at any time, though they are probably more common with an incoming tide and are frequently associated with offshore storms. Boaters should also be aware of surge channels—narrow inlets in rocky shorelines. Even small waves gain force when confined between the rock walls, and currents can suck sea kayaks and other small craft into such channels without warning.

Swimmers and boaters should watch for rip currents, where water is channeled off the beach and rushes out to sea through the surf. Rip currents form when water piles up on the beach as waves come in. All this water has to go somewhere. If the shape of the beach and ocean floor offer a channel for it, water can gather in a strong current. Heavy surf creates stronger rips. Rip currents can form any time— watch for foamy or "dirty" water drifting seaward and a gap where the waves just fall over or lie down rather than forming the classic curl.

If caught in a rip, stay calm and swim parallel to shore. Don't try to fight the current and don't over exert yourself. Most rips weaken within two hundred yards offshore, and most are fairly narrow. Swim along the shoreline until you pass out of the rip, and then work toward land.

Also pay heed to local tides. Some areas of the North American coast experience tidal variations of as much as forty feet. Notable tidal basins include the Bay of Fundy between Nova Scotia and New Brunswick, Hudson Bay, Cook Inlet near Anchorage, Alaska, and Bristol Bay on the north side of the Aleutian Chain. Tidal rips and currents are also strong enough to capsize small craft—or carry them out to sea— along much of the Alaskan and British Columbian coasts from Yakutat Bay south to

Puget Sound. Land travelers should monitor tides to prevent being cut off at the base of cliffs or on sand spits, jetties, or offshore rocks. Many foot trails on the West Coast (including the West Coast Trail on Vancouver Island and the wilderness coast hike from Oil City to Ozette on Washington's Olympic Peninsula) contain sections that run between headlands and the ocean and are passable only during low tide.

STAYING FOUND

When Franz Kafka said, "You are free and that is why you are lost," he probably had in mind losing your way in some dark, existential landscape of the soul. But the same cause-and-effect relationship applies equally well to getting lost in wild country—we are most apt to get lost when traveling through new terrain, enjoying "the freedom of the hills."

On familiar ground, we may become disoriented or temporarily confused, but we can count on a recognizable landmark to soon appear to set us straight. Wandering in new territory, however, requires a few skills beyond a sharp memory and keeping our eyes open. Especially in dense timber, maze-like canyons, foggy or snowy weather, or in the vast Arctic, it pays to know how to read a map and use a compass.

Map and Compass

Detailed topographic maps are available from the U.S. Geological Survey and, in Canada, through the National Topographic Series. Sporting goods stores usually sell local and sometimes regional maps. Natural features such as mountains, cliffs, rivers, lakes, and springs are shown on topo maps, as are roads, rail lines, towns, and some backcountry buildings. Contour lines indicate changes in elevation, and a light green shading is used to show forested areas. Maps come in different scales; the most popular ones range from 1:250,000 (one inch equals four miles) to 1:24,000 (one inch equals 2,000 feet). The smaller the second number in the ratio, the more detailed the map.

The easiest way to learn to read a topo map is to buy the map quadrangle (or "quad") that covers your favorite local landscape. Take the map along on your next visit and compare its contour lines to the terrain right in front of you. With a little practice the landscape of a topo map will jump out at you like a 3-D model.

Another feature of most topo maps is a note or schematic indicating *declination*, or the difference (in degrees) between true north and magnetic north. Compass needles always point to magnetic north—a spot in the high Arctic with a strong magnetic field—while maps are oriented to true north or the North Pole. The difference between these points varies depending on your position on the globe. In Maine, magnetic north is as much as twenty degrees west of true north, but in Alaska, the compass needle points nearly thirty degrees east of true north. Refer to a local topo map for the declination in your region, and remember to factor in the degrees east or west when lining up compass directions on the map.

Even without a map, a compass is good insurance against getting lost, and using one needn't be complicated. At the trailhead, take out your compass and line up the needle with 0 degrees north. Look at the surrounding landscape and note any prominent features or terrain patterns and their positions relative to north, south, east, and west. Taking the lay of the land—and doing it frequently—is often enough to keep you from getting lost in the first place. Also look at your general direction of travel. If your route leads southwest (225 degrees), then a return bearing 180 degrees opposite (northeast or 45 degrees) will get you back to your starting point.

Other Preventive Measures

◆ Always let someone know where you're going and how long you plan to be in the backcountry. If possible leave a map with your itinerary marked on it. Register with the local ranger or at the trailhead.

◆ While traveling in the backcountry, pay attention to your direction in relation to the sun, landscape features, and trail junctions.

◆ Make sure everyone in your group knows the planned route, campsite locations, and general direction of travel. Discuss your plans if the group decides to split up, and honor your commitments for agreed-upon meeting times and places. If possible, give each person a map of the area

◆ Learn to gauge the distance you travel. Some people judge distance by knowing their approximate pace and keeping an eye on their wristwatch. Others are able to keep a running total of shorter distances between rest breaks or landmarks. Still others rely heavily on maps and the scale bar. At first, it may help to rely on a combination of the three.

◆ Some landscape features, particularly streams, mountain ridges, and lake or ocean shorelines, serve as excellent handrails to guide your way. Take note of their shape and general orientation to the cardinal compass points and your direction of travel.

◆ Look back over the way you've come to see what the terrain would look like on the return trip. Do this frequently even if you plan to take a different route out. Plans can change and retracing your steps may be the surest way out, especially in an emergency.

◆ Refer to map and compass often, before you get lost. Stop to identify prominent landmarks and all trail junctions.

◆ If confused or disoriented don't hesitate to ask a passerby for help.

If You Become Lost

◆ Stop and take your bearings. Look for a landmark and scan your map for that feature. Stay calm—sit down and enjoy a snack. Be rational and recall how much you were enjoying the trip—scenery, fresh air, wildlife and wildflowers—before you realized you were lost. Other than not knowing where you are, nothing else has changed so why stop enjoying the experience? Remember: this is a temporary circumstance. Only panic can keep you permanently lost.

◆ Take stock of your condition. Beautiful scenery notwithstanding, are there any immediate threats—weather, dangerous terrain, a medical problem—that take precedence over merely being lost? Are you injured, tired, ill, or overly cold or hot? Do you have adequate clothing, water, food, and shelter to survive for a while on your own? Set your priorities and cope with one thing at a time.

◆ If separated from your group whistle or shout. Sets of three are a widely known distress signal. If there's no response after several tries save your breath. If it's a short distance backtrack to the last place you and the others were together and wait there.

◆ When traveling alone (or if the whole group gets lost together), carefully backtrack to familiar ground. If that doesn't work try to orient yourself to a familiar landmark. Climb to a nearby vantage point to scan your surroundings. In most places, following a river downstream will lead to a road, outpost, or some other piece of civilization. If nothing looks familiar stay in one place.

◆ If you can't find your way back stay put and remain calm. Conserve energy. Take care of your basic needs for water, food, and shelter. Place a bright, visible object (a tent, backpack, that one safety-orange shirt at the bottom of your pack) out in the open to attract attention. Sit tight and wait for help to arrive.

Finally, serious explorers willing to part with $600 to $1,000 can take advantage of the Global Positioning System (GPS) to track their location in the backcountry anywhere on the planet. The GPS relies on data from orbiting satellites, transmitted to a hand-held receiver, to pinpoint your location to within one hundred yards. Some GPS units also continuously calculate altitude, speed, and direction of travel.

TRAVELING SOLO

Though traveling through the backcountry alone is generally discouraged, some folks wouldn't have it any other way, at least once in a while. They echo the sentiments of eighteenth-century historian Edward Gibbon, who once wrote, "I was never less alone than when by myself." Certainly, going solo confers a wonderful freedom on the individual trekker—you can go where you want, when you want, and stay as long as you want. But with the freedom comes a necessary responsibility. You owe it to yourself, as well as to friends, family, and potential rescuers, to take every precaution to make your trip a safe one.

◆ Only highly experienced backcountry travelers should attempt trips solo. What kind of experience? Years of actual backcountry travel and camping across different types of terrain, in all weather, and preferably leading groups. You should possess excellent skills in reading map and compass, route selection, first aid, tracking, use of all personal equipment, and leaving no trace. It is doubly important to be highly proficient at your chosen mode of travel (skiing, horsepacking, mountain biking, etc.).

◆ Know your limits. Maintain a high level of physical and mental fitness. Learn beforehand (in safe, familiar surroundings) whether you are comfortable with prolonged solitude and whether you have the skills to thrive alone in the wilderness.

◆ Leave a detailed description of your itinerary with a friend, relative, or ranger. Promptly notify this person upon your return to civilization to avoid an unnecessary "rescue."

CRIME IN THE BACKCOUNTRY

No one likes to think about crime in the backcountry. After all, we go there to ease our minds, to escape for at least a few days the uglier side of civilization. Nonetheless, crime sometimes tags along. According to Forest Service surveys, crime in the backcountry is fairly rare, with only three percent of designated wilderness areas reporting cases of theft in the backcountry. But fully twenty-seven percent reported incidents of trailhead break-ins. Some regions of the country are worse than others. In California, theft and vandalism occurs at thirty-eight percent of that state's trailheads into designated wilderness areas. The problem is also prevalent in the Northeast, Midwest, and in Oregon and Washington.

Losing your belongings to a common thief is aggravating enough, but when it happens far beyond road's end it can turn a fun outing into an unwelcome test of the victim's endurance and survival skills. In 1993 a church group left a cache fifteen miles from the trailhead in Montana's Mission Mountain Wilderness in preparation for a Sunday school camping trip that weekend. They marked the duffle as essential food and hung it in an obvious spot. When the kids and their chaperones arrived, the entire cache was gone. After a meager lunch (snacks they'd carried with them), the weary group hiked back out the fifteen miles. In 1989 a lone backpacker in Oregon's Three Sisters Wilderness returned to basecamp at sunset after climbing a nearby peak only to find his tent and sleeping bag stolen. Temperatures dipped below freezing that night and he was forced to huddle by a fire until dawn before hiking out.

Theft and vandalism may be the most common type of crime committed against backcountry recreationists, but not the most serious. Sadly, each year outdoor enthusiasts are assaulted, kidnapped, even killed while recreating in the backcountry. In separate incidents in 1993, while hunting in a remote area of north-central Florida, two hunters were stalked, killed, and robbed of their valuable guns and other equipment. Between 1989 and 1992, an Ohio serial killer shot five people while they were hunting, fishing, or jogging. In 1988 two women backpacking the Appalachian Trail were shot; one was killed, one wounded. These killings brought the murder count on the Appalachian Trail to three in the previous fifteen years.

We offer these tragic facts not to frighten anyone away from their favorite backcountry playground, but to bring the problem to light, and to put it in perspective. Frankly, your chances of being victimized by crime are far greater in your own home town than at any backcountry campsite. But the *possibility* does exist, even in wild country. That possibility is all the more potent because help (or law enforcement) is usually far away; you can't simply pick up the phone and dial 911. The best way to protect yourself is to be aware, stay alert, and minimize your risks.

◆ Ask a local land manager about any recent problems. Have there been break-ins at the trailhead? Do the authorities regularly patrol the trailhead? Any crimes reported in the backcountry?

◆ At the trailhead, lock your vehicle. Check each door before you leave the car. Roll all windows tightly shut. Any valuables that aren't going in the pack should have been left at home. Never leave notes on the vehicle describing your itinerary or expected date of return. Also never leave keys stashed under the bumper or "hidden" nearby and use a locking gas cap.

◆ There's safety in numbers—criminals are less likely to strike large groups. Think twice before traveling solo.

◆ Be inconspicuous. Keep valuable equipment out of sight, in your pack or tent, unless using it. Never leave gear unattended. If you've set up a basecamp and plan to leave for a day-trip assess the likelihood of theft. You may decide to carry most of your gear with you, leave a sentry, or stash everything in a well-concealed spot. (This last is difficult to do—if you feel compelled to hide your gear, it's probably best to carry it with you.)

◆ Personal confrontations in backcountry are rare, though in some areas conflicts between different types of trail users have escalated into yelling matches and fist fights. Play it safe and back down from any provocation. Walk away and let the other guy stew in his own juices. The writer André Gide summed it up best: "Sometimes you have to let other people be right. It consoles them for not being anything else."

◆ Encounters with mushroom pickers, marijuana farmers, squatters, and prospectors on their claims can also turn ugly. These folks may be a bit jumpy, and are often armed. Do your best to convince them that you're not a competitor and that you're eager to leave and let them get back to work. If you encounter any illegal activities leave the scene immediately and report them to the local authorities.

◆ One last caution: avoid obnoxious drunks. Too much alcohol (or other drugs) can lead to trouble anywhere, but impaired judgment is particularly risky around firearms, axes and knives, packstock, and campfires.

SPECIAL ENVIRONMENTS

Most of the no-trace and safety practices outlined in chapters 3, 4, and 5 can be used no matter where in the North American backcountry you travel. But there are a few places—special environments such as deserts, Arctic and alpine tundra, regions of snow and ice, coasts, rivers and lakes, and wetlands—where the standard practices aren't always appropriate. For example, the standard setback for camping near water is a minimum of two hundred feet. But on remote coasts, rivers, and lakes it is often best to camp on the beach, below the high water or monthly high tide line when it is safe to do so. This way, trampling and other damage is confined to the sand or gravel shore, and any sign of your stay will be washed away by the next ebb and flow in water levels.

Certain hazards are also more prevalent in these special environments. Avalanches occur only where snow accumulates; the Mojave rattlesnake lives only in desert habitat; protecting food from bears presents special difficulties on the treeless tundra, and so on.

The following section is designed for quick reference for anyone planning a trip to the desert, Arctic or alpine tundra, regions of snow and ice, on the coast, on rivers and lakes, or through a wetland. Specific no-trace techniques and safety concerns are given for each of the six special environments. Bear in mind that some recommendations apply in more than one place—choosing a campsite on a remote coast is similar to choosing a campsite along a remote river; sunburn is a significant concern not only in the desert but also at high altitudes and wherever sun is reflected off snow or water. And these environments also frequently overlap. Read both relevant sections, for instance, when planning a river trip through the Arctic tundra.

Finally, when in doubt rely on the standard practices and recommendations given in chapters 3, 4, and 5 for basic guidance. Applied with common sense and resourcefulness, they will see you through almost any situation that might arise.

DESERTS

North America contains a variety of arid lands, from arctic barrens that receive less than three inches of snowfall a year to Great Basin salt flats, from the slickrock of Canyonlands to the bone-dry arroyos and cactus plains of the Sonoran Desert. All of these regions suffer a scarcity of water and a poverty of soils, but our focus in this section is the true deserts of the American Southwest, from southern Texas through New Mexico, Utah, Arizona, Nevada, and southern California. Some of the camping and travel methods recommended here may also apply to other arid lands; look for leave-no-trace techniques and safety issues that may apply equally well in southeast Alberta's badlands, Wyoming's dusty sage country, or eastern Washington's scablands.

Leave No Trace

People are drawn to desert oases, particularly if drinkable water is present. Recreational use often concentrates around water in an otherwise sparsely used area. Minimizing impacts is crucial because most forms of life here are already stressed by temperature extremes, lack of water, and a scarcity of food. Any added stress—such as trampling plants or spooking wildlife away from shade—reduces the margin for survival. Desert plants and soils also grow and develop slowly. Though some plants and soil types may be fairly resistant to damage, they are all slow to recover from impacts; scars from a single incautious person will greet other visitors for years to come.

The most important ways to leave no trace in the desert are to:
◆ Concentrate use on existing trails and campsites in popular areas, or on hard or barren surfaces that are resistant to impacts.
◆ Tread lightly around water; keep soap, human waste, and other pollutants far away (at least two hundred feet) from water sources.
◆ Use a stove for cooking and build no fires.

Trip Planning

Planning a backcountry trip in the desert often centers around water—how to carry enough of it and where to find fresh supplies. Remember that human use, and hence impacts, tend to concentrate around desert streams and pools. If possible, use maps to locate potential campsites near but not immediately next to water sources. For example, if you know of a good campsite a mile or two beyond a spring, you can plan to top off your water bottles at the spring, and then move on to the campsite. Pack enough containers to carry water for the evening's cooking and drinking, plus a quart for the morning.

Many popular desert areas have designated backcountry campsites. Camping permits may be required and the number of backcountry visitors allowed into any one area may be limited. Call ahead to ask about peak-use periods and any relevant regulations.

Route Selection

Concentrate use on existing trails and campsites in popular areas, or on hard or barren surfaces that are resistant to impacts. Keep cross-country travel to a minimum, and then stay on routes that follow dry washes, gravel or salt flats, or slickrock. Where no trails and no trample-resistant routes exist, spread out and try to step on bare soil as much as possible.

Some desert regions are home to a particularly fragile layer of soil known as cryptobiotic crust (sometimes referred to as cryptogamic soil). This crust is actually a living layer of algae, fungi, lichens, and mosses. As this microscopic community of plants grows, it slowly builds a crust of miniature black towers and ramparts on the ground's surface. The crust protects against wind and water erosion, enhances the soil's ability to absorb and retain moisture, and acts as a storage for nutrients and a seedbed for bigger plants. Cryptobiotic crust sets the stage for plant growth in soils that might otherwise remain barren.

Yet one foot step can crush the crust, and it will take years to regenerate, even longer for the foot print to disappear. When traveling through areas of cryptobiotic crust stay on established trails or slickrock. If you encounter cryptobiotic crust while traveling cross-country, skirt around the area; if necessary, backtrack and seek another route.

Choosing a Campsite

Desert camping is a relatively recent phenomenon, but long-term damage has already begun to show up in heavily used areas. Remember that once damaged, the desert landscape is extremely slow to recover.

The presence of potable water most often determines where to camp in desert country (though with careful planning and enough water bottles this need not always be the case). But precisely because water is so scarce here, campers must take extra care to protect its quality and to reduce the social impacts of crowding around a watering hole. Camp at least two hundred feet from any water source (in narrow canyons with streams this may not be practicable). An even greater setback from water may be needed to ensure that wildlife is not frightened away from the watering hole or to preserve some semblance of solitude despite heavy human use.

Whenever possible camp on barren soil or rock. Free-standing tents can be pitched on slickrock; stow gear inside or tie guy lines to large rocks to hold the tent in place if the wind picks up. Foam or inflatable sleeping pads offer comfort on even the hardest surface.

Campfires

Trees and shrubs grow slowly here; downed wood is scarce and slow to be replenished. What little dead wood there is provides important food and shelter to insects, birds, and other wildlife. Deserts (along with arctic and alpine tundra) are the least appropriate environment for building campfires. Use a stove for cooking and boiling water. Boaters (especially rafters) may opt to carry charcoal briquettes and a fire pan. Bag cold ashes and pack them out with the rest of your garbage. Burying ashes and charcoal is not effective—wind will blow the sand away, revealing an unsightly mess.

Waste Disposal

Garbage, even food scraps, decomposes slowly in dry desert conditions. Burying garbage may only slow the process more, or animals may uncover it. Pack out all trash and left-over food.

Human waste also decomposes slowly here. Cat holes may prolong the process. The preferred method is to use a poop tube (described on page 70) and pack out all human waste. For on-site disposal in areas with very little human use, it's best to scatter feces in small pieces on the surface of the ground. The sun's rays and high heat at the surface will "cook" waste faster than it would decompose. Sprinkle sand on the feces to discourage flies. Choose an out-of-the-way spot and avoid water drainages. In more popular areas, dig a cat hole six to eight inches deep and immediately cover all waste. Avoid leaving human waste in dry stream beds or on the floors of narrow canyons. Tomorrow's thunderstorm may flood the channel, washing the waste downstream to someone else's watering hole.

Also think before urinating just anywhere. Hard desert soils can channel even a piddle's worth of runoff into a nearby water source. Around camp, avoid urinating repeatedly in the same areas. Urine-saturated sand retains a strong odor and salt residues may attract unwanted animals.

Bathing and Laundry

Follow the guidelines given on page 48. Remember that wildlife and people tend to concentrate around water in desert environments. Where water is scarce, it should be used only for cooking and drinking. Small bodies of water, especially those with little inflow, are highly vulnerable to contamination. Stirring up silt, adding soap or other pollutants, or removing too much water can dramatically reduce water quality. Using a lot of water from a small hole may deprive wildlife of a crucial drink. Take water for bathing only from larger sources—lakes, flowing streams, and rivers.

Watching Wildlife

As anyone who travels in desert country quickly learns, exertion here carries with it a heavy price—overheating and dire thirst. Desert wildlife may be wonderfully adapted to its environment, but all animals heed the same bottom line: stay cool and conserve body fluids or perish. To avoid causing any unnecessary exertion give animals plenty of room. When approaching water or food sources or isolated oases of shade scan ahead to see if any wildlife is resting nearby. Detour or wait, if possible, to leave wildlife undisturbed..

Safety

Deserts have a reputation as one of the most hostile environments for human habitation. Mention the Mojave, Sevier, or Sonoran desert and people conjure up a withered, half-baked prospector crawling across a parched and thorny wasteland, buzzards overhead, the only water in sight a cruel mirage. Indeed, lack of water and exposure to sun and extreme temperatures are important concerns to any desert traveler. But heeding a few simple precautions can prevent a death march and provide instead an enjoyable, even comfortable, outing.

To prevent **dehydration** an average adult needs three to six quarts of drinking water a day. Sustained intense exercise in temperatures over 100 degrees F. (not recommended) may require three gallons or more. Always carry extra water and restock supplies at every opportunity. Supplement your fluid intake with fresh fruit, especially apples, oranges, and bananas. Fruit provides potassium and other nutrients to help ward off muscle cramps. Drink before you get thirsty. Infrequent urination, muscle or stomach cramps, fatigue, and dizziness are signs of serious dehydration—stop, drink some water immediately, and find a shady place to relax for a while. Guard against heat exhaustion and heat stroke. (See signs and treatment chart on page 101).

Sunburn can be a nuisance or severely debilitating. It's possible to suffer extensive second-degree burns, and long-term repeated exposure may lead to skin cancer. Apply a sun screen with a Sun Protection Factor (SPF) of fifteen or higher. Water- and sweat-proof lotions are available; reapply as needed through the day. Wear a long-sleeve shirt, a hat, and UV-protected sunglasses. Solar radiation is most intense between the hours of 10 a.m. and 3 p.m.; limit exposure during these hours.

Flash floods occur when heavy rains or runoff are not absorbed by hard desert soils. A distant thunderstorm may send walls of water rushing down once-dry washes or high-walled canyons. Check the weather forecast before you leave. Don't camp in dry washes or canyon streambeds, and look for lines of debris or other evidence of periodic flooding before you pitch the tent. Listen for distant thunderstorms. Never wade into floodwaters to cross them. Wait until the water subsides or find another route.

Be alert for **poisonous snakes**. Rattlesnakes and the Arizona coral snake are generally reclusive but will bite if cornered or provoked; the Mojave rattler is more aggressive than most and also packs a more potent venom. The Gila monster, a lizard found in Arizona, is rarely encountered but should be avoided because of a toxin in its saliva. Snakes seek shade during the heat of day and bask on sun-heated rocks during the cool of morning and evening. Watch where your step and sit, and don't put your hands in crevices or on ledges without looking first. Sleep in a tent with a sewn-in floor and zippered mesh doors. Use a flashlight when moving around at night. For information on how to treat a snake bite, see page 129.

Spiders, scorpions, and **centipedes** are common desert residents. Most are more active at night and hole up under rocks or in shady crevices during the day. Watch where you put your hands and feet, and look before you sit. Sleep in a tent with a sewn-in floor and zippered mesh doors. Shake out shoes, socks, and clothing before putting them on.

Give **cacti** and other prickly plants a wide berth. Cactus spines can penetrate through shoes and clothes, causing pain, irritation, and infection. Most cactus spines bear tiny barbs that make them hard to pull out—it's best to let a doctor remove them. A tetanus shot may also be warranted. Some cacti and the century plant produce a caustic sap that burns the skin and can cause blindness if rubbed in the eyes. Don't break open stems or leaves.

Desert water is a haven for life, including microscopic bacteria and pathogens. *Giardia, campylobacter, E. coli,* and hepatitis A may live in pools, lakes, streams, and rivers. Treat all drinking water by boiling it for five minutes or purifying it with an approved filter. You may need to pre-filter silty or muddy water, or set it aside to settle out silt before filtering. Also avoid water high in salts, which can cause stomach cramps and dehydration.

ALPINE AND ARCTIC TUNDRA

High alpine and Arctic environments share many characteristics, the most obvious of which are a relatively cold climate and a short growing season. Tundra plants grow slowly, low to the ground, and put much of their energy into extensive root systems where soils are developed enough to support it. Not surprisingly, the same plants that have adapted well to the tundra environment thrive wherever similarly harsh conditions occur. Whether high in the Wind River Mountains of Wyoming or near sea level on Alaska's North Slope, you will find kindred dwarf willows, heather, lichen, low-bush huckleberry, and cranberry.

A few important distinctions should be made, however. Alpine tundra tends to support a wider variety of plants than is found in the Arctic, probably because invading species arrive from surrounding habitats. Alpine zones typically receive more snow than the Arctic, and it lingers later into early summer. Finally, permafrost—permanently frozen soil—underlies much of the Arctic tundra.

Snowmelt, rain, and other water can't percolate into deeper layers because of this ice barrier. Eventually, the upper soil layer becomes saturated with water and extremely vulnerable to disturbance.

These fragile regions saw comparatively little human use for eons, but our penchant for remote places is rapidly ending that seclusion. Many of our designated wilderness areas and national parks were established to preserve high alpine regions, but wilderness and park status tends to attract more visitors. And trekking across the Arctic has also grown more popular—also due in large part to the publicity garnered by the Arctic National Wildlife Refuge and Gates of the Arctic National Park. As with other environments, recreation on the tundra places both the land and the people drawn to play in it at risk.

Leave No Trace

Of all environments tundra may have the lowest ability to recover once damage has occurred. Cold temperatures and a short growing season combine to preserve damage to plants and soil—a museum of past mistakes with masterpieces on view for decades or even centuries. Veteran Arctic travelers know this well...it is not unusual to stumble across a small circle of smaller plants on the open tundra—evidence of a Thule encampment one thousand years ago. Alpine tundra is also slow to heal. In one particularly fragile area, researchers in Colorado's Rocky Mountain National Park estimated that seventy to one hundred years may pass before a high meadow would recover from just one season of off-trail foot traffic.

The effect of trampling on plants and soil varies from alpine to Arctic regions, but the end result is equally disastrous. In an alpine meadow, if a few plants are crushed the soil is left vulnerable to freeze-thaw cycles and erodes with every runoff. Roots of neighboring plants are then exposed and the plants die. More soil is left open to the elements and the cycle continues. In the Arctic, when plant cover is removed from the soil overlying permafrost, the result may be "thermokarst-ing"—uneven thawing and melting that leaves islands of plants atop ice surrounded by water-filled holes and gullies. In either case, damage spreads to areas far beyond the site that was initially trampled.

The most important ways to leave no trace in alpine or Arctic tundra are to:
◆ Stay on established trails. If no trails exist, seek routes on bare mineral soil, rock, cobble streambeds, snow, or other durable surfaces.
◆ Use a cookstove and build no fires. Leave what scant wood there is to return much-needed nutrients to the soil.

Trip Planning

Alpine tundra occurs in relatively small pockets along the crest of our continent's major mountain chains. Winter dominates the calendar at these elevations, and snow and ice are prevalent here (see page 161). Bear in mind that spring arrives late and soils remain muddy (and vulnerable to trampling) well into summer. Some alpine areas also receive heavy rains or wet snows through summer, periodically saturating soils. Winter travel, when snow protects the ground and plants, causes the least disturbance but brings other hardships (numbing cold and avalanche risk chief among them). Fall, after the first hard frost at elevation, is also a good time to visit alpine zones—soils are drier and grasses and sedges are more resistant to long-term damage at this time.

Whenever possible, plan to camp below the alpine zone. Look at maps to find likely sites for base camps down in the timber. Plan day hikes into alpine areas, preferably along established routes.

When planning an Arctic expedition, remember that travel here can be extremely challenging. Muskeg and peat bogs are notorious for sucking the boots off of unsuspecting hikers, destinations appear deceptively close, and weather can abruptly turn severe. Anticipate delays and slow going—pack extra food and warm clothing to prevent the need for emergency actions such as building fires or camping in poor sites.

Route Selection

Because of the potential for trampling and long-term damage, off-trail travel requires extra care. In pristine areas look for routes on durable surfaces or spread out to avoid walking in one another's footsteps. When walking on talus or across boulder fields avoid stepping on moss, lichen, or succulents growing between rocks. Also avoid wet or saturated ground and steep slopes, particularly slopes covered with low shrubs. In popular areas stay on established trails.

There are few trails in the Arctic. Instead, follow streambeds and gravel outwash plains. Dry ridges are tempting, but mats of lichen favor dry ground above permafrost—often on ridges—the same terrain favored by hikers in this otherwise

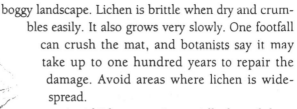

boggy landscape. Lichen is brittle when dry and crumbles easily. It also grows very slowly. One footfall can crush the mat, and botanists say it may take up to one hundred years to repair the damage. Avoid areas where lichen is widespread.

Avoid "short-cuts," especially through low-lying areas. Hiking across muskeg, especially with a backpack, can take much more time than expected. It's also hard work and more trouble than it's worth unless you enjoy repeatedly falling down into cold water and testing your ankles' range of motion. Most point-to-point trips during Arctic summer are best made by boat, following a river. Hikers are better off setting up a base camp on a durable surface for the duration of their stay and then exploring the surrounding landscape on day hikes. Winter travel by ski, snowshoe, or dog sled allows a far wider choice of routes.

Choosing a Campsite

Tundra plants and soils are especially susceptible to wear and tear from repeated foot traffic around camp. To prevent such damage, head down below timberline to camp each night whenever this is possible. If you're willing to confine cooking, group meetings, and sleeping to a few well-chosen sites, it is possible to find durable campsites within the alpine zone. Look for outcrops of bedrock or patches of sand. A snowbank offers a protective platform for a tent or kitchen area; and dry, grassy areas make good sleeping sites for a night.

In the Arctic bear in mind that weather is harsh enough on the plains and downright ruthless at higher elevations at these latitudes. Colder, north-facing slopes receive less sunlight and winds may funnel along mountain flanks. Plan your itinerary to avoid camping at elevation in the Arctic. Look for sites along gravel streambeds (but beware of flashfloods) or on slumps of bare mineral soil. Avoid dense lichen colonies. Limit your stay in any one site to two nights or less, and keep foot traffic to a minimum.

Wherever you camp, don't move rocks to make a flat space for sleeping. Rocks provide shelter from the wind for many small plants, which contribute to soil development and stability. Remove the rock and the plants die, leaving a permanent scar. And if you can't camp on a durable surface watch every step you take. Limit foot traffic and avoid stepping in the same place more than twice. Stay one night only, or move the tents to a new site far enough away to avoid trampling the same ground.

Campfires

Of all the landscapes in North America, tundra is perhaps the least-suited to campfires. Fuel is scarce or nonexistent, the scars from a single fire will endure for decades, and, during Arctic spring and summer, there's an abundance of daylight and no need for firelight. In alpine regions, the trees that grow at timberline are on the edge of survival. Growth is slow here and dead wood contributes essential nutrients to the soil. Those nutrients can come from no other source—burn them in a campfire and the next generation of trees goes without a meal. Use a cookstove and postpone the campfire for the next night in the forest below.

Plan ahead to do without a fire. Carry extra socks and dry clothes, and prevent hypothermia so an emergency fire won't be needed. But if disaster strikes and a fire becomes necessary, use as little wood as possible. DO NOT dig a fire pit. Use a fire pan; or make a mound fire of sand or gravel on a large rock.

Waste Disposal

Tundra can be thought of as cold storage for human waste—in this climate, feces take years to decompose. Researchers at Montana State University and also in the Sierra Nevada found that fecal bacteria and protozoans survived a year or more in alpine zones, even when buried "properly" in a cat hole. For this reason, it is especially important to NOT use group latrines; a large pile, frozen much of the year, could take decades to decay. Also, a cat hole only disturbs plants and soil; where permafrost exists, disturbing the upper layer of soil may cause thermokarsting.

In popular places, carry a poop tube (page 70) and pack out all human waste. On longer trips where packing it out may not be practical, particularly in remote Arctic regions, you can smear waste on a rock or on the surface of bare ground where no one else is likely to discover it. Choose a site well away from surface water, or—if surrounded by bog—in a low-lying area unlikely to leach into nearby drainages. Sun and weather will break it down faster than if it were buried.

Because alpine tundra soils may be shallow and are prone to erosion, use extra care when disposing of waste water. Sprinkle it over a wide area or pour it onto a large rock at least two hundred feet from any water source.

Watching Wildlife

Tundra inhabitants face an extremely short foraging season, so keep a respectful distance and leave all wildlife undisturbed. In this open landscape an animal may not tolerate close approach, especially around denning or feeding sites. For example, Denali National Park recommends staying a quarter mile from bears and at least one mile from any known wolf den. Rely on binoculars, spotting scopes, and zoom lenses to bring you close.

Safety

In both alpine and Arctic tundra, the main safety concern is always **weather**—sudden storms can bring heavy snows any time of the year, extremely high winds, and white-outs. Plan ahead; bring extra food and a storm-proof shelter. Be alert for signs of hypothermia (see page 98) and frostbite (see page 99).

Bears may pose a special problem for those who camp on the tundra—there are no trees suitable for hanging food out of a bear's reach. Instead, carry your food in bear resistant food containers (see page 122). Cache the food downwind one hundred yards or more from camp, preferably with a vantage so approaching bears can be seen at a distance. Don't camp in dense brush or on obvious game trails.

Rodents—lemmings, pikas, ground squirrels, and voles—are abundant. Keep food covered and stored in hard plastic or tin containers. Reduce your risk of disease or sleepless nights listening to the scurry of little paws by camping well away from dens or nests.

Mosquitoes are a bane of both alpine country and the Arctic. Though transmission of disease is unlikely, sheer numbers of these bloodsuckers can cause depression, irritability, and even panic. Multiple bites may weaken a person or cause an allergic reaction in sensitive individuals. Wear a head net, long pants, gaiters to cover your ankles, gloves, and bug jacket saturated with repellant. Pray for wind. But when choosing campsites with a sought-for breeze in mind, weigh the tendency of breezy passes to turn into overnight wind tunnels.

Snow and Ice

The advent of synthetic fabrics has brought about a dramatic increase in cold-weather outdoor recreation. Today, people are better able to dress for comfort in extreme conditions, layering fast-wicking fibers and pile for insulation with high-tech, laminated outer shells to shed wind, rain, and snow. The result is that more and more people are heading outdoors and playing on snow and ice.

Of course, more people means an increase in impacts on formerly unvisited snowfields and during what was once the "off" season. We can also anticipate an increase in rescue operations during winter or wherever permanent snow and ice are found. Park and forest rangers are just now beginning to prepare for the predicted avalanche of winter visitors; we can help by modifying our leave-no-trace techniques to fit the winter environment, and by playing it safe in the snow, ice, and cold.

Leave No Trace

A thick mantle of snow or ice acts as a buffer between backcountry travelers and the plants and soil underneath. Consequently, trampling and turfing up the soil are less of a concern to winter travelers. But winter also leaves other parts of the wilderness more exposed and vulnerable, notably wildlife and watersheds. As win-

ter use increases, encounters (and potential conflicts) among recreationists also become a concern.

The most important ways to leave no trace on snow and ice are to:
◆ Avoid disturbing wildlife and skirt around or minimize time spent in critical wildlife habitat (such as feeding and denning sites).
◆ Pack out all garbage and human waste.
◆ Be inconspicuous to other people; disperse use in popular as well as pristine places.

Trip Planning

Generally, safety issues (such as extreme weather or avalanche risk) guide most people's decisions about where and when to recreate on snow and ice. But the winter traveler also faces several important leave-no-trace concerns that may influence the timing of a trip, route selection, or planned destination.

Plan your route and likely campsites to avoid critical wildlife habitat. Elk, deer, moose, and other animals typically move onto winter range where they can find forage despite severe weather. Favored areas include wind-blown slopes and ridges, lower elevation valleys, and streams and lakes that remain open when others freeze out. In the mountains, south-facing slopes receive more sun and are clear of snow earlier in the spring than their north-facing neighbors. These open hillsides attract winter-hungry grazing animals as soon as grass pokes through the snowpack. Plan your route to skirt around or avoid these areas. If you must pass through wildlife winter range minimize the amount of time spent in the area.

As more people head for the outdoors to play on snow and ice, opportunities for solitude decrease and the chance of an unpleasant encounter between motorized and non-motorized travelers goes up. Backcountry use tends to be concentrated on popular or safe routes in places with permanent snow and ice, while in winter more route choices are available. Before planning your trip find out whether your intended route is heavily or lightly used, and whether it's favored by snowmobilers, skiers, or both. If solitude is important choose untracked areas and go during mid-week. Bear in mind that the kind of people who seek out remote icefields or who enjoy winter camping typically place a high value on solitude, peace and quiet, and the challenge of living in the cold and snow.

Route Selection

Conflicts on the trail can occur among cross-country skiers, snowshoers, and snowmobilers because of the differing types of tracks each leaves behind. Snowshoes poke big holes in ski tracks, and snowmobiles can create odd bumps, ruts, and slants in the snow that wreak havoc with a skier's balance. Ideally, ski tracks should be followed only by other skiers. When snowshoers or snowmobilers follow a ski route, they will encounter many more friendly skiers if they travel off to one side and cut across the ski tracks as little as possible. And remember, as long as you avoid disturbing wildlife and stay out of avalanche-prone areas, snowcover is your ticket to wandering off trail without worries of trampling fragile plants.

Do, however, stay off exposed plants and soil particularly when temperatures are warm and soils are wet. Choose a route either at lower elevations where snow has long ago melted and the soil has had a chance to dry out, or at higher elevations where snow still covers the ground. On snow, avoid cutting tracks over the exposed tops or branches of young trees, sagebrush, or other shrubs.

Use brightly colored duct tape instead of plastic surveying tape to mark route wands (and other equipment). Survey tape rips easily and blows off in the wind, littering the snowscape.

Snowmobilers should be aware that wildlife will take advantage of the hard-packed trails their machines create. The possibility of moose, bison, or elk trotting down the trail is reason enough to slow down around blind curves or when visibility is limited.

Choosing a Campsite

When choosing a no-trace snow camp, look for a site where you won't disturb wildlife and other people. Also look for a good site to dispose of waste water (from cooking) and human waste (if packing it out is impractical). Avoid obvious water drainages and terrain likely to be used by other people.

Camp at least four hundred yards from existing trails, including game trails, and obvious food sources for wildlife. Also stay away from south-facing slopes (particularly at lower elevations) and wind-blown ridges, where elk, deer, and other animals come to feed on exposed plants.

Camp in the lee of trees when possible. Trees provide shelter, block the wind, and screen your camp from other visitors.

Dismantle all snow structures when breaking camp, unless you plan to return soon and reuse them. For extended stays, many experienced snow campers dig out a snow cave to sleep in and a kitchen area, complete with cooking platforms and "counter tops" to work on. Break down the snow cave and any windbreak walls, and fill all large holes.

Campfires

Deep snow or a hard crust of ice makes obtaining downed firewood a difficult chore at best. People are sometimes tempted to take branches from standing trees, above the snow's surface, simply because they are accessible. Then when summer arrives, the trees are full of gaps from the broken branches far above the ground. Aside from the aesthetic concern, green wood burns poorly, producing lots of smoke and little heat. If downed wood can't be found, do without a fire.

Today's winter traveler is generally better off relying on good clothes, a sleeping bag, and plenty of food to keep warm. Fires are notoriously difficult to build on snow without causing a meltdown. The heat creates a sinkhole, and the fire is swallowed up and extinguished. It's also hard to properly disperse ashes in snow.

Waste Disposal

Winter conditions are a hinderance and a help when it comes to disposing of human waste. Usually, the ground is inaccessible—and would be frozen solid if you could get to it—so digging a cat hole is out of the question. But sub-freezing temperatures make it far easier (and less odorous) to collect and carry out all waste in a poop tube or in plastic bags. Whenever possible carry out all human waste.

If packing it out is impractical, you will have to choose from one of several on-site disposal methods, none of which are flawless. The standard method is to dig a cat hole deep into the snow and cover the waste with more snow immediately. The waste will not decompose until warmer temperatures return, and any bacteria present will survive. It is important to choose a site well away from water drainages so that snowmelt does not carry the waste or germs directly into surface water. Also avoid concentrating waste in one spot. And try to choose a site unlikely to be discovered by other people. Climbers at Denali National Park are told to toss their plastic bags of human waste into deep crevasses traveling on glaciers in the high country. But in similar terrain in North Cascades National Park, the recommendation is to smear waste on the snow surface where the sun will bake it. What to do? Weigh the risk of contaminating drinking water supplies (including snow melted for drinking and cooking) and the likelihood of discovery by later parties. Do the best you can, and always pack out all used toilet paper. Kick snow over urine sites, making sure first to choose a spot that no one is likely to sit (or fall) in.

Items dropped or lost in snow become litter after spring thaw. Pack out everything. If using candles at night collect melted wax in a metal cup and pack it out.

Pour all waste water (from cooking) into one hole in the snow in an out-of-the-way spot. Cover the hole with snow when breaking camp.

Some mountaineering and polar expeditions have abandoned equipment in midtrek. The trekkers' routes can be easily retraced by following the trail of sleeping bags frozen solid with body vapor, soiled clothes, and broken snowshoes or skis. Better planning can prevent such emergency measures. Frozen sleeping bags can be cached for later retrieval. Cache near a landmark, and mark the site accurately on a map.

Watching Wildlife

Watching wildlife during winter offers wonderful insights into how animals adapt to survive such harsh conditions. But it is doubly important to allow wildlife to feed, rest, and move about as needed. Remember that animals may be less accustomed to people in the backcountry during winter, and that the fight-or-flight response may be triggered at greater distances than during other seasons. Keep at least a quarter mile—preferably downwind and concealed—from elk, deer, pronghorn antelope, caribou, and other large prey species. Predators, small birds, and mammals may actually come closer to investigate or obtain food from people, but such behavior should be discouraged.

Safety

Wherever snow and ice are present the backcountry traveler must be prepared to cope with cold conditions and the slippery, unstable nature of frozen water. Exposure to cold and the risk of falls and avalanches are the main concerns. Bear in mind that these hazards are not limited only to the winter environment but may be encountered wherever snow and ice linger year-round.

Hypothermia occurs when a person loses body heat faster than he or she can generate it, resulting in a decline in core body temperature. Common causes are exposure to cold, physical exhaustion, and too little food intake. Contributing factors may include exposure to wind, rain, or snow; wearing damp or wet clothing; or prolonged inactivity. Temperatures need not be below freezing for hypothermia to be a threat; most cases occur at temperatures between 40 and 50 degrees F., often coupled with windy or wet conditions. (See the chart on page 100)

Frostbite is the freezing of living tissue. Exposed skin is particularly vulnerable, as are the extremities. Most cases of frostbite involve fingers, toes, ears, noses, and cheeks. These parts are more often exposed to cold, and blood flow to them may be reduced as a person's body struggles to keep its internal vital organs warm. To prevent frostbite, avoid exposure to extreme cold and severe windchills. Keep your entire body warm—if your feet are cold put on a hat and extra clothes to reduce overall heat loss. Eat high-calorie foods and carry extra food with you. Always dress in loose-fitting, insulating layers, and carry spare clothes to change into when the first set becomes damp. See the chart on page 100.

To prevent **snow blindness** always wear sunglasses that block one hundred percent of UV sunlight. Leather eyeguards over the nose and along both temples help shield the eyes from glare reflected off snow and ice. A hat with a dark-colored visor also helps. Wear sunscreen on all exposed skin to prevent sunburn.

Winter storms may force a delay in your travels, so carry extra food, stove fuel, and a stormproof shelter. High winds that presage or accompany a storm create dangerous windchills and often add to avalanche risk by loading dense, heavy snow onto unstable layers in the snowpack. Blowing snow can also cause a white-out or ground blizzard, reducing visibility to near zero. Check the forecast before you go and keep an eye on the weather at all times. If caught in a strong storm find a site safe from avalanches and wait it out in your shelter (or in a snow cave). Be aware that the avalanche hazard may be high for several days after a storm—postpone travel or stay on safe routes.

Avalanches can occur wherever snow gathers on a slope. Read the section on avalanche safety that begins on page 105. Key points to bear in mind are:

◆ Stay off slopes greater than thirty degrees.
◆ Avoid travel during snow storms. Most avalanches occur during or immediately after a snowfall. Rapid accumulation (an inch or more per hour) or large amounts of snowfall (a foot or more) point to a high risk.
◆ Stay out of avalanche starting zones, tracks or paths, and runout zones. Learn to recognize avalanche terrain and choose routes and campsites in safe areas.
◆ Watch for signs of avalanche hazard—sluffs and previous slides, cracks and hollow noises radiating from the snow as you travel across it, and sudden settling of large blocks or slabs of snow. Dig a snow pit to evaluate the snowpack and avalanche risk.
◆ Never travel alone, but never expose more than one person at a time to a slide-prone area. Ideally, all group members should wear radio transceivers and know how to use them. Carry snow shovels, probe poles, and avalanche cords.

In many mountainous areas of the far north, large glaciers offer the most convenient routes through rugged terrain. But travel on a glacier requires special skills and equipment—never attempt a glacial traverse alone. All groups must have an experienced leader. The two major hazards are large gaps or cracks in the ice called crevasses and steep sections that may require technical climbing skills. Crevasses may be concealed by fresh snow or snow bridges that give way when someone walks onto them. A fall into a crevasse can be deadly—some are hundreds of feet deep and it is difficult if not impossible to climb back out on the sheer, icy walls of the crack. All members of the group should practice self-arrest and crevasse rescue before attempting a glacial route. While traveling, rope together in groups of two or (even better) three so at least one person is on belay should another fall into a crevasse. Do not attempt ice climbs or slopes steeper than thirty degrees without an ice ax and the training to use it properly.

Acute Mountain Sickness and related high-altitude illnesses often strike in the alpine zone, where permanent snow and ice are prominent features. Though the effects of altitude are thought to be the primary cause of acute mountain sickness, exposure to cold may also play a part. Watch for signs of acute mountain sickness, climb slowly to allow time to acclimate to higher elevation, and descend at the first sign of trouble.

COASTS

The United States and Canada combined boast over 45,000 miles of coastline, the continental fringe where urban, rural, and wild landscapes give way to a vast and restless wilderness, the sea. Though our coasts display a wide variety of climates and habitats—from the desert shores of the Baja to the icy snouts of Alaska's glaciers, and from Florida's reef and mangrove shallows to the fogs and fifty-foot tides of Canada's cool maritime provinces—one aspect is nearly constant: recreation in wild coastal areas is on the rise everywhere. Open beaches and shoreline trails have long been popular for hiking and backpacking, but the advent of sea kayaking has brought occasional heavy use to remote offshore islands and pristine reaches of coast.

When traveling along a coast, we have a tendency to watch the waves and gaze out to sea. But bear in mind the terrain, climate, and habitat type of the adjacent inland region. Leave-no-trace and safety concerns for the coastal traveler will vary depending in large part on the character of the land and its plants and wildlife.

Leave No Trace

One part of the coastal environment sets it apart from all other regions, especially when considering its vulnerability to trampling, erosion, and other recreation-caused damage. The *intertidal zone*—that strip of beach or rocks between daily low and high tides—is probably the landscape most resistant to recreational damage. The changing tides erase footprints and most other signs of use, and bare sand is nearly impervious to harm from hiking and camping. Even the life forms here are fairly hardy, adapted as they are to the pounding surf, wide temperature ranges, and daily flooding by tides. The intertidal zone also includes a portion of beach above daily high tide, where monthly and seasonal high tides, plus annual storm tides, periodically reach to rearrange the landscape.

On the other hand, land above the intertidal zone can be highly sensitive to trampling and other damage. Here are land plants and animals—and soils—clinging to the edge of suitable habitat. Damage to plants gives wind and water a crack to hammer away at, increasing the threat of erosion. Dune-dwelling plants—most of which are early colonizers—are especially vulnerable to trampling. In many regions, coastal dunes afford the only protection for inland areas against storms and flooding.

The most important ways to leave no trace in coastal areas are to:

◆ Concentrate use and activities on sand and gravel beaches between the low and high tide lines.

◆ Keep a respectful distance from marine mammals and other wildlife and their nesting, resting, and feeding sites.

◆ In popular places encourage a sense of solitude by camping in secluded coves rather than on long beach strands or headlands, and avoid high-use times and seasons.

Trip Planning

Coastal travel tends to be linear—up coast or down coast. The tides, weather, and terrain will dictate many of your choices, but a few other considerations should also enter into planning your trip.

If solitude is important write or call ahead to local land managers to find out what season brings the fewest visitors. Ask if there are any special hazards (weather, tides, etc.). And request a local tide table for the month(s) of your visit (and navigational charts if boating). Where tides are extreme, beach space limited, or land-route choices are dependent on low tides, schedule your trip to coincide with the monthly low tide.

Use maps to locate all coastal access points along your route. Recreational use is highest near towns and roads, somewhat less between trailheads, and least along "dead-end" reaches of coast that are accessible only from one trailhead.

Route Selection

Coastal hikers usually face only two choices of direction, and route selection may be settled with the flip of a coin. But within the confines of following a shoreline, consider the finer points of route choices.

Walk below the daily high tide line as much as possible; timing most of your travel to coincide with low tide. This offers the widest expanse of beach for hiking, and your tracks will be washed over by the incoming tide. Low tide is also best for rounding headlands that may be cut off during high tides, and for seeing the greatest amount of intertidal wildlife, shells, and assorted flotsam. When the tide is high, try to stay below the monthly high tide line—again, it's best to schedule beach hikes during periods of low tides.

If you cannot go around a headland on its seaward side look for an established inland trail. Failing that, spread out and gently bushwhack over the top to the other side. Whenever inland travel is necessary look for routes on trails, fingers of sand, river banks, or trample and erosion-resistant grasses. Avoid areas of pioneer plants in loose soils, tall grasses (such as sea oats), and low-growing shrubs and bushes.

Boating along a coast offers considerably more freedom than hiking, and a few important responsibilities. Stay at least two hundred yards from kelp beds and offshore rocks, where marine mammals and sea birds may rest or feed. Many offshore islands and sea stacks are wildlife refuges—important rookeries for birds, safe haulouts for seals and sea lions, and precarious outposts for rare or endangered plants. Ask local land managers which areas are off limits. Power boats should throttle down near shore and in shallows to avoid running aground or creating strong wakes. Use extra caution around coral reefs—keels and anchors can cause extensive damage to these living habitats (see page 73). In popular areas be alert for other boaters and swimmers, snorkelers, and divers in the water.

Choosing a Campsite

The ideal campsite on the coast offers a sandy or rocky beach below the monthly high tide line but safely above the daily high tide line. As much as possible do all your cooking, lounging, and group meetings on the lower beach and reserve a small site on the upper beach for sleeping. Pitch the tent on a durable surface; sand is the most comfortable. Stay off sand dunes that have plants growing on them. If you have to camp above the beach follow the guidelines in Chapter 3. Look for inland sandy sites or patches of short grasses.

Campfires

A sandy beach may be the most resistant site of all for building a campfire, and a fire's glow is particularly poignant against a black ocean at night. These are reasons enough for most people...campfires are highly popular in coastal areas.

But before you build a fire, make sure that driftwood is abundant and local regulations allow fires. Build the fire below the daily high tide line, directly on the surface of the sand. If the wind is blowing strong and onshore, keep the fire small to prevent embers from sailing inland into dry grasses and brush. Some people like to dig a shallow pit for a windbreak. Collect only as much driftwood as you need. Rather than burning the ends of large logs use sticks and other small pieces.

Once the fire is out, crush the charcoal and scatter the ashes in the surf. If you dug a fire pit, backfill it once the ashes are cleaned out.

Waste Disposal

Proper disposal of human waste in coastal regions can be either remarkably easy or stupendously difficult, depending on whether the area is remote or heavily visited. In truly remote areas, where few other people pass through, some authorities recommend depositing waste directly on the beach well below the high tide line. The ocean swarms with bacteria that will quickly decompose fecal material. Avoid tidepools and choose a beach with sufficient wave action and tides to break up and scatter the waste. This may sound repulsive to some, but oceans are particularly good at absorbing organic waste. Think of all the marine mammals and coastal creatures that defecate into the water each day—a heavy load that is handled very well by a dynamic system of wave action, dispersal, and bacterial decomposition. As long as we do not concentrate large quantities of sewage—as some coastal urban sewage outlets do—the ocean is as good or better a place to deposit waste as dry land. Use moist sand to wipe with; if using toilet paper, pack it out in a zippered plastic bag with the other garbage.

Realize that human use of once remote coastal regions is on the rise; as areas become popular, this method may no longer be practical. And in already popular places, there's no good way to dispose of human waste on site. The best answer here is to pack it all out in a poop tube (page 44). If you have to leave waste on-site in a popular area, bury it in a cat hole in the soil above the highest tide line. Waste buried in sand may be quickly uncovered by wind or waves and present a health hazard to other people.

Some garbage can be burned if you have an occasional campfire, but burn only paper and light trash that won't leave residues or solid wastes in the ashes. Don't bring glass containers to a beach because of the risk that it can break and injure barefoot beachcombers. Plastic garbage also poses high risks, this time to wildlife. Plastic grocery bags and six-pack rings can snare birds and small mammals, and plastic line and old fishing nets easily tangle around fins, flukes, and necks. Too often the animal drowns or suffers a slow amputation as the plastic saws through the entangled body part.

Pack out all other waste, but think twice before dumping it at the nearest fishing village or island hamlet. Many small coastal towns do not have adequate landfills or waste management systems. Rather than carry garbage around for a week only to see it dumped in the town trash heap, or spilled off the end of a pier, pack garbage out to a larger town or city. Rule of thumb: if public trash cans or dumpsters are available, there is probably a modern landfill nearby.

Watching Wildlife

Marine mammals common to North America's coasts include whales, orcas, dolphins, walrus, sea lions, seals, sea otters, and manatees. These animals are protected by the Marine Mammal Protection Act, which prohibits the harassment, feeding, or touching of marine mammals on shore or in the water. Other animals such as sea turtles and some crabs. When watching marine wildlife, it's best to stay back at least one hundred yards; remember: if the animal changes its behavior because of your presence, you're too close.

Sometimes people come across seal or sea lion pups alone on the shore. Do not assume that they have been abandoned—mother is likely feeding in the water nearby. Leave pups alone. Human interference with a pup may cause the mother to abandon it. More rarely, dolphins and whales may strand themselves on beaches. If you find a stranded marine mammal do not approach it. Immediately call the National Marine Fisheries Service or the U.S. Fish and Wildlife Service and direct them to the animal's location.

Shellfish—especially clams and abalone—tend to be susceptible to overharvesting. Gather only what you can eat, and only when species are locally abundant. Ask first about local regulations.

Safety

Land and sea combine to give coastal areas an array of hazards found no where else. Ask locally about safety issues such as strong currents or extreme tides unique to each area.

Walk slowly and watch your step when beachcombing or wading to avoid an unpleasant encounter with one of any number of **spiny or stinging creatures**. Fire worms, which look like large underwater woolly bears or hairy centipedes, live in shallow waters along the Gulf of Mexico. They favor reefs, pilings, and sandy bottoms strewn with rocks or debris, often along the low-tide line. One species, the green fire worm, grows to ten inches long. All species come armed with bristles that pierce the skin, break off, and release a painful toxin. The pain and itching may last several days. Skates, scorpion fish, and saltwater carp frequently swim and rest in shallow waters; all are armed with spines. Sea urchins also bristle with venom-filled spines that can cause difficulty breathing, weakness, and collapse. Watch for sea nettles and jellyfish when swimming.

Paralytic shellfish poisoning (PSP) occurs when people eat mollusks—mussels, clams, and oysters—tainted with toxins from certain species of plankton and bacteria. The patient soon grows numb and tingly in and around the mouth, light-headed, weak, and incoherent. Symptoms progress to include drooling, difficulty swallowing, clumsiness, headache, thirst, diarrhea, stomach pain, blurred vision, sweating, and rapid heartbeat, ending in paralysis. Provide rescue breathing as needed, and take the patient to a hospital immediately.

Boaters should be aware of **dangerous currents** at all times. Watch for surge channels—narrow passages or coves where even a modest swell gains power as it is confined on either side. Also learn to recognize and avoid rip currents, strong tidal currents, and areas with extreme tides. Use nautical charts for all off-shore boating and consult a tide table frequently. Hikers should also carry a tide table to avoid being cut off by a rising tide while rounding a headland or walking far out on mud-flats.

Always check the **weather** forecast before beginning a trip. Extended coastal trips call for carrying a small radio to monitor weather forecasts. Severe storms and hurricanes often give little warning of their approach until it's too late to evacuate. High winds, heavy surf, and storm surges (when a wall of water is driven inland by a storm) typically accompany severe storms and may overwhelm coastal areas. Strong thunderstorms sometimes generate water spouts—tornadoes at sea—that can capsize small boats. Water spouts are most common in the Gulf of Mexico.

RIVERS AND LAKES

People are drawn to water, not only out of physical thirst, but to quench our aesthetic and recreational thirsts as well. Streams and rivers across the continent are important recreational corridors, and lakes of every description and locale serve as popular destinations for backcountry travelers. Boating, whether by canoe, kayak, raft, sailboat, or motorboat, continues to be one of the fastest growing forms of out-door recreation. This section examines some of the special leave-no-trace and safety concerns and techniques associated with backcountry boating, though many of the same suggestions will work for hikers or other land lubbers when traveling or camping near rivers and lakes as well.

Leave No Trace

Perhaps more than any other type of wild country, pristine rivers and lakes are limited in number. Heavy recreational use threatens to strip many once-wild water-ways from that list. The number of people floating rivers is till rising astronomical-ly. Even the Yukon's remote Tatshenshini River has seen visitation more than triple from 326 people in 1984 to nearly 1,000 in 1993. Campsites along the Tats are no longer pristine. Rivers and lakes demand extra care to preserve the few remaining wild waterways.

When we travel by boat we tend to bring more stuff with us, but it's also easier to pack out more stuff—all our garbage, human waste, and even other people's

trash. This "pack it in, pack it out" mentality becomes even more important when traveling on or near water because garbage—litter, sewage, and other contaminants—also travel easily by water. Rinse a potful of phosphate-laden soap into a stream, and the effects are quickly carried downstream. Deposit human waste too near a lakeshore, and disease and unwanted nutrients soon find their way into the lake. If enough people make the same mistake, the aquatic ecosystem won't be able to absorb the effluent. Recreation-caused harm to water quality is already a concern in most popular places and one that looms on the horizon wherever use is on the rise.

The most important ways to leave no trace on rivers and lakes are to:
◆ Keep all contaminants out of the water. Pack out all human waste.
◆ Tread extra lightly around campsites, which often suffer repeated use even on relatively pristine rivers and lakes.

Trip Planning
River trips are usually scheduled to coincide with particular flow levels—too much water and the river is dangerous; too little and you wear out the bottom of your boat. Where water levels vary widely, a river may be jammed with boaters during the two weeks or month of optimal flows and empty the rest of the year.

Repackage all food into plastic bags and take no glass bottles or containers.

Route Selection

On larger bodies of water, land below the level of regular flushing flows (tides, seasonal floods) is typically resistant to damage and also resilient—plants regrow rapidly thanks to plentiful water and nutrients. Gravel or sand bars below the high water mark are similar to the intertidal zone of coastal areas (page 167) in their capacity for absorbing and recovering from recreational use, though the time interval between cleansing floods on a river is typically much longer than the daily changes of an ocean's tides.

Stay off lush plants on banks and shores. Use boulders and gravel or sand beaches for access to water, whether launching a boat or simply dipping a pot for cooking water.

Choosing a Campsite

On rivers, choices for campsites are often fairly limited: a sandbar, the tip of an island, a beach beside a deep pool. On popular rivers, the managing agency usually institutes a permit system and designated campsites to promote a sense of solitude. If everyone abides by the rules, a surprisingly high number of groups can travel down the same river one or two days apart and never run into one another.

Lakes on the other hand allow travel in all directions, often with easy access to the entire shoreline. Here it is more difficult to ensure solitude.

Popular campsites may give the impression of overuse in an otherwise pristine setting—there may be few impacts in the surrounding backcountry or on the river or lake itself, but each night's campsite is a worn out patch of dirt.

Camp on a shoreline where sand, gravel, or bedrock beaches are found to prevent trampling of inland plants. But consider solitude—your own and others. Are other boaters likely to pass by? Can other campers see your camp from across the lake? Remember that sound carries well over open water.

Campfires

When traveling by boat, take advantage of the ease with which extra gear can be carried on board if you want the luxury of a campfire. Use a fire pan, consider bringing in your own supply of firewood (or charcoal), and haul out all ashes (cold). You can reburn ashes and charcoal in each night's fire, so there's little accumulation by the end of the trip. Be especially careful to keep ashes out of the water. Ashes are rich in nitrogen, which can cause unwanted algae growth, and charcoal floats, typically landing on some downstream beach for all to see.

Waste Disposal

Because the risk of contaminating a water source is so high, human waste should not be disposed of on-site during river and lake trips. Box latrines are fast becoming standard equipment for most paddlers, even in pristine areas where regulations do not yet require them. Kayakers and canoeists trying to travel light can use a poop tube (see page 44 for details). If waste (including urine) must be disposed of on-site, the preferred method is to hike well away from camp and from the river or lake. At heavily used campsites along large canyon-bound rivers, urine build-up in the sand may cause odor and sanitation problems, even attracting undesirable wildlife into camp. Here it may be best to pee directly into the water where any impurities are quickly diluted

Small amounts of waste water from cooking can be filtered through a bandanna and the water poured back into a river. On lakes, it's best to scatter waste water on land at least two hundred feet from the water source. Put filtered food remnants into a plastic bag and pack them out with the other garbage. Bathe without soap and use extra care to keep lotions, cleansers, fuels, and oils out of water sources

Safety

Be careful when **crossing streams** on foot—avoid areas of deep water and strong currents. Look for wide, shallow fords and cross diagonal to the current, facing the opposite shore. Loosen packstraps so you can ditch the pack if you do happen to fall in. See page 143 for more tips on fording streams.

Keep an eye on the **weather** at all times. Strong winds can blow up suddenly, creating dangerous waves on rivers and lakes. Attempt crossings of open water only when skies are clear and the water is calm—early morning is often best.

Boating in **whitewater** requres skill and experience. Know the limits of crew and craft, and familiarize yourself with the river beforehand by reading maps and guidebooks. Ask local authorities about particular rapids and other hazards. Never let desire or enthusiasm override good sense when deciding whether to run a rapid. When in doubt, portage around rapids or line your boat through from shore.

In areas where both are allowed, conflicts often arise between motorized and non-motorized boaters. Motorboats must slow down when passing or overtaking canoes and kayaks—wakes can capsize other boats.

Remember that **bears** like to travel along river bottomlands and lakeshores just as people do. Watch for tracks and other signs along shorelines. Choose campsites far from areas of bear activity; consider moving inland to camp when bear traffic is heavy near the water. Follow the guidelines beginning on page 111 when traveling in bear country.

Water hemlock is the bane of boaters who mistake it for water cress and add it to salads. Water hemlock is highly toxic—a single bite may kill an adult. Do not eat wild plants unless they are positively identified by an expert.

Treat all **drinking water** by boiling or filtering it, regardless of how clean the source appears. All streams, rivers, and lakes in North America should be considered suspect for supporting *Giardia lamblia* and other pathogens.

Pollutants and contaminants can spread easily through water. A small source can affect a large area.

WETLANDS

Wetlands serves as a catch-all term for a wide variety of landscapes that are inundated by water during all or part of the year. This includes swamps, bogs, bayous, fresh and saltwater marshes, everglades, and pothole ponds. All of these habitats share four important characteristics: lots of shallow, slow-moving water; more mud or boggy terrain than dry ground; dense plant cover; and a rich menagerie of migrant and resident wildlife.

More people are choosing to recreate in wetlands, perhaps for a change of pace from mountain trails, but also because society at large seems to have a new-found appreciation for wetlands and their wildlife. And because travel through wet-lands—particularly through true swamps and marshes—has always been fairly dif-ficult, many of these areas remain wonderfully wild and untrammeled. It's impor-tant to preserve this wildness by leaving no trace of our passing, and also to protect ourselves from a few hazards peculiar to wetlands.

Leave No Trace

Most wetland recreation is done either in a boat or on foot—other forms of trav-el aren't practical in this soggy environment. Canoeing offers the most freedom while perhaps causing the least amount of disturbance to the surroundings, but paddlers should still be mindful of approaching too close to wildlife or other visi-tors and of stirring up silt and crushing plants when running aground or landing. Hiking here also demands special caution, especially around wet or saturated soils and plants. As more people visit wetlands, the need to practice the leave-no-trace ethic will also grow.

The most important ways to leave no trace in wetlands are to:
◆ Plan your travels to avoid disturbing wildlife, especially migrating or nesting waterfowl.
◆ Prevent waste and cooking or cleaning residues from entering water.
◆ In popular places, stay off wet or muddy trails—plan visits to coincide with dry conditions.

Trip Planning

Most wetlands in North America undergo seasonal fluctuations in water levels. Summer and early fall tend to be drier and winter and spring bring precipitation or increased runoff, but each area has its own cycles. Call or write the local wetland manager to learn which season would be best for your visit. Hikers should aim for the driest months, while boaters will favor the wettest. Bear in mind that migrant waterfowl and other wildlife are present only at certain times of the year, and many wetlands (including national wildlife refuges) set specific hunting seasons or area closures. Depending on your reasons for visiting an area, you may want to choose dates to coincide with or avoid such special events.

Exotic Plants

To prevent undesirable plants from spreading to new areas, always inspect your boat, boat trailer, and other equipment for hitch-hiking weeds before you leave home. Do another quick check before putting the boat into the water. Especially in the Southeast and Midwest, be on the lookout for hydrilla and water hyacinth. Undesirable animals can also spread from one waterway to the next. In Florida, walking catfish have escaped from fish farms by dragging themselves over dry ground to neighboring swamps. More worrisome was the pet piranha let loose in

Paradise Lake near Reno, Nevada. Thankfully it was a surprised angler and not a swimmer who first encountered the two-pound Amazonian.

Route Selection

Foot travel in wetlands is often limited to established trails on high ground or boardwalks across bogs and open water. Wherever such trails exist, use them. If possible stay off wet or muddy trails, especially where foot traffic is moderate to heavy. Where cross-country hiking is possible (and not prohibited), spread out and avoid wet ground as much as possible. Stay out of overgrown thickets and sloughs.

Choosing a Campsite

Campsites in wetlands are often hard to find. Level ground may be submerged or saturated with water, and dense vegetation may cover any remaining land. Insects also abound, making some sites inhospitable. Finally, wetlands offer few if any sites for cooking, cleaning, and toiletries that are far enough from water to protect water quality. Consider yourself fortunate to find a dry piece of ground large enough to sleep on. In smaller wetlands, it's best to move to surrounding uplands for campsites.

♦ Camp on sand or gravel beaches where available.
♦ Avoid areas with wet soils, particularly if the ground slopes. Streambanks are often muddy and are quickly torn up by foot traffic.
♦ When traveling by boat, consider sleeping in it. Even a canoe can pass for a bed for a night or two. Find a calm, sheltered place to anchor or tie up. Stay self-contained in the boat and you will leave no trace of your visit.
♦ In the South, many areas provide chickees—wooden platforms on stilts in the water. Use a free-standing tent when camping on chickees—tent stakes won't work here, and nails are not allowed. Fires are also prohibited on chickees, due to the risk of burning down the campsite.

Campfires

Building a campfire in a marsh or swamp can be more trouble than it's worth. Downed wood is often wet or water logged, and dry sites on which to build a fire are few and far between. Boaters can carry a fire pan and their own fuel if regulations and conditions allow open fires. Use punk sticks rather than a campfire to smoke out mosquitoes and other bugs.

Waste Disposal

In wetlands, it is practically impossible to dispose of human waste away from water sources. Much of the land area may be seasonally inundated, and the water table is typically very near the surface, so burying waste is not a good option. A few developed wetlands (such as parts of Everglades National Park) provide backcountry toilets, but these are rare.

Because most wetlands travel is by boat, visitors are usually encouraged to use a portable latrine. Double bag all waste and pack it out. Also pack out all toilet paper. Travelers on foot should also pack out all waste whenever possible using a poop tube (see page 44).

With so much surface water around, travelers must be extra careful to keep soap and wash water out of the natural system. Do without soap, and use as little water as needed for washing and cooking. Strain out food particles and residue and pack them out with other garbage. Scatter waste water over plants and soil when possible so that nutrients can be filtered out before reaching surface water.

Watching Wildlife

Many wetlands offer exceptional wildlife viewing opportunities, particularly during seasonal waterfowl migrations and breeding, nesting, and fledging periods. Bear in mind that these are critical times for birds—there's no energy to spare from migrating or parenting. Yet even the slightest disturbance may set off an entire flock or cause an adult to leave an egg or fledgling exposed to the elements and predators. Keep a respectful distance—at least one hundred yards—from all migrating flocks and nesting areas.

Where plant cover is dense, move slowly and try to avoid inadvertently sneaking up on wildlife, especially when canoeing (which can be remarkably quiet).

Safety

Compared to mountain peaks or desert canyons, wetlands are relatively gentle landscapes with few spectacular dangers. The two main areas of concern are water hazards and encounters with wildlife.

Hypothermia is a risk whenever wet conditions combine with temperatures of 70 degrees F. or colder. See the chart on page 100.

In salt marshes and estuaries, beware of **extreme tides** and powerful currents. Consult a local tide table when hiking below the high tide line or boating. Always play it safe around water, but be extra cautious where hazards may be hidden by murky water.

When collecting **drinking water** watch for flukes, worms, and leeches. Always pre-filter dirty water and let silt settle out before treating. Boil or filter all drinking water to eliminate bacteria and other pathogens.

Two species of **poisonous snakes** favor wetland habitats. In the southeast United States, the cottonmouth or water moccasin grows to four or five feet long on a diet of fish and frogs. The swamp rattler or massasauga is a small rattlesnake found from the coastal swamps of Texas to the marshes of the Great Lakes region. Both are excellent swimmers and will bite if provoked.

Alligators live in the warm waters of southern rivers and swamps, ranging from the Carolinas, Georgia, and Florida, west through Mississippi, Louisiana, and Texas to the Rio Grande. Gators avoid people when possible, though pets and small children are fair game. Even an adult is in trouble if a gator is surprised or cornered. Do not swim in muddy or tannin-stained water where visibility is limited. Where alligators are more common, stay alert when near water, especially at night and during mating season (April and May). Keep children in sight at all times and do not let them wade or swim alone where alligators may be present. Get out of the water immediately if an alligator is present. On land, back away slowly. If pursued run or climb a tree.

Flies and mosquitoes are abundant during warmer months. Wear a long-sleeved shirt and long pants, and use repellant as needed. Yellowjackets also favor wetlands—beware of nests in dirt banks and tree branches.

SOURCES

The following organizations represent specific interests within the wide spectrum of outdoor recreation. All promote backcountry ethics or safety, or both. Listing here does not necessarily imply endorsement, by the author or publisher, of any organization's bylaws, creeds, or educational programs.

Adventure Cycling
P.O. Box 8308
Missoula, MT 59807
(406) 721-1776

American Alpine Club
710 10th St., Suite 100
Golden, CO 80401
(303) 348-0110

American Avalanche Institute
Box 308
Wilson, WY 83014
(307) 733-3315

American Birding Association
P.O. Box 6599
Colorado Springs, CO 80934
(800) 634-7736

American Canoe Association
P.O. Box 248
Lorton, VA 22079

American Cave Conservation Association
131 Main and Cave St.
P.O. Box 409
Horse Cave, KY 42749
(502) 786-1466

American Fisheries Society
5410 Grosvenor Ln.
Bethesda, MD 20814
(301) 897-8616

American Hiking Society
1015 31st St. N.W.
Washington, D.C. 20007
(703) 385-3252

American Littoral Society
Sandy Hook
Highlands, NJ 07732
(201) 291-0055

American Rivers
801 Pennsylvania Ave. S.E.
Suite 303
Washington, D.C. 20003-2167
(202) 547-6900

American Trails
1400 16th St. N. W.
Washington, D.C. 20036
(202) 483-5611

American Wildlands Alliance
7500 E. Arapahoe Rd.
Suite 355
Englewood, CO 80112
(303) 771-0380

Appalachian Mountain Club
5 Joy St.
Boston, MA 02108
(617) 523-0636

Appalachian Trail Conference
P.O. Box 807
Harpers Ferry, WV 25425
(304) 535-6331

Backcountry Avalanche Institute
Box 1050
Canmore, AB TOL OMO
(403) 678-4102

Back Country Horsemen of America
P.O. Box 1192
Columbia Falls, MT 59912

The Backcountry Llama (newsletter)
2857 Rose Valley Loop
Kelso, WA 98626
(206) 425-6495

Canadian Llama Association
Box 476
Bragg Creek, AB TOL OKO
(403) 949-2955

Canadian Parks and Wilderness Society
160 Bloor St. E.
Suite 1150
Toronto, Ontario M4W 1B9

Canadian Recreational Canoeing
 Association
P.O. Box 500
Hyde Park, Ontario NOM 1ZO

Coastal Conservation Association, Inc.
4801 Woodway
Suite 220 W.
Houston, TX 77056
(713) 626-4222

Defenders of Wildlife
1244 19th St. N.W.
Washington, D.C. 20036
(202) 659-9510

The Desert Protective Council
P.O. Box 4294
Palm Springs, CA 92263

Ducks Unlimited
One Waterfowl Way
Long Grove, IL 60047
(708) 438-4300

GreenPeace USA
1436 U St. N.W.
Washington, D.C. 20009
(202) 462-1177

International Council for Outdoor
 Education
P.O. Box 17255
Pittsburgh, PA 15235
(412) 372-5992

International Llama Association
P.O. Box 37505
Denver, CO 80237
(303) 756-8794

International Mountain Bicycling
 Association
P.O. Box 412043
Los Angeles, CA 90041
(818) 792-8830

Izaak Walton League of America
1401 Wilson Blvd. Level B
Arlington, VA 22209
(703) 528-1818

Llama Association of North America
P.O. Box 1882, Dept. L
Minden, NV 89423
(702) 265-3177

League of Conservation Voters
1150 Connecticut Ave.
Suite 201
Washington, D.C. 20036
(202) 785-8683

Leave No Trace
288 Main St.
Lander, WY 82520
(800) 332-4100

National Audubon Society
950 3rd Ave.
New York, NY 10022
(212) 832-3200

National Avalanche School
2638 Dapplegray Ln.
Walnut Creek, CA 94596-6699
(415) 937-9338

National Marine Fisheries Service
Silver Spring Metro Center 1
1335 East-West Hwy.
Silver Spring, MD 20910
(301) 427-2239

National Organization for River Sports
314 N. 20th St.
P.O. Box 6847
Colorado Springs, CO 80934
(719) 473-2466

National Outdoor Leadership School
288 Main St.
Lander, WY 82520
(307) 332-6973

National Parks and Conservation
  Association
1015 31st St. N.W.
Washington, D.C. 20007
(202) 944-8530

National Safety Council
444 N. Michigan Ave.
Chicago, IL 60611

National Ski Patrol
133 S. Van Gordon St.
Suite 100
Lakewood, CO 80228
(303) 988-1111

National Speleological Society
Cave Ave.
Huntsville, AL 35810

National Wildlfie Federation
1400 16th St. N.W.
Washington, D.C. 20036-2266
(202) 797-6800

The Nature Conservancy
1815 North Lynn St.
Arlington, VA 22209
(703) 841-5300

Rocky Mountain Llama Association
168 Emerald Mtn. Ct.
Livermore, CO 80536

Sierra Club
730 Polk St.
San Francisco, CA 94109
(415) 776-2211

Student Conservation Association
Box 550
Charlestown, NH 03603
(603) 826-4301

Tread Lightly!
298 24th St.
Suite 325-C
Ogden, UT 84401
(801) 627-0077

Trout Unlimited
501 Church St. N.E.
Vienna, VA 22180
(703) 281-1100

Wilderness Canoe Association
P.O. Box 496, Station K
Toronto, Ontario M4P 2G9

Wilderness Medical Society
P.O. Box 2463
Indianapolis, IN 46206
(317) 631-1745

The Wilderness Society
1400 I St. N.W. 10th Floor
Washington, D.C. 20005-2290
(202) 842-3400

World Wildlife Fund
1250 24th St. N.W.
Washington, D.C. 20037
(202) 293-4800

BIBLIOGRAPHY

HISTORY OF THE LEAVE-NO-TRACE CONCEPT

"Park Eyes Limits: Yellowstone May Cut Back Winter Visitors." Associated Press. In *Helena Independent Record*. Lee Enterprises. January 1, 1994. p. 1-A.

"The Public Lands." Robert H. Nelson. In *Current Issues in Natural Resource Policy*. Paul R. Portney, editor. Resources for the Future, Inc. 1982. p.14.

Wilderness and the American Mind. Roderick Nash. Yale University Press. 1982 (third edition). 425 pp.

Wilderness Management. John C. Hendee, George H. Stankey, and Robert C. Lucas. North American Press. 1990, second edition. 546 pp.

"Wilderness Use and User Characteristics: A State-of-Knowledge Review." Joseph W, Roggenbuck and Robert C. Lucas. In *Proceedings—National Wilderness Research Conference: Issues, State-of-Knowledge*, Future Directions. Compiled by Robert C. Lucas. USDA Forest Service, General Technical Report INT-220. 1987. p. 204.

Wilderness: The Way Ahead. Vance Martin and Mary Inglis, editors. Findhorn Press and Lorian Press. 1984. 319 pp.

LEAVE NO TRACE: ETHIC OR ETHOS?

"Here's to the Winners." Anna Quindlen. In *San Francisco Chronicle* (syndicated). August 4, 1992.

"Minimizing Conflict Between Recreation and Nature Conservation." David N. Cole. In *Ecology of Greenways: Design and Function of Linear Conservation Areas*. D.S. Smith and P.C. Hellmund, editors. University of Minnesota Press. 1993. pp. 105.

The Pursuit of Wilderness. Paul Brooks. Houghton Mifflin. 1971. 220 pp.

A Sand County Almanac and Sketches Here and There. Aldo Leopold. Oxford University Press. 1949 (1971 reprint). 226 pp.

"Seven Principles of Low-Impact Wilderness Recreation." David N. Cole and Edwin E. Krumpe. In *Western Wildlands*. Spring 1992. p. 39.

Should Trees Have Standing? Toward Legal Rights for Natural Objects. Christopher D. Stone. Tioga Publishing. 1988. 102 pp.

Thinking About Nature: An Investigation of Nature, Value and Ecology. Andrew Brennan. University of Georgia Press. 1988. 235 pp.

"Wilderness is All in Your Mind." Roderick Nash. In *Backpacker*. February/March 1979.

LEAVE NO TRACE: TECHNIQUES

Assessing and Monitoring Backcountry Trail Conditions. David N. Cole. USDA Forest Service, Research Paper INT-303. 1983. 10 pp.

"Attitudes Toward Wilderness and Factors Affecting Visitor Behavior: A State-of-Knowledge Review." George H. Stankey and Richard Schreyer. In *Proceedings—National Wilderness Research Conference: Issues, State-of-Knowledge*, Future Directions. Compiled by Robert C. Lucas. USDA Forest Service, General Technical Report INT-220. 1987. p. 246.

Backcountry User's Guide: Waterton Lakes National Park. Canadian Parks Service, Ministry of the Environment. 1987. Brochure.

Changes on Trails in the Selway-Bitterroot Wilderness, Montana, 1978-1989. David N. Cole. USDA Forest Service, Research Paper INT-450. 1991. 5 pp.

Disturbance and Recovery of Trampled Montane Grassland and Forests in Montana. David N. Cole. USDA Forest Service, Research Paper INT-389. 1988. 37 pp.

"Elder of the Tribe: Grandma Gatewood." Louise B. Marshall. In *Backpacker.* April 1977. p. 28.

Evaluating Your No-trace Camping Experience. USDA Forest Service, Informational Pamphlet N 66. 1990. 2 pp.

"Florida, Noah's Ark for Exotic Newcomers." Rick Gore. In *National Geographic.* October 1976. p. 538.

How to Shit in the Woods. Kathleen Meyer. Ten Speed Press. 1989. 77 pp.

Keeping the "Wild" in Wilderness. USDA Forest Service. 1983. Pamphlet R1-83-07.

Leave No Trace! USDA Forest Service. Government Printing Office. 1992. Two booklets: FS-520 (17 pp.), FS-521 (25 pp.).

Leave No Trace: Outdoor Skills and Ethics. National Outdoor Leadership School. 1992. 16 pp.

Low-impact Recreational Practices for Wilderness and Backcountry. David N. Cole. USDA Forest Service, General Technical Report INT-265. 1989. 131 pp.

Managing Campfire Impacts in the Backcountry. David N. Cole and John Dalle-Molle. USDA Forest Service, General Technical Report INT-135. 1982. 16 pp.

Managing Wilderness Recreation Use: Common Problems and Potential Solutions. David N. Cole, Margaret E. Petersen, and Robert C. Lucas. USDA Forest Service, General Technical Report INT-230. 1987. 60 pp.

The New Complete Walker. Colin Fletcher. Knopf. 1978. 470 pp.

NOLS Wilderness Mountaineering. Phil Powers. National Outdoor Leadership School and Stackpole Books. 1993. 241 pp.

Problems and Practices in Wilderness Management: A Survey of Managers. Randel Washburne and David Cole. USDA Forest Service, Research Paper INT-304. 1983. 56 pp.

Reading the Outdoors at Night. Vinson Brown. Stackpole Books. 1972. 191 pp.

Recreational Trampling Effects on Six Habitat Types in Western Montana. David N. Cole. USDA Forest Service, Research Paper INT-350. 1985. 43 pp.

Rules for Visitors to the National Forests. USDA Forest Service. August 1986. Pamphlet PA-1381.

"She Knows if You've Been Bad or Good." Elizabeth Royte. In *Outside.* April 1992.

Soft Paths. Bruce Hampton and David Cole. Stackpole Books. 1988. 173 pp.

"Stop Walking Away the Wilderness." William M. Harlow. In *Backpacker.* August 1977. p. 33.

Trends in Campsite Condition: Eagle Cap Wilderness, Bob Marshall Wilderness, and Grand Canyon National Park. David N. Cole. USDA Forest Service, Research Paper INT-453. 1992. 40 pp.

The 2 oz. Backpacker: A Problem Solving Manual for Use in the Wilds. Robert S. Wood. Ten Speed Press. 1982. 128 pp.

Visitor Characteristics, Attitudes, and Use Patterns in the Bob Marshall Wilderness Complex, 1970-82. Robert C. Lucas. USDA Forest Service, Research Paper INT-345. 1985. 32 pp.

Walking Softly in the Wilderness. John Hart. Sierra Club Books. 1977. 436 pp.

Weeds. Alexander C. Martin. Golden Press. 1972. 160 pp.

Wilderness Campsite Impacts: Effect of Amount of Use. David N. Cole. USDA Forest Service, Research Paper INT-284. 1982. 34 pp.

Wilderness Campsite Monitoring Methods: A Sourcebook. David N. Cole. USDA Forest Service, General Technical Report INT-259. 1989. 57 pp.

Wildland Recreation. William E. Hammitt and David N. Cole. John Wiley & Sons, Inc. 1987. 341 pp.

LEAVE NO TRACE: TAILORED FOR DIFFERENT MODES OF TRAVEL

All About Llamas. Taylor/Gavin Communication. 1986. "Llama Basics, No. 1." Videotape.

The Amateur's Guide to Caves and Caving. David R. McClurg. Stackpole Books. 1973. 191 pp.

Backcountry Skiing. Lito Tejada-Flores. Sierra Club Books. 1981. 306 pp.

Backcountry Touring and Camping. BLM Utah, Minimum Impact Guide. USDI. BLM-UT-GI-92-030-8000. 1992. Pamphlet.

The Basic Essentials of Mountain Biking. Mike Strassman. ICS Books. 1989. 67 pp.

Cave Exploring. Robert J. Traister. Tab Books. 1983. 184 pp.

The Complete Mountain Biker. Dennis Coello. Lyons and Burford. 1989. 170 pp.

"Dogs on the Trail." Guy and Laura Waterman. In *Backpacker.* August 1977. p. 29.

"Fat Tire Fever: Mountain Biking Montana." Robert Ekey. In *Montana Magazine.* August 1991. p. 5.

Florida's Coral Reef Ecosystem. DeeVon Quirolo and Marydelle Donnelly. Reef Relief Environmental Education Center. 1993. Brochure.

Grizzly Country: Mountain Biking. Published jointly by the Interagency Grizzly Bear Committee, Wyoming Game and Fish Department, and US Fish and Wildlife Service. No date. Pamphlet.

"Horsepackers: Can the New West Tolerate an Old Tradition?" Perri Knize. In *Backpacker.* January 1987. p. 34.

If You're Boating in John Pennekamp Coral Reef State Park. Florida Department of Natural Resources; Coastal America, U.S. Navy. No date. Brochure.

Llamas on the Trail: A Packer's Guide. David Harmon and Amy S. Rubin. Mountain Press. 1992. 170 pp.

Mountain Bikes on Public Lands: A Manager's Guide to the State of the Practice. K. Keller. Bicycle Federation of America. 1990. pp.

"Mountain Bikes: The Gnarly Question of Knobby Tires." Jim Chase. In *Backpacker.* January 1987. p. 36.

Mountain Biking. BLM Utah, Minimum Impact Guide. USDI. BLM-UT-GI-92-028-8000. 1992. Pamphlet.

Mountain Biking Skills. Editors of Bicycling magazine. Rodale press. 1990. 122 pp.

Mountain Manners. Back Country Horsemen of Montana. No date. 20 pp.

"National Parks Grapple with Rock Climbing." Laura P. McCarty. In *National Parks.* September/October 1993. pp. 22.

Off-Road Vehicle Use: A Management Challenge. Richard N.L. Andrews and Paul F. Nowak, editors. USDA Office of Environmental Quality; School of Natural Resource, University of

Michigan; University of Michigan Extension Service. 1980. 348 pp.

The Outward Bound Canoeing Handbook. Paul Landry and Matty McNair. Lyons and Burford. 1992. 130 pp.

Packin' In on Mules and Horses. Smoke Elser and Bill Brown. Mountain Press. 1980. 158 pp.

Packstock in Wilderness: Use, Impacts, Monitoring, and Management. Mitchel P. McClaran and David N. Cole. USDA Forest Service. General Technical Report INT-301. 1993. 33 pp.

Reef Etiquette. National Marine Sanctuary Program. National Oceanic and Atmospheric Administration, U.S. Department of Commerce. No date. Flyer.

Song of the Paddle: An Illustrated Guide to Wilderness Camping. Bill Mason. NorthWord Press. 1988. 186 pp.

"Squabble Over Heli-Skiing." Michel Beaudry. In *Snow Country.* March/April 1993. p. 26.

Treading Lightly with Pack Animals: A Guide to Low Impact Travel in the Backcountry. Dan Aadland. Mountain Press. 1993. 140 pp.

Yosemite Climbing. Written and published by The Access Fund. 1992. Brochure.

SAFETY

The ABC of Avalanche Safety. E. R. LaChapelle. The Mountaineers. 1985. 112 pp.

AMA Handbook of Poisonous and Injurious Plants. Dr. Kenneth F. Lampe and Mary Ann McCann. American Medical Association. 1985. 432 pp.

Avalanche Awareness. Betsy Armstrong and Knox Williams. Alliance Communications. 1988. Videotape. 30 min.

The Avalanche Book. Betsy R. Armstrong and Knox Williams. Fulcrum. 1986. 240 pp.

Avalanche Handbook. Ronald I. Perla and M. Martinelli, Jr. USDA Forest Service, Government Printing Office. 1975. 238 pp.

The Basic Essentials of Map and Compass. Cliff Jacobson. ICS Books. 64 pp.

Be Expert With Map and Compass. Bjorn Kjellstrom. Charles Scribner's Sons. 1976. 214 pp.

Bear Attacks: Their Causes and Avoidance. Stephen Herrero. Winchester Press. 1985. 287 pp.

The Bears of Yellowstone. Paul Schullery. Yellowstone Library and Museum Association. 1980. 176 pp.

"Bears on Attack." Hartt Wixom. In *Western Outdoors.* June 1983. p. 34.

Bear Us in Mind. Center For Wildlife Information. No date. Brochure.

"Been There, Done That." Jerry Adler, Daniel Glick, Patricia King, Jeanne Gordon, and Alden Cohen. In *Newsweek.* July 19, 1993. pp. 42.

Draft Special Order (minimizing grizzly bear/human conflicts). Northern Region, USDA Forest Service. July 30, 1993. 2 pp.

"Finding Your Way." Tom Huggler. In *Outdoor Life.* October 1992. pp. 34.

Give Wildlife Room to Live. Center for Wildlife Information. No date. Folio. 6 pp.

Grizzly Country—Bear Necessities: How to Avoid Bears. Interagency Grizzly Bear Committee. No date. Brochure.

Grizzly Country—The Big Game Hunter: Storing Your Food and Game Meat. Interagency Grizzly Bear Committee. No date. Brochure.

Grizzly Country—Fishing. Interagency Grizzly Bear Committee. No date. Brochure.

Grizzly Country—Grizzly Bear Encounters: Getting Out Safely. Interagency Grizzly Bear Committee. No date. Brochure.

Grizzly Country—Hunter Safety: Avoiding Bear Confrontations. Interagency Grizzly Bear Committee. No date. Brochure.

Grizzly Country—Women in Grizzly Country. Interagency Grizzly Bear Committee. No date. Brochure.

"High Altitude Sickness." Dr. Charles Houston. In *Backpacker.* June/July 1978. p. 38.

"How to Cross a River." Bill March. In *Backpacker.* April/May 1979. p. 72.

Lightning. Martin A. Uman. McGraw-Hill, Inc. 1969. 264 pp.

"Lightning: Nature's High-Voltage Spectacle." William R. Newcott. In *National Geographic.* July 1993. p. 83.

Living with Wildlife: In Lion Country. Colorado Division of Wildlife. No date. Pamphlet.

Medicine for the Outdoors. Paul S. Auerbach. Little, Brown and Co. 1986. 347 pp.

Mountaineering First Aid. Martha J. Dentz, Steven C. Macdonald, and Jan D. Carline. The Mountaineers. 1985, third edition. 112 pp.

Outdoor Emergency Care. Warren Bowman, M.D. National Ski Patrol. 1993. 546 pp.

River Rescue. Les Bechdel and Slim Ray. Appalachian Mountain Club Books. 1989. 238 pp.

River Rescue. Anne R. Ford and Les Bechdel. Gravity Sports Films, Inc. No date. Videotape. 55 min.

Safety. Alton L. Thygerson. Prentice Hall. 1986. 331 pp.

Storm. A.B.C. Whipple. time-Life Books. 1982. 176 pp.

Weathering the Wilderness. William E. Reifsnyder. Sierra Club Books. 1980. 276 pp.

Wilderness Medical Society Position Statements. Kenneth V. Iserson, MD, editor. Wilderness Medical Society. 1989. 20 pp.

Wilderness Medicine. William Forgey, M.D. ICS Books. 1987, third edition. 151 pp.

The Wilderness Route Finder. Calvin Rutstrum. MacMillan. 1967. 214 pp.

Yellowstone Today. USDI National Park Service, Newsletter. Summer 1993. 16 pp.

You are in Bear Country. Parks Canada. Ministry of the Environment. 1984. Brochure.

SPECIAL ENVIRONMENTS

Low-impact Recreational Practices for Wilderness and Backcountry. David N. Cole. USDA Forest Service, General Technical Report INT-265. 1989. 131 pp.

Soft Paths. Bruce Hampton and David Cole. Stackpole Books. 1988. 173 pp.

DESERTS

Hiking the Desert. Dave Ganci. Contemporary Books. 1979. 78 pp.

ARCTIC AND ALPINE TUNDRA

Arctic and Alpine Environments. Jack D. Ives and Roger G. Barry, editors. Harper and Row. 1974. 999 pp.

Land Above the Trees: A Guide to American Alpine Tundra. Ann H. Zwinger and Beatrice E. Willard. Harper and Row. 1972. 489 pp.

National Wildlife Refuges of Alaska. U.S. National Fish and Wildlife Service. U.S. Department of the Interior. 1987. Brochure.

Timberline. Stephen F. Arno. The Mountaineers. 1984. 304 pp.

Vanishing Arctic. T.H. Watkins. Aperture Foundation, Inc., and The Wilderness Society. 1988. 87 pp.

SNOW AND ICE

The Complete Snow Camper's Guide. Raymond Bridge. Charles Scribner's Sons. 1973. 390 pp.

Climbing Ice. Yvon Chouinard. Sierra Club Books. 1978. 192 pp.

"Winter Crowds Prompt Study." Associated Press. In *Helena Independent Record.* Lee Enterprises. January 11, 1994.

Wrangell-St. Elias. National Park Service. U.S. Department of the Interior. 1988. Brochure.

COASTS

Camping on a Wilderness Island. Gulf Islands National Seashore, USDI National Park Service. No date. Pamphlet.

The Coastal Kayaker. Randel Washburne. Pacific Search Press. 1985. 214 pp.

Florida Keys National Marine Sanctuary: Past, Present, Future. G. Multer. Florida Institute of Oceanography. 1993. Brochure.

Gwaii Haanas/South Moresby Archipelago Information Package. Canadian Parks Service and Haida Gwaii Watchmen. 1991. 11 pp.

Kachemak Bay State Park. Alaska Department of Natural Resources. 1988. Brochure.

Protecting Marine Mammals. Amy Broussard. Seagrant College Program, Texas A&M University. 1992. Pamphlet.

Sea Kayaking Gwaii Haanas/South Moresby Archipelago. Canadian Parks Service. No date. 10 pp.

RIVERS AND LAKES

Song of the Paddle. Bill Mason. NorthWord Press. 1984. Videotape. 40 min.

Song of the Paddle: An Illustrated Guide to Wilderness Camping. Bill Mason. NorthWord Press. 1988. 186 pp.

WETLANDS

Backcountry Trip Planner. Everglades National Park. 1993. Brochure.

National Parks and Preserves of South Florida. Bob Showler and Peter Allen, editors. Florida (National Parks and Monuments Association. Winter 1993-94. Newsletter. 12 pp).

Wilderness Canoeing in Okefenokee National Wildlife Refuge. U.S. Fish and Wildlife Service, Department of the Interior. No date. Brochure.

GENERAL READING

Arctic Dreams. Barry Lopez. Charles Scribner's Sons. 1986. 464 pp.

Backpacking One Step at a Time. Harvey Manning. Vintage Books. 1986, fourth edition. 475 pp.

Bears of the World. Terry Domico. Facts On File. 1988. 189 pp.

Beyond Fair Chase. Jim Posewitz. Falcon Press. 1994. 128 pp.

Crossing Open Ground. Barry Lopez. Vintage Books. 1989. 208 pp.

Desert Solitaire. Edward Abbey. Ballantine Books. 1968. 303 pp.

The Ecology of North America. Victor E. Shelford. University of Illinois Press. 1965, fourth edition. 610 pp.

Fieldbook of Natural History. E. Laurence Palmer. Second edition revised by H. Seymour Fowler. McGraw Hill. 1975. 779 pp.

Grizzly Country. Andy Russell. Knopf. 1967. 302 pp.

Grizzly Years: In Search of the American Wilderness. Doug Peacock. Henry Holt and Company. 1990. 288 pp.

In the Spirit of Crazy Horse. Peter Mathiessen. Viking Press. 1983. 646 pp.

The Meadow. James Galvin. Henry Holt. 1992. 230 pp.

Mountaineering: The Freedom of the Hills. Ed Peters, editor. The Mountaineers. Fourth edition, 1982. 550 pp.

A Natural History of the Senses. Diane Ackerman. Random House. 1991. 331 pp.

Pilgrim at Tinker Creek. Annie Dillard. Harper's Magazine Press. 1974. 271 pp.

Prairy Erth. William Least Heat-Moon. Houghton Mifflin. 1991. 624 pp.

Roadless Area. Paul Brooks. Sierra Club, Ballantine Books. 1942 (1964 reprint). 242 pp.

Walking Down the Wild. Gary Ferguson. Simon and Schuster. 1993. 204 pp.

Where the Grizzly Walks. Bill Schneider. Mountain Press. 1977. 191 pp.

The Wild Bears. George Laycock. Outdoor Life Books. 1986. 272 pp.

The Wilderness Handbook. Paul K. Petzoldt. Norton. 1974. 286 pp.

The Wilderness Reader. Frank Bergon, ed. Mentor, New American Library. 1980. 372 pp.

INDEX

AUTHOR BIO

Will Harmon traces his love for the outdoors back to a childhood spent rummaging through the undergrowth of a 140-acre hardwood forest in southeastern Pennsylvania. More recently (disguised as an adult), he earned a Bachelor of Arts in English from the University of Montana and has enjoyed working as a backpacking, skiing, and rafting guide; wilderness ranger and trail builder for the USDA Forest Service; and writer specializing in nature, outdoor recreation, and natural resource management. He is the author of *The Hiker's Guide to Alberta* and numerous educational articles and handbooks. Will lives in Helena, Montana, with his wife Rose and their two sons, Evan and Ben.

OUT HERE THERE'S NO ONE TO ASK DIRECTIONS

Let Falcon Be Your Guide

The **FALCON**GUIDES series consists of recreational guidebooks designed to help you safely enjoy the great outdoors. Each 6 x 9" softcover book features up-to-date maps, photos, and detailed information on access, hazards, side trips, special attractions, and more. So whether you're planning you first adventure or have enjoyed the outdoors for years, a **FALCON**GUIDE makes an ideal companion.

For more information about these and other Falcon Press books, please visit your local bookstore, or call or write for a free catalog.

Falcon Press • P.O. Box 1718 • Helena, Montana 59624
1-800-582-2665

FALCON™

FALCONGUIDES *Perfect for ever*

FISHING
Angler's Guide to Alaska
Angler's Guide to Montana

FLOATING
Floater's Guide to Colorado
Floater's Guide to Missouri
Floater's Guide to Montana

HIKING
Hiker's Guide to Alaska
Hiker's Guide to Alberta
Hiker's Guide to Arizona
Hiker's Guide to California
Hiker's Guide to Colorado
Hiker's Guide to Florida
Hiker's Guide to Georgia
Hiker's Guide to Hot Springs
  in the Pacific Northwest
Hiker's Guide to Idaho
Hiker's Guide to Montana
Hiker's Guide to Montana's
  Continental Divide Trail
Hiker's Guide to Nevada
Hiker's Guide to New Mexico
Hiker's Guide to North Carolina
Hiker's Guide to Oregon
Hiker's Guide to Texas
Hiker's Guide to Utah
Hiker's Guide to Virginia
Hiker's Guide to Washington
Hiker's Guide to Wyoming
Trail Guide to Glacier/Waterton
  National Parks
Wild Country Companion

MOUNTAIN BIKING
Mountain Biker's Guide to Arizona
Mountain Biker's Guide to
  Central Appalachia
Mountain Biker's Guide to Colorado
Mountain Biker's Guide to New Mexico
Mountain Biker's Guide to Northern
  California/Nevada
Mountain Biker's Guide to Northern
  New England
Mountain Biker's Guide to the
  Northern Rockies
Mountain Biker's Guide to the Ozarks

Mountain Biker's Guide to
  the Southeast
Mountain Biker's Guide to
  Southern California
Mountain Biker's Guide to Southern
  New England

ROCKHOUNDING
Rockhound's Guide to Arizona
Rockhound's Guide to Montana

SCENIC DRIVING
Arizona Scenic Drives
Back Country Byways
California Scenic Drives
Colorado Scenic Drives
New Mexico Scenic Drives
Oregon Scenic Drives
Scenic Byways
Scenic Byways II
Trail of the Great Bear
Traveler's Guide to the Oregon Trail
Traveler's Guide to the
  Lewis and Clark Trail

WILDLIFE VIEWING GUIDES
Arizona Wildlife Viewing Guide
California Wildlife Viewing Guide
Colorado Wildlife Viewing Guide
Florida Wildlife Viewing Guide
Idaho Wildlife Viewing Guide
Indiana Wildlife Viewing Guide
Montana Wildlife Viewing Guide
Nevada Wildlife Viewing Guide
New Mexico Wildlife Viewing Guide
North Carolina Wildlife Viewing Guide
North Dakota Wildlife Viewing Guide
Oregon Wildlife Viewing Guide
Tennessee Wildlife Viewing Guide
Texas Wildlife Viewing Guide
Utah Wildlife Viewing Guide
Washington Wildlife Viewing Guide

PLUS—
Birder's Guide to Montana
Hunter's Guide to Montana
Recreation Guide to
  California National Forests
Recreation Guide to Washington
  National Forests